The Mother of All Minds

Leaping Free of an Outdated Human Nature

DUDLEY LYNCH

For Ian

my stand-in
for all the
tomorrows

A human said to the universe, "Sir, I exist."

"However," replied the universe,
"the fact has not created in me a sense of obligation."

Stephan Crane

But things that fall hopelessly apart
    in theory lie close
together without contradiction
    in the paradoxical soul of the person . . . .

Carl Gustav Jung

We hold the future still timidly, but perceive it for
the first time, as a function of our own action. Having
seen it, are we to turn away from something that
offends the very nature of our earliest desires, or is the
recognition of our new powers sufficient to change
those desires into the service of the future which they
will have to bring about?

J.D. Bernal

O my soul, do not aspire to immortal life, but exhaust
the limits of the possible.

Pindar

(The above quotations may have been slightly
altered to reflect both genders.)

Contents

The Mother of All Minds

Introduction

WITHOUT THE "I," there would be few books. And certainly not this book. When we speak of the "I," we are speaking primarily about the ego, of course. As you are about to discover, I couldn't have written this work without an outrageously healthy ego because an outrageously healthy ego is pretty much the whole point of *The Mother of All Minds*.

There is a new kind of audacious attitude in town, yes. It is outrageously self-affirming, yes. But it is also outward-looking, forward-thinking and all-encompassing. And, yes, it is my own attitude. But the new flavor of ego being focused on here has implications and uses that go far beyond one mortal's enthusiasm at finding himself a guinea pig rooting around the frontiers of human thinking skills.

I realize that a term like "outrageously healthy ego" may not settle all that well with those who possess academically trained minds or prefer less exuberance in their descriptions. Commenting about this topic in a strictly bookish, externally focused, hands-off academic fashion is, of course, the best way to avoid having to attempt a hands-on, experiential, internally focused look at what's been happening. But please don't misunderstand me. I have no real qualms with professorial types sounding like professors. It's simply that I have no intention of trying to sound like *them*. It serves no one's best interest to wait any longer for a more interior view of an extraordinary development under way at the cutting edge of our human thinking capabilities.

All this to explain that one of the chief motivations behind my writing of *The Mother of All Minds* has been to provide a hands-on, "experienced from the inside" view of this outrageously healthy new ego's arrival and prospects.

I *know* this is happening because it has happened to me. I *know* that it has happened to others. And as I observe what is happening to humanity and other living things on the planet because this kind of knowing is still only an embryonic force in the human tool kit of thinking qualities, I *know* it is important and needs to be encouraged.

However, there was something I *didn't* realize until I began the serious legwork for this book. And that's the extent to which the outrageously healthy ego phenomenon is a "third rail"-like episode for some of the very people who *should* know how important this development is. It is important, first, for the individual's psychological growth. And, second, for the hope of speeding up the maturation of our species and the injection of greater degrees of sanity and progress on our increasingly beleaguered planet.

I call this a third-rail phenomenon because of the qualities it shares with the third rail on the subway line. The topic is charged, electrified, off-putting! Scary! I know this because in my research I frequently bumped into evidence of such a reaction.

There were individuals who have undergone an impressive shift in their thinking capabilities. Anyone who has been around them for any duration and knows what to look for can see that they have. But after agreeing to talk with me about changes in their life and thinking and how these alterations came about, when the time came to chat, they got cold feet and withdrew. Others claimed to have experienced such a transition—but really couldn't point to the kind of sustained, next-level-up results in their thinking and behavior that I found persuasive. And some individuals adamantly insisted that they can't think this way and yet, by my observation, they can and they do.

One possible explanation is that most of these individuals are simply shy or inordinately private. But I don't think that is the whole explanation or even the most likely one. I encountered this kind of uncertainty and reticence so many times that I have this robust hunch: much more than we have previously suspected, taking the wraps off an outrageously *healthy* ego is a serious gut-check-and-soul-searching assignment for anyone who might be a candidate for it. In fact, it wasn't until a more personal hindsight became available—when I could look back at my own third-rail encounter—that this realization struck fully home.

As the outrageously healthy ego I now freely and cheerfully acknowledge that I am, let me say it flat out: there is a force field that a person must push through to get to where this new version of the ego takes on its character and its competence. And this force field is formidable. If a person becomes aware of this obstacle, the individual's psyche often places one weighty, difficult-to-bulge counter-resistance after another in the midst of any path that would put the individual beyond this antagonistic force, *even if the opportunity is begging to be acted on*. I can only speak for myself, but it is surprising to me to discover counter-progressive, counter-productive forces of such strength and tenacity in our psyches at such a late stage in our human development.

The "barrier reef of the mind" phenomenon that I'm writing about is keeping many humans from developing the new thinking skills we need to deal with the kind of world we are now experiencing. A world increasingly clogged and choking on its own detritus and wastes. A world hugely vulnerable to the mass-destruction weaponry available to anyone nutty enough or morally adrift enough to deploy it. A world where the greedy, arrogant, indifferent and amoral have a hammerlock on far more than their fair share and don't give a damn about the damage this does to the countless, powerless legions of highly susceptible have-nots. A world still all too often witness to behaviors more suited to the old animal brains than to the newer human versions. A world so starved for competent, mature, visionary leadership at the moment that one can be forgiven for thinking that there's only one thing that might possibly salvage the mess that we've made so quickly in the twentieth and twenty-first centuries. And that would be the near-spontaneous appearance of large—or at least adequate—numbers of, well, outrageously healthy egos acting in the service of outcomes where we have traditionally expected the ego to be sublimated. As we are about to see, this is a possibility that shouldn't be ruled out.

Having set that stage, we will now proceed to explore a psychological milestone in the development of our species about which most people who have ever lived have been totally ignorant. That you and I know of such a possibility in itself puts us in uncommon company. If the circumstance hasn't already occurred for you, the fact that it may be possible for you to make such a leap is an exceedingly rare privilege and exciting prospect. We're going to look at that possibility closely.

Chapter by chapter, here's a thumbnail look at the approach we'll be taking:

CHAPTER 1

In Chapter 1, "Out of Alpha," we'll survey our new realities: an explosive rate of change, ongoing across-the-board revolutions on many technological fronts, high-speed growth in information processing and delivery, growing social and political challenges on a global scale (not to mention growing challenges for each of us personally)—and a mind with a storied history of changing itself at the cutting edge to keep up. How is it responding this time? Well, not the way the mind change forecasters were expecting. We might still be wondering what is going on were it not for the discoverer of this outrageously healthy ego we are discussing. The American psychologist the late Dr. Clare W. Graves just happened to be looking in the right time, place and way. He was astute enough to realize that the mind was once again shifting at the leading edge. And he was gutty enough to publicize his discovery, controversial though he knew it was destined to be.

And if you are wondering, "Alpha" is what I call the first great mind of our species. Understandably, "Beta" is what I call its successor.

CHAPTER 2

Beta commands our attention in Chapter 2, "A Return to Agency." What is it like to begin using a mind that is "a leap apart" from all others currently available. Is your IQ going to soar? (No.) Will you friends no longer recognize you? (They may notice something and even begin to withdraw from you but won't know exactly why they're doing it.) Does using the Beta brain/mind "homogenize" your thinking, equipping you as a kind of "every-mind" that can think all over the human skills map? (Not really.) Beta's thinking characteristics have appeared to fill specific needs at a particular time in history and a categorical place in our psyche's development, so they are distinctive and explicit, not homogenized and all over the map (although they do often make use of thinking skills developed earlier in uniquely effective ways).

CHAPTER 3

"Beta Blockers" is the title to Chapter 3. The blockers, or enforcers, are powerful emotions. For each of us, the advance through Alpha comes in stages, and each stage has its own special identifying emotional "signature." In this chapter, we identify these "Beta blockers" for each of Alpha's six developmental stages, or levels. We are particularly interested in the emotional blockers of the final stage of Alpha, Level 1.6 (using the numbering system employed in *The Mother of All Minds*), because they are instrumental in making the "leap to Beta" such a third-rail issue.

CHAPTERS 4 AND 5

In these two chapters, we take up the challenge of how to be effective and strategic, each of us personally and progressively, in dealing with the barrier to Beta.

In Chapter 4, "The Ways of the Will," I propose this bomb-shell possibility: that over the eons our species has been doing much more than merely building a mind (so as not to spoil the surprise, I prefer not to reveal what exactly until you get to that chapter). If we play our cards right in response to this develop-ment, at the end of Alpha, we may finally have a chance to say "yes, but there is more" to the powerful forces keeping us from enjoying a more mature psychology. In Chapter 5, "Accepting the Power," I get very specific about choices that, made manifest and made committedly, can initiate the progress we each must gener-ate before we can put the wraps on one great undertaking in our personal psychology and inaugurate an auspicious, outrageously healthy, ego-centered new one.

CHAPTERS 6 AND 7

Then comes an important part of my effort to provide my reader with an interior view of all this, as opposed to another out-side-looking-on version. Chapters 6 and 7 are autobiographical. "A Story of One" (Chapter 6) narrates my travels through the first five stages of Alpha. As is true for all of us, there were significant hurdles for me to overcome. And, one by one, hurdle them I did. Right to up the point where, at the end of Alpha, I hit the "third rail" wall. That encounter provides the focus of Chapter 7, "Free to Be." There's no way around it; moving on was painful. Problematic. Uncertain. Scary. The key to getting it done? In hind-sight, it appears to have been finally deciding deep in my being to strap on that outrageously healthy ego. What triggered this deci-sion? Well, so as not to let the cat out of the bag before you have a chance to read the chapter, let me just say that it involved an OK Corral-type showdown at the highest levels of big-time corporate power. (A showdown which, by the way, I lost.) As will become obvious, all along the way, there were choices to be made, and self-defining moments and issues to be faced and finessed. But no pre-cise script to follow, other than the path of the levels. Just a yard forward and a cloud of dust, sometimes followed by a yard or two backwards, and a cloud of dust. And then, belatedly and unexpectedly, as I will suggest elsewhere in these pages, the feeling arrived that one had just been born full grown.

CHAPTERS 8 AND 9

Early on in the planning of this book, I not only determined that I would offer a decidedly interior view of Beta. I also decided that of the two great minds whose story was available, I was going to concentrate on Beta's story, not Alpha's. But in the end, that simply wasn't feasible. Because Alpha is the chassis on which Beta runs. In fact, that's the title to Chapters 8 and 9: "Alpha's Chassis" and "Alpha's Chassis, Con't." You might want to read these chapters while listening to Ravel's "Bolero," because the drama of Alpha's development in you and me just builds and builds.

CHAPTER 10

Chapter 10 is one of my favorite chapters. Maybe the reason was that it was perhaps the most challenging of all to write. I can't tell you how many points of view I sampled on the question of what the mind *is* and how it works. Most of them were learned and thorough. And there was major disagreement among them. Are we simply meat machines? Is the self only an illusion cast by our amazing brain? At what point should we quit thinking about the brain and start thinking about the mind? (One scientific wit has noted that the challenge is not unlike that of deciding when a man you have been handing pennies to has just become rich.) In the end, I sought to invent my way out of the morass. My invention: the "Neinja," which is also the name of this chapter.

CHAPTER 11

The plot thickens when you understand that the neinja is the mind's latest significant replicator, the first two being the gene and the meme. At the Beta level of the mind, it is also the anchor of that outrageously healthy ego I keep mentioning. You can think of it as a smart-cookie integrator of our brain skills. Or as a perceptive sleuth capable of searching out the parameters needed to begin with to make a new kind of mind functional and worth crowing about. Those are precisely the investigative qualities we need to turn loose in order to understand Beta, and in Chapter 11, "Across the Great Divide," that's what we do. In the hands of the Beta neinja, this new mind's distinctive thinking characteristics quickly begin to take on defining character and depth.

CHAPTER 12

Few qualities of the Beta mind have more constant utility— or require more careful handling—than its people-reading skills. As I note in Chapter 12 ("People Clues"), "knowledge of *how* people think is an invaluable clue to *what* they might be thinking. So is knowledge of how they are behaving. And knowledge of how they see things is a dependable insight again and again into what they probably *can't* see." It's clear to the Beta thinker that the world of Alpha is not at all a WYSIWYG ("What You See Is What You Get") kind of place. This chapter takes a close, careful look at getting the best uses from the Beta user's ability to zero in on the mind levels that others may be using and understand their possible consequences, quotidian or otherwise.

CHAPTER 13

Since activating Beta, I've changed how I play the game. You will, too. The game touches, and often consumes, everything. The game is what happens when, to get your desires and needs met, you must go to, through, around or away from someone else who is trying to get his or her needs and desires met.

In Chapter 13, "The Game," I argue that "more than anything else, excelling at game strategy and execution is what makes achieving the leap out of Alpha worthwhile." Game *theory* has increasingly captivated researchers from economics and management studies to anthropology and biology. Now, game theory is beginning to break out of academia as experts realize just how useful mapping the games people play can be to knowing what to watch out for. In this chapter I suggest that how the Beta thinker plays the game is the most revealing single feature of the Beta thinker's mind. So this is a subject that we linger over.

CHAPTER 14

I do not attempt to suggest an agenda to you for using your Beta mind skills. You'd have every right to be insulted if I tried (and to doubt how much I actually understand about how your mind functions). But as I note in Chapter 14, "Crossings," I expect us to bump into each other repeatedly in the days ahead. Our crossings are much more likely to come in Alpha than Beta, because Alpha is where the peoples and the other species of the planet will continue to suffer from an immaturity on the part of humans that is little short of astonishing given what we now know about ourselves and the amazing technological capabilities in our hands.

The closing chapter to *The Mother of All Minds* could have been an encyclopedia of contemporary circumstances in need of better thinking and more maturity. But that's another book by itself. So I pick and choose, seeking to convey a flavor for how a Beta thinker might go about assembling and responding to a list of "critical issues and assignments."

Attitudes about the future get a look-see (with an assist from the Pilgrims!). We sample a short list of "abysmally soul-searing, gravely hazardous, immeasurably wretched or unspeakably dumb activities" that cry out for more appropriate responses. We spend a few moments with psychological sharks and scorpions, noting that they are merely among the most dangerous manifestations of our species' "cruel and egocentric capability for being the cause of others' suffering or for being indifferent to their fate." We briefly visit the growth-industry world of neuroscientific research and end up agreeing with Dostoevsky that yesterday's world is too cruel to be good enough for our tomorrows. And there's more.

This summary may make it all sound too overwhelming to contemplate, or maybe simply too morbid. But for an outrageously healthy ego, it's only another day at the office. Once you get the gap behind you, very little remains as it once appeared, including your understanding of what can be done with the world as you find it.

It has been an adventure to write this book. And I'm sure the adventure is just beginning. Though this account is a nonfictional one, I will be writing much of the way from that decidedly *interior* stance, and, as you are going to see, when you open yourself up in this manner, there is little left to hide behind. This kind of book can't be written without putting yourself in full view of the world as a marked target.

What makes it all worthwhile is the possibility that my efforts can play a constructive role in helping a Beta mind arrive in your near future (if one isn't already here for you.) Any time we can add another Beta mind to the population of the planet, we have registered a net gain for the world-at-large. Once again, new wealth has been created expressly because the sum of the whole is again exceeding the reach of the parts!

On that note, let me say that it is my fervent and enthusiastic hope that you find much personal benefit in these explorations!

Plano, Texas
November 11, 2003

Chapter 1: **Out of Alpha**

YOU MAY BE SO nascent to the scene that you can't remember a world without skateboards, diamond ear studs or Angelina Jolie. Or you may be a member of Tom Brokaw's Greatest Generation and wish you still could live in a world with none of the above, and much else. Or you may be one of the fabled baby boomers— and therefore perhaps also a parent of many years standing of Gen-Xers or Gen-Nexters. Or you may be such a spanking new arrival that no one has yet hit on an apt moniker for your cohort or decided what your generation is to be remembered for. But wherever you fit, you have been alive and witness to a time during which the mind of humans has been extraordinarily inventive in its own behalf.

Even so, I don't expect you to spot a bumper sticker anytime soon showboating this message: *Equipped to think at the leading edge!* Generally, people are more circumspect about their personal abilities, even if the evidence eventually becomes as obvious to keen-eyed, in-the-know observers as...well, a showboating bumper sticker. I'm sure you will be, too.

Nevertheless, this is a book about individuals who are entitled to make such a claim. There are probably more of these persons than you realize, though not nearly as many as our complex societies and economies have already begun to need. Nor is it at all farfetched that you may already be one of them—or will soon be. Beginning halfway through the final century of the just-ended millennium and showing no signs of abatement, the mind of humans has been unprecedented in taking strides in its own self-interest.

I can tell you this. If you find yourself more than a few pages deep in this account and feel yourself responding energetically and approvingly to the chemistry of these ideas, you are almost certainly someone who has completed the historic leap to this emergent new thinking dimension I'm describing. Or, else, you are likely to be someone who is about to. *Nothing is more self-selective than voluntarily opening yourself up to the possibility of undergoing massive changes in how you think.*

I believe this is a reasonable assumption: that with each great epochal advance in our technological capabilities, particularly related to the development of tools and the processing and transmission of information, the brain is eventually called on to respond with a technological leap of its own. And that over the eons, each time this unrivaled quart-sized agglomeration of wired switches (neurons) and chemical moats (synapses) in our heads has been challenged to do so, at the leading edges of the envelope, it has responded with an intensity and ingenuity available nowhere else in nature.

Therefore, I am about to present extensive evidence that there is a new-sprung way to think. I will argue that this new aggregation of mental capabilities is more competent, conscientious and attuned to contemporary needs than any previously available sum of mind abilities. For in a matter of only a few decades, it appears that this mind of ours has done a wrap on a design it spent all of conscious history constructing and has undertaken an abrupt migration into groundbreaking new territory.

The mind's leap this time is easily its greatest ever—in no small part because of the fierceness of the winds of alteration propelling it forward. Change is bubbling around us like fresh lager. And the challenges it is creating are as thick as pea soup. What else but a deeply original and agile new mental calculus operating at a leapfrogged new threshold of engagement could be expected to contend seriously with the conditions of complexity and the speeds of change that the mind is being asked to respond to? *How can we possibly expect our mind to keep up with an explosively changing world if our thinking faculties themselves are frozen in time and brain tissue?*

To me, the answer seems clear: We can't.

And, we haven't.

Do you remember when the leading home computer was a scrawny, weak-kneed device with a permanent memory maxing out at a measly 256 bytes? Probably not. Very few people ever owned an Altair, which was marketed in the mid-1970s as a hobbyist kit. The personal computer I'm writing this on has a beefcake storage capacity of approximately 2,048,000,000 bytes—or two gigabytes. It operates at speeds that render the word "blur" obsolete. Supercomputers, moreover, leave all this far in the distant dust. And with each generational "Moore's Law" advance in computer-processing performance capacity, the price of the technology has dropped. Never has the myth of King Midas come closer to being a true story than in the world of bits and bytes—in the relentless, fast-paced advance in calculating-power-available-per-dollar-invested. In the ever-declining cost of copying and recombining information.

In the period roughly (although not totally) paralleling the technological revolution known as the Age of Computers, the brain has been called on once again to go beyond itself in operating capabilities, and once again, at the leading edge, it has met this challenge. Spectacularly!

A UNEXPECTED TURN

Consequently, this is what has occurred within most of our lifetimes: Urged on—egged on!—by the exponential, near-overnight revolution in information-processing technologies and by the prairie fires of interrelated hi-tech innovation and tools that cheap computer power has fueled, the cutting edge of the mind has evolved much swifter than anyone expected. And, additionally, it has headed in directions that very few mental handicappers anticipated.

From neo-Darwinians and other hard-edged materialists to New Agers and other lean-to-the-left mystics to highly practical mind-as-computer modelers and other engineering-minded metaphor-makers—and to holders of numerous viewpoints removed or in between—human skills trackers generally failed to anticipate a startling development.

They failed to foresee that the latest emergent version of the mind would not, as some observers were expecting, act to down-grade its earth-bound "mental" interests and qualities so as to be able to focus more completely on—be closer to—more non-earthly "spiritual" interests and qualities. That is, focus more on the nature and life of the soul than the nature and life of the mind. (Although, let us be swift to observe, the new kind of mind I have begun to describe is quick to acknowledge that it lives in a uni-verse of profound, often seemingly unfathomable mysteries.)

They failed to understand, as others had guessed, that the next great "critical mass" version of the self would not be tailored to serve as a single processing node plugged into a "global brain" expected to be far better equipped to handle the rising flood waters of complexity than one mind acting alone. (Not that this emergent new thinking skills processor is any stranger to the idea and value of interdependence. As we shall soon see, it simply doesn't want group-think to be used as an excuse by anyone to avoid *personal* responsibility and responsiveness.)

And they didn't see an alternative to the expectations of still others that the mind would take an overwhelmingly rational turn, producing, as one noted philosopher has called them, people deserving to be called "brights."[1] (Now, this does appear to be happening in part. But the more potent the mind's ability to inte-grate emotions and reason [that is, old and new brain processes] becomes, the less interested it seems to be in obscure, perhaps unanswerable philosophical or mechanical questions. Any attraction to arguing endlessly over the postmodern equivalent of "how many pins can dance on the head of an angel" is absent.)

Instead, to the surprise of nearly everyone, the mind has done just the opposite of much of this. It has made a U-turn. Instead of plowing headlong into exotic new dimensions, it has headed right back into its most familiar earth-bound, non-spiritualistic domains, into its mind-bound origins, its staircase history, its stage-by-stage development—into its first great haunts.

Though it is not averse to rolling out provocative new thinking skills, the latest version of our mind appears just as determined to put to bold, productive new uses the totality of its most familiar thinking skills, honed during millions of years of painstaking assembly. For the first time, it appears that the species has good reason to lay claim, at least in those who have moved to this new mental staging area, to a more "total thinking package" than ever. In a startling design that we've barely begun to assess, we are beginning to witness the best components of a mind whose origins are cloaked in the mists of genesis as it scurries to discover what it can make of itself when these "parts" work together in better coordination in a single personality. One Beta thinker told me: "I don't think that my thinking has changed from the earlier levels—it's more than I can stay detached enough to operate in the most effective way to move projects forward and can bring all my past experiences to bear on my current activities."[2] This is also fits with my own experience.

RUN-UP TO A RUBICON

Making the leap to a new level of human capability and performance—one worthy of a pressing new era of complexity and challenges—is, of necessity, an enterprise for a selected few at first. For pioneers, and it is their story, most of all, that we'll be pursuing.

If you have already made the changeover, I cannot know until you tell me exactly what the experience was like for you. But if your experience was anything like mine, I strongly suspect that your mind suddenly threw on the brakes, halting your world in mid-stride. And that the experience was not unlike suddenly being born full grown.

I know that, in part, the switch-out has been perceptual. Your post-hiatus world looks palpably different from the former one. How you see reality is noticeably more complex, penetrating, observant. You can now quickly notice and characterize patterns where before you might have intuited only vague stirrings or noticed nothing at all. Part of the newness has to do with your powers of interpretation. You have quickly noticed new assumptions in your head about how the world works that are at once more astute, pliant...mature. And there have been changes in your predictive instincts. You apprehend that many of your expectations, from private to planet-wide, have been markedly altered. Things that used to spook that mind of yours no longer do. In hindsight and in total, this most private of experiences has assumed the contours of an unprecedented, life-altering Rubicon in your personal history.

I'm comfortable calling this a secular epiphany of sorts. But it is much more concrete than something aimed at satisfying the ephemeral needs of the soul. In the mutative moment that I am describing, the mind makes you aware that it has been at work— probably for some time—fundamentally reorganizing and reconstituting itself. What you've just registered, if you have had such an experience, is the news that your mind is ready for you to know what's been going on backstage. The memorable hiatus you went through was primarily a "pay attention" announcement of what your mind has already achieved in its leap to stay relevant in a restless, ever-changing world!

What you now see when you look about you is no longer the ghost of a stalking, threatening tiger waiting behind every expression of cultural distinction from people unlike you or anything that is different or alien to you. But rather you see more clearly than ever before a fecund global community that, to use Ben Franklin's apt observation, must hang together, else we all end up hanging separately. You represent a twenty-first century embodiment of that eighteenth century Enlightenment ideal—that we are all together in this. In doing so, you are managing to envision all else in the world drawn closer than you imagined was possible.

No longer must you agonize over when to put your self interest up against your "better self" interest. That kind of self-serving interrogation is suddenly recognizable as the sanctimonious stop-gap, feel-good cop-out that it is. Instead, cued by Mohandas Gandhi's Möbius strip of an observation, you find yourself asking, "How do I become the change I want to see in the world?" You have begun to know yourself more as the process and not mainly as the vehicle.

When things don't work out, you reject the mantle of personal failure that the former "you" might have tried to cloak your shoulders with. This time, you turn to Thoreau to put issues and developments in a more manageable perspective: "The sun is but a morning star; there is more to day than dawn." You are now able to acknowledge that the incalculable complexity of the universe is beyond anyone's dictatorial predictive or scheduling efforts, including yours.

When you think about your weightiest concerns, the cardinal issue is no longer only how to survive as a human. Frequently, the survival answers come almost automatically for you now. That is, more than at any time before, you now have the ability to spot danger and match it with a patterned response shaped to deal with the issue or the occasion. This new quality allows you to focus on finding the most functional, realistic and appropriate ways *to be human*, given the contemporary circumstances and demands on your humanity. To paraphrase Ralph Waldo Emerson, your rallying cry has become, "Ride, humankind, ride!" To the fullest extent possible, you now want to know what can be made of the fact and circumstances of your humanity, during the time that you are alive, for those around you who are alive and for those whose lives are still to come.

NITRO IN THE NEURONS

Since virtually all the minds that have made the leap to this new style of mind are still living today, this is an incipient development. But I hope through the suggestions and observations offered in this work to help increase the number of minds making the move. And to encourage others to do what they need to do and what they can do to take advantage of this great new watershed in human thinking abilities.

This being the case, I think we should take a much closer look at this new level of the mind, its origins and its implications.

How do we know about this remarkable development?

Why should we care about such a development?

Why is it happening now?

How is it different from anything that has happened before?

Is it something you'd choose for yourself? Is it something you *can* choose for yourself? If you can, how would you go about choosing it?

And if you are successful at choosing it, what will this mean for you? For others? For the planet?

I believe that you and I can build a solid case for the claim that the most momentous verb of our time is the verb *evolve*. To call forth, to call out. To move out. You live in, you are a part of, you are yourself part of an evolving world. You are a verb in motion. As we are about to see, you may very well be one of the most active "verbs in motion" of all time, or on the verge of becoming so. For at the outer edge of the envelope, we are pushing back limitations of the mind that we've long acquiesced to in our human nature.

The pages ahead spell out a vision and an opportunity that I believe psychologically responsive and responsible people will find compelling and realistic. One they will want to be in the thick of, with every ounce of nitro their neurons can muster.

My argument is that the world needs as many people who can think this way as it can get, and it needs them now. What better reason does any intelligent person with psychological awareness and ambition, an empathic conscience and a dream of betterment on Earth for the greater good and the greater numbers need to commit to seeking out and discovering if it is possible for them to travel the road I'm about to map?

Let's take up the story, then, beginning with how we came to know that such a development was underway, and check in with the acutely observant sleuth of the mind who was responsible for the discovery....

*T*O A SURPRISING extent, his facial features reminded me of the somber, dignified Abe Lincoln who stares back at you in Matthew Brady's daguerreotypes.

In the Newton, Mass., restaurant on that cantankerous, wintry day, I could instantly fit Lincoln's craggy face, with the dark, hedgerow eyebrows, onto a gangly body not unlike the late actor Jimmy Stewart's, though not quite so tall.

Most people who ever met Dr. Clare W. Graves also remembered his black-rimmed eyeglasses, possibly in part because of their proximity to a pair of watchful, deep-set eyes. Dr. Graves, an American psychologist, was the pioneering researcher and theorist who was the first to realize that a major new watershed in human thinking abilities had been breached.

At his last public appearance—in 1984, before a confab sponsored by the World Future Society in Washington, D.C.—lanky, energetic Clare Graves unfolded himself from his chair, strode to the podium and lost no time informing the crowd of futurists, "I call my point of view The Emergent, Cyclical, Double-Helix Model of Adult Biopsychosocial Systems Development."

The audience reacted as you might expect. Certainly, it reacted as Dr. Graves was expecting. Laughter, giggles, mutterings, a few audible—and cynical-sounding—"oh, no's!" When the tittering quieted down, he stuck out his jaw and said, "Well, damn it, that's what it is!"

This time, nearly everyone laughed.[3]

On several occasions, Graves summed up his provocative model of human psychological realities this way:

"The psychology of the mature human being is an unfolding, emergent, oscillating, spiraling process marked by progressive subordination of older, lower-order behavior systems to newer, higher-order systems as man's existential problems change….Each successive stage, wave, or level of existence is a state through which people pass on their way to other states of being. When a person is centralized in one state of existence, he has a psychology which is particular to that state. His feelings, motivations, ethics and values, biochemistry, degree of neurological activation, learning system, belief system, conception of mental health, ideas as to what mental illness is and how it should be treated, conceptions of and preferences for management, education, economics, and political theory and practice are all appropriate to that state."[4]

Translation: there is no single accurate way to describe a mature human because, in the truest sense, there is no such thing. Human maturation, Graves concluded, is an ever-ongoing process! There is no single *correct* description of a mature human. Already, there have been several, with hopefully others to come. Maturity is as maturity does.

AGENDA FOR GROWN-UPS

The *healthy* psychological journey is, therefore, calibrated to aim forward. According to Dr. Graves' research data, as we make this journey, our mind oscillates. First, it veers toward one philosophical extreme, then reverses itself and moves toward an opposing one. That is to say, from a world-view with expressive, individualistic values, we subsequently migrate to a world-view with sacrificial, group-oriented values, and then we reverse the process. And, disaster or stalemate notwithstanding, we do it again and again, back and forth, climbing a spiral staircase of stages of psychological and mental development, for as long as personal and environmental circumstances permit.

Following such a pattern, a healthy person's psychology always tends to be moving toward increasing complexity and more openness to nuance. One reason is because the mind is forever taking its cues from its surroundings, which are themselves growing ever more tangled and demanding over time.

But there was one level of the mind that excited the tenaciously inquiring, academically rigorous mind that discovered the "biopychosocial" basis of the mind more than the others. This was the latest one.

Dr. Graves had not gone looking for such a mind. It had simply shown up one day as a blip on the radarscope of his psychological research. It was as if, at the leading edge of human nature, the mind had suddenly decided that it was done with various, older, fraying-at-the-edges and often destructive versions of itself. It had decided to open for business elsewhere, at a location where its foremost desire was that humanity act significantly more grown-up. Self-police itself much more effectively. Take its responsibilities more seriously. And exert new control over rambunctious, irresponsible and hooded aspects of its interiority that have long since been allowed too free a rein because more competent, conscientious and compassionate aspects of its interiority have not quite been able to assemble a critical mass of influences amid all the firings in the neurons.

Was human nature turning goodie-two-shoes? Did it want us all to act like we were novitiates at the nunnery gates? Was it losing its stomach for bold forays and risk-taking and pushing the envelope of the unknown, even if, as frequently happens when this occurs, blood is shed and lives are lost?

Not where Graves was looking and gathering data.

CHALLENGING ABE MASLOW

What the mind out on the point had gotten a bellyful of was the constant phenomenon and consequences of the species' still all-too-animal-like mental and emotional behaviors. This cutting-edge mind was fed up with the often singular inattention of older levels of itself to the impact of one's personal policies and decisions and actions on the planet's various life forms, particularly the variety called *homo sapiens sapiens*. Of course, the problem was that such activities have characterized human conduct forever! What was it that this new mind was thinking and proposing—that it could simply snap its fingers and change the whole of reality, including its own? Well, if it could, it certainly would snap its fingers and change a lot of things. But its new outlook was hardly so frivolous or naïve. What it knew it *could* do, based on new capabilities abruptly and unexpectedly within its reach, was make a conscious decision to quit aiding and abetting an increasingly strained, outmoded and stalemated basket of thinking skills. The next step was to set up shop personally in a more competent psychological space where humans had not hung out before. It knew this could be done because it had already done it.

At Newton that day, I asked Dr. Graves why his "biopsychosocial" theory spotlighting this new, emerging psychological space had provoked such a strong revulsion in his fellow and sister psychologists, for that turned out to be the case. "Probably because I went up against Abe Maslow's view of the self-actualizing human," he replied.

Dr. Abraham Maslow was famous for his theory concerning a hierarchy of human needs. He called the fifth stop in his five-stage theory of human psychological development "self-actualization" and said it was the *ne plus ultra* of his theoretical levels.

After this stage, Maslow believed there was no further hierarchical arrangement to a person's psychological development. With basic needs taken care of, a person could now concentrate on aesthetic needs like beauty, order and symmetry (perhaps in art, music and literature) and on encouraging truth and justice, not to mention simplicity and playfulness. With the actualization of one's self, Maslow argued, the "quantitative" quest for psychological maturity was at an end. That was because one's culture, basic needs, fears of their own destiny and fears of maximizing their own potentialities had been transcended. From now on, he thought, personal development, should it occur, would be all "qualitative."

At first, Dr. Graves' ideas on human development paralleled Maslow's. In fact, he began by trying to rationalize Maslow's research data. But that was before some of his own research subjects suddenly began to describe moving into a new psychological reality—a new stage, a new "quantitative" environment!—that lay *beyond* Maslow's domain of self-actualization. What *his* data was suggesting, Graves reported, was that psychological development was open-ended. It was cap-less. There was no arbitrary ceiling to the hierarchy of self-growth stages—not for each of us personally nor for the species as a whole. Not with this large brain of ours. There is, or so it would appear and so Dr. Graves concluded, always room for improvement.

Graves went further. He said his research data had captured almost the precise moment that some of the first humans had managed to move beyond Maslow's stage of self-actualization. A moment when they had begun to reveal that they had experienced a rebalancing of their brains' operating formulas, a reprogramming of themselves, and had moved on into a new universe of personal possibility. When they had become equipped with a substantially new thinking space—in short, a new kind of mind bringing with it an amazingly apropos new world-view in light of humanity's developing challenges.

"The biggest surprise of my life," he told me in Newton, "was the day in 1959 when I realized that some of the people I'd been testing were claiming that they had moved beyond self-actualization. One day they were saying that Abe Maslow's description fit their idea of maturity perfectly. Now, here they were telling me, 'No, that's the way I used to think. But that's not the way it is any more.'"

"A momentous leap," he called it.[5]

In the years since, nothing quite so insightful in matters of the mind has managed to supercede his discovery and explanations. Nothing, for that matter, has even come close.

ISSUES OF THE GAP

I have dubbed this extraordinary, newly arriving mind "Beta." After the second letter of the Greek alphabet. And, secondarily, after the computer programmer's meaning of the word: a test version of a new software program. The mind that precedes it is, naturally enough, "Alpha," which the dictionary says means "beginning." If Beta is freshly minted, largely untested and not all that well-known to most of us, Alpha is as familiar as an old shoe to everyone. Alpha—or as computer geeks might prefer to style it, Mind 1.0—has primarily been about one thing, and one thing only: survival. The trek to Beta—Mind 2.0—has come in steps, Alpha-directed steps. Steps leading to six variations or levels of the Alpha mind—Levels 1.1 through 1.6—all generally focused on that tenaciously singular theme: how to stay alive.

Alpha is where you begin to leave the animal in you behind. Beta, it appears, is going to be where you can learn to bring the human in you more fully, demonstrably, effectively alive.

Beta is possible because we humans have at long last begun to experience some success in deactivating and reconstituting some really messy processes left over from the way nature causes us to be assembled. As we are about to see, this has made it possible to take the protective tarps off important new uses and competencies available in our rich, innate supply of human possibilities.

Dr. Graves felt that something unexpected and exponential happened to the thinking qualities of the human creature when it availed itself of the Beta mind. This decampment extended far beyond just the empathetic. He said a sudden and remarkable change in human behavior occurred upon the crossing of "a chasm of unbelievable depth of meaning." In the quote that follows, I have substituted the terms I am using for the old mind and the new mind for his more academic terms. He observed:

"The gap between Alpha and Beta is a gap between getting and giving, taking and contributing, destroying and constructing. It is the gap between deficiency or deficit motivation and growth or abundance motivation. It is the gap between similarity to animals and dissimilarity to animals, because only man is possessed of a future orientation.

"Once we are able to grasp the meaning of passing from the level of 'being one with others' to the *cognitive* level [Beta] of knowing and having to do so that all can be and can continue to be, it is possible to see the enormous differences between man and other animals [italics his]. Here we step over the line which separates those needs that man has in common with other animals and those needs which are distinctly human.

"Man, at the threshold of Beta...is truly becoming a human being. He is no longer just another of nature's species."[6]

To be present as the brain, one more time, effects a new kind of mind is the equivalent, or better, of being present at the birth of a promising new nation. Or watching at the precise moment that some spectacular event in the heavens first becomes visible. Or witnessing from close up the rise of a great leviathan from the sea. As we are about to see, there is much that takes getting use to as a result of being witness to the emergence of this new category of human phenomenon. This is particularly true if your head has been selected as a staging area for its arrival.

Chapter 2: **A Return to Agency**

*F*OR ALL OUR GIDDY excitement over Beta's arrival, we don't want to be so gauche as to ignore the fact that Alpha deserves a hearty round of applause. Several rounds, in fact. Maybe a round of drinks on the house, too.

The first great mind of the species took us by the hand back when we were primates scarcely dry behind the ears and has delivered us to the Digital Revolution.

We may turn up at an Alpha-mobilized adulthood somewhat banged up or befuddled in certain areas, a bit misshapen or maladroit in others. Yet, as the century just ended demonstrated to an unprecedented degree, moseying through Alpha to an admirably high level of functioning is not only a possibility for hundreds of millions but is actually a likelihood if certain basic things—food, shelter, love, an education, job opportunities and a modicum of personal freedoms—are made available. Before we know it, we are, thanks to Alpha, grown, involved, contributing: civilized.

Moreover, the scientific and technological advances made under Alpha's aegis will be vital bedrock to a superstructure of discoveries and breakthroughs in the physical and life sciences for many decades, and probably centuries, to come. It is not at all unlikely that the greatest uses for many of Alpha's key discoveries—antibiotics, nuclear power, the silicon chip, DNA, even liberal democracy—still lie ahead. As we will see again and again in this work, Alpha has been no slouch.

On the other hand, its slow progress has often come at great cost and pain. For every successful story of relentless persistence and aspiring vision, the history of Alpha offers an untold number of stories of searing setback and appalling misevaluation and misjudgment. And the testing and travail continues.

Moreover, as I've already noted, getting from Alpha to Beta is proving to be no romp in the park, either.

Because seeing the need for Beta isn't the same as being there. Talking the talk of Beta doesn't equip you to walk the Beta walk. Getting close to Beta isn't any guarantee that you'll be able to arrive there.

Upon entering Beta, you have left behind a world you spent all your life getting to know and learning to cope with. Now, you are engrossed and enveloped by this experience where you are—let's call it for what it is—something of a stranger in a strange land. It will take some getting use to.

None of this means that you are suddenly going to qualify for Mensa or Intertel. Not unless your "dipstick" intelligence, as Dr. Howard Gardner, the multiple intelligence authority, jocularly refers to what used to be known as simple IQ, was conspicuously high to begin with. Achieving Beta has nothing to do with making non-geniuses into geniuses.

And yet here you are suddenly possessed of a new slate of thinking skills that includes qualities and capabilities a Hypatia of Alexandria, an Aristotle, a Cicero, an al-Khwarizmi or a da Vinci—arguably some of history's great minds—might have gazed at in amazement and some envy.

Activating Beta is what happens to you when you wade out into a world of strangeness and challenge, of great need and near-endless possibility—the world of the twenty-first century, for example—and don't get spooked, sidetracked, beleaguered or consumed by old programming from Alpha.

This turn of events has everything to do with what I have come to call "the lens capacity" of your mind.

In a manner of speaking, your mind has an aperture that polices the degree to which the world's chaos and diversity will be allowed to register in your awareness. How big is this aperture? How much information is your mind capable of admitting? And how widely is your mind's lens permitted to range on the directional tripod of reality? Can it move only a little ways, a fair distance or virtually a full 360-degree sweep? That is, just where in an essentially infinite world can your mind take aim to receive raw input? And finally, at what focal length is your mind currently set? That is, how much of what is potentially visible between you and the outer limits of what you might be capable of seeing is it seeing plainly? How well, and how deep, can it focus?

Of course, when the mind changes levels, there is much more than merely a "lens" effect.

TWO-PRONGED GOAL

With each increase in "aperture power"—in the amount of the world's data and complexity that your mind can functionally admit—there is a corresponding behind-the-scenes-and-the-screens' compensation in processing power. With each advance, your mind is maturing. Things that used to spook it no longer do. The world becomes a wider stage. With each augmentation toward the horizon, more people, more systems, more and different ideas can now be assigned a role and permitted a say in the outcomes you are open to. Emotionally, you are growing up. Your ability to decide becomes more adroit. You are growing wiser. Now, with the arrival of Bea, there has been an immoderate widening of the abilities of your mind that monitor and make sense of the surrounding world.

More than anything else, activating Beta is about gaining proficiency at handling yourself and your mind as you pursue a two-pronged goal for your life that overshadows all others: (1) being an expressive, assertive, make-it-happen-when-it-needs-to-happen kind of individual (2) with a paramount concern for the well-being of other lives, regardless of the species, when it can be done appropriately in the larger scheme of things. And doing so regardless of whether people approve or they don't, and whether they assist or don't, or whether they even notice.

To help with the task, Beta often brings with it the ability to stay in relationships high on the scale of the paradoxical as well as the ability to handle issues simultaneously that, for all intents and purposes, may appear incompatible. This is a skill at juxtaposing that most any contemporary executive, manager, political leader or a lengthy slate of other occupations would pay dearly for. And yet the odds are not high that they'll succeed in moving to Beta and pull it off. Repeatedly, we can expect that users of the Alpha mind will simply "pass through" the Beta mind like a neutrino passing through the earth without so much as a moment's recognition or pause. *Whereof one has no inkling, thereof one cannot anticipate or acknowledge!* Simply put, Beta is too big and too complex a place.

How big?

In presentations that have lent themselves to such a hands-on, close-up demonstration, I've often illustrated Beta's capaciousness and other crucial thinking qualities using a set of bowl-like items—plastic, metal, some actual food bowls from the kitchen—and several handfuls of red and blue marbles.

ASSAYING (BRAIN) SIDES

The basins come in ascending sizes. The first is quite small, no larger across than a silver dollar. The next one is more the diameter of a nice-sized orange you'd buy at the grocery store. Then comes a bowl about the width of a Frisbee. And so forth, each one larger than the one before. Seven basins or bowls in all, which I keep under wraps—under a cloth, actually, like a magician's props—until I'm ready to bring each one into view.

The first bowl is placed on the left (brain) side of the table and receives red marbles because—as Level 1.1—it represents the first stage of the mind to be expressive and individualistic in character. The next bowl goes on the right (brain) side and forward a little, and, as Level 1.2, receives blue marbles because it represents the first sacrificial, group-oriented thinking system. And so I proceed, back and forth, level by level, to the final stage of Alpha—Level 1.6—which is on the blue-marble, sacrificial, group-oriented right side of the model.

The first six basins are now out in full view. The three on the left contain red marbles. Those on the right, blue marbles.

I then reach beneath the edge of the cloth and bring out another basin. At this point, almost without fail, there is a preternatural, "you can hear a pin drop" quietness in the room. Why? Because this basin easily dwarfs all the others. This basin is *huge*.

Laconically, I announce, "Beta."

Immediately, it is obvious that we are in another dimension altogether.

One by one, I reach for the basins already in place and deposit each one within this new basin. They all fit easily, with room to spare. Then I do something that tends to raise eyebrows even higher among the more observant of my participants. I set the new entry down some distance away from the original six bowls.

And I do something else, something with big implications. I place the oversized new basin—the one representing Beta—on the red-marbles side.

Why? Because that's where it goes!

Beta is not only "a momentous leap" removed from Alpha. *It is also a return, design-wise, to the other side of our mental developmental pattern: to the leadership of the left-brain side, with all the intimations that this raises for this newly emergent cycle of the mind and the uses for which it is destined!*

The left brain/right brain phenomenon was one of the most surprising medical discoveries of the past century.

Rapidly accumulating evidence now suggests that the left side (hemisphere) of the brain—which among a myriad of functions controls key mechanics of language in most individuals—houses the processes that provide a general search-and-conquer quality to our thinking: this half of the brain is a parser and break-er and reshaper of information as it seeks to find more (often effi-cient and effective) ways to do things and explain things. Also, this side acts as a brake on the dark, depressing moods that, if left to themselves, can be triggered by the opposing hemisphere. As such, the left side is a major contributor to sunnier, more upbeat outlooks.

In contrast, the right side is much more heavily involved with shapes and spaces, geometries and geographies, continuities and connections, sometimes old ones, sometimes new ones. It also acts as a brake on manic, runaway moods to which its opposite hemisphere can be vulnerable if left without a governor. The right side moderates outlooks and reduces wild spikes in excitement, thus contributing to more level-headed outlooks.

You might say, generally speaking, that the right brain is a cohesion-building, let's-respect-the-integrity-of-the-whole yin to the left brain's more bumptious and assertive let's-take-it-apart-and-see-if-it-barks yang.[1]

And all this fits exceptionally well with Dr. Graves' theory. He interpreted his data as showing that mind levels on the "cool" (right-brain-like) side of the developmental spiral—levels 1.2, 1.4 and 1.6 in Alpha—work diligently to bring their users' inner worlds closer to an external standard or set of expectations. We can say that these levels, operating as they do from an outer-directed locus, are inwardly focused. And that levels on the "hot" (left-brain-like) side of the spiral—levels 1.1, 1.3, 1.5 and now Beta—work diligently to change the outer world to match their users' personal desires, goals and visions. So we can suggest that these levels, operating as they do from an inner-directed locus, are outwardly focused.

In overall orientation, then, Beta is another of those levels of the mind oriented toward expressive, individualistic, take-it-apart left-brain-like kinds of thinking. *It is a return to agency*—to the action side of our being. The progenitors to Beta, the users of the kinds of minds previously shaped on this side of the model, have been the world's Lone Eagles. Its Winner-Take-All Conquerors and its Marchers to a Different Drumbeat. Its Far-Flung Frontier Scouts and Venturers Far From Home. Its Risk-Taking Entrepreneurs and Put-It-All-On-The-Line Moguls. Its Empire-Building High-Muck-a-Mucks and its Steely-Eyed-and-Toothed Powerbrokers. That is to say, during its numerous sweeps through space/time over the centuries, the left-brain-oriented side of our mental development has generated plenty of outrageous egos. What it hasn't been doing, though, is generating egos nearly as "healthy"—as mature, conscientious, competent, caring and far-sighted—as we might have hoped.

Now, there is a case to be made that this might be changing. We can still expect Beta to show a kinship and a direct line of descent with its expressive-side counterparts who have operated down through the ages from the left-brain-influenced levels of Alpha. This development isn't in question: Beta definitely signals a return of our personal psychology to the dominion of the strong ego—a return from a wilderness of often inadequate (especially for our times), self-effacing, sacrificial values and behaviors. But we should and can expect to see a great deal more. This time, as I've already indicated, in Beta, we can expect the "healthy" to be conjoined to the "outrageous" in the ego. Oftentimes, outrageous-ly so!

FINGERING BETA'S PULSE

In summary, after your arrival in Beta, we should be able to use terms like these to describe you: paradoxically both ego-dampened and ego-emboldened (whichever is appropriate), conscientious, trustworthy, real-time, pragmatic, realistic, functional, gratification-delaying, wide-angled and Teflon-like (in the sense that, more than most, you are more psychologically equipped to confront people's emotions—unless you choose to do otherwise—without finding yourself attached or in reaction to them). But there is much more to your Beta thinking qualities, as you are about to see.

For more than two decades, I've supplied assessment tools capable of recognizing Beta thinking skills in an individual. These instruments have been used by the tens of thousands in six languages and several dozen cultures. But unless a person was enrolled in one of my seminars, I've not had access to the outcome. This was a deliberate result of our "change-to-gain-quickly" approach to product design and use at Brain Technologies. We didn't want our clients having to wait for the new self-knowledge our tools could provide them by having to wait for these instruments to be scored. So we've traditionally made them self-scoring and self-interpreting. Recently, however, I've begun using more elaborate methods of both assessment and processing that permit me to collect and analyze the scoring results.

My sampling of Beta using this new approach is already more than adequate to buttress three conclusions: (1) Users of the Beta mind are now materializing in many countries, cultures and careers/professions, (2) a sizable cohort of pre-Beta thinkers (individuals positioned to "make the leap," whether they ever do or not) is in the pipeline that I have sampled and (3) even in a sample as biased toward Beta or pre-Beta conditions as mine, the Beta mind is still a relatively scarce specimen.

In all, I've analyzed the Beta-tracking scores of 1,655 persons from eighteen countries—from Australia and Austria to Brunei and Brazil to Ireland and Holland to Saudi Arabia and Singapore to the U.K. and the U.S. The ages of these individuals have ranged from the early twenties to the late sixties. Their primary activities at the time they responded to my self-appraisal instrument were quite varied: from secondary school and college/graduate school enrollment to professional educational involvement to business to government to the law to politics to medicine to the ministry to training and consulting and other forms of change agentry.

Of this number, 156 individuals scored in the range I've designated as Beta. They indicate ownership of a mind attracted to the novel and the complex—and to thinking about the future. A mind comfortable in ambiguous situations that can change rapid-ly. A mind that will listen to reason, if it is truly sensible and informed, even if it is coming from a mind not heavy outfitted with formal credentials. A mind that welcomes diverse sources of information. A mind with a knack for spotting patterns and sig-nificant relationships between things and people, things and things, and people and people. A mind not inclined to be sacrifi-cial for the sake of being sacrificial. A mind that prefers to team with a handful of others who are competent, stimulating and committed to systematic improvements as opposed to a sizable organization or else a mind that prefers to work alone.

In addition, in my sample, I have identified another 335 per-sons (out of the 1,655 who have responded to my self-appraisal) who, in my opinion, are in late Alpha. I can cite evidence that these individuals possess thinking qualities that if combined with the sufficient "escape velocities" of psychological awareness and ambition and supportive environmental conditions could propel them to Beta. Maybe it will happen, maybe not.

Not infrequently, I get to meet these individuals. Spend time with them in a workshop. Maybe do lunch, or do dinner. But unless I already have their Alpha/Beta scores in hand, I've not been able to spot anything totally dependable in their body lan-guage or dress, language habits or ordinary draughts of conver-sation that says to me immediately: *This is a Beta thinker*. It is only as I get to observe them and listen to them, as I get to know them better, as I learn more and hear more about their personal inter-ests, their personal projects, their life tactics and strategies, their agendas and priorities and genuine "take" on human and non-human matters big and small, that their "Beta-ness" starts to become vivid and real for me. Beta, like God, is in the details, the planning, the strategy, the reasons, the maneuvering, the respon-siveness, the execution and the results. *And as much in what people don't do—and the reasons why—as in what they do.*

But generally, as we are about to see, this is what Beta thinkers do: think audaciously, live strategically and act wise-heartedly.

BETA'S NEIGHBORHOODS

It was my original intent in thinking about this book to use the experience gained during many years as a journalist and narrative author to profile the lives of Beta thinkers in great detail. I've written political biographies (including one about President Lyndon B. Johnson). And a book of highly vivid profiles of tornado disaster victims and survivors that promoters of "storm chaser vacations" say they often read to their clients as they drive through the southern Great Plains in search of storm clouds. Not to mention many dozens of newspaper and magazine people-oriented feature stories. But as I researched the lives of bona fide Beta thinkers I've tested and know well, I came to realize how difficult Beta is to describe from the outside looking on. It's a story, a condition, a state of mind that makes sense mainly—perhaps in a realistic sense, *only*—to those capable of knowing how it is lived because they are living it. So I abandoned my plans to saturate my book with *Reader's Digest*-like vignettes of Beta thinkers on call and on duty. Because they are so often at work in an Alpha world and are frequently utilizing aspects of their former Alpha mind levels, it is difficult for the external observer to pinpoint precisely where Alpha thinking leaves off and pure Beta thinking kicks in. Even so, I want us to kibitz in a few Beta neighborhoods because I think you'll enjoy observing the energy, imagination, outreach and impact of such a mind at work:

■ *There is the Beta thinker I know who insists on minimizing his footprint in many aspects of his life. He'll carry his garbage home to recycle it instead of putting it in the nearest bin for convenience' sake. When he goes camping he makes sure he leaves the area better than he found it by cleaning up garbage left by others. He turns off lights to minimize his electricity consumption and makes sure he uses energy efficient bulbs in his lamps.*

He purchased a hybrid (part gasoline-driven, part electric) Toyota Prius to minimize the impact of his car on the environment. He even went so far as to urge one of the local supermarkets to supply recycling bins for its outside dining areas where people often eat what they've just purchased from the busy deli counters. He also treats people "environmentally," I'd have to say, having watched him at the process for many years.

He almost never criticizes people publicly, and when pushed, his responses are frank and honest. He just seems to be incapable of playing wasteful, deceptive games. He almost never imposes his views on others. Doesn't admit to his own brilliance and can talk knowledgeably, or so it seems, about almost anything.

I'll call our profile subject Tim (though that's not his real name). Much of what I'm telling you about Tim came from an interview I had with his significant other and business partner, a Beta thinker in her own right.

"Tim thinks of me as another person and has never treated me as an assistant, secretary or anything lesser," she said. "True equality requires this. One of the markers of more complex thinking in our culture is in the way a man treats a woman. As a woman, this is always the tell-tale sign of presence or lack of more complex thinking in men. It takes a truly conscious human to get past the pervasive socialization of women as 'lesser beings' in more than just talk. How they behave always gives them away."

Another reason she loves Tim is because of how he loved and treated Edge, her Russian wolfhound and best friend and constant companion for ten years.

"Although always friendly, Edge never particularly cared for men," she told me. "He had a mind of his own and although fully obedience trained, he did his 'dumb blond' routine when most people told him what to do. 'Do you mean me? Huh? What?'

"Tim was the only male that I ever saw Edge light up for and obey fairly consistently. Edge loved him, and our 'family' seemed to blend together easily, naturally and organically as if we'd always been together. When we would make choices about travel, outings and what to do for an evening, Tim always treated Edge as an equal.

"Being a former dog professional (trainer/breeder/showperson), I had particular ways of dealing with Edge. These were more dog-like. Tim regarded Edge as another living being and treated him as if he were another human that he liked and respected.

"This was annoying at times. Because Edge had a history of separation anxiety, we had to keep arriving and leaving the house low-key and ignore him for the thirty to forty-five minutes before leaving and after returning. It took a long time to convince Tim that he didn't have to say hello and goodbye every time.

"I wouldn't say that this was particularly different from most doggy lovers and pet owners. What makes it uniquely different is how he regarded Edge. Tim saw Edge as no different than any other human being except he had fur and ate food from a bowl on the floor. Edge returned the love and respect in his gentle way and treated Tim like any other human being, an honor few received."

I couldn't help but realize that, Beta thinker that he is, Tim is characterized as much by what he doesn't do—and why—as by what he does.

■ *Then there is the Beta thinker who in recent years has been involved with a highly unusual episode in American environmental history. Picture a nondescript motel literally in the middle of nowhere—in the vast emptiness of the American West. That's where he was, exhausted but level-spirited as usual, when he called me one evening not long ago.*

A few blocks away from where he was staying, in one of the few towns with any population to speak of in one of America's least populated states, sat what used to be one of the dirtiest swatches of soil in the country's industrial past. That's the bad news. The good news is that this patch of a few hundred acres is becoming one of the country's cleanest parcels, especially given its soiled and sordid history and reputation.

The property sits on the banks of a river. In another era, one with few safeguards for the environment, a refinery was operated there. To its credit, the current owners of the old refining company—one of the world's largest oil companies—chose to fund a new type of approach to cleaning up the property in what may be the nation's largest refinery cleanup ever.

The approach was called the Collaborative Process, and for good reason. Every government agency from federal to local and all the private parties involved in the cleanup were asked to send a representative to a monthly governing council one day a month for three years. Sitting in one big room, they hashed out the issues of remediation, which were tangled and unbelievably complicated. The work was tiring and tedious. Tempers could easily fray—and sometimes did. But this group accomplished in three years what normally takes ten to twelve years, in no small part, I'm convinced, because the person facilitating the council meetings was, by my measure, a Beta thinker.

He's a character, this one. At times, his personality and his mannerisms so closely resemble those of Columbo, Peter Falk's rumpled TV detective, that it's amazing and amusing to watch.

I think I might have seen him in an executive-styled suit. Once.

On another occasion, I remember walking into his office one morning and sitting there quietly, totally ignored by him though he knew I was there, for nearly fifteen minutes while he finished reading his e-mail. (At least I was the priority next in line!) He went to college for nine years but never graduated. As you might expect of the successful facilitator of one of the toughest remediation processes in the history of the American environmental era, he has almost infinite patience with people when there is any prospect of any progress happening at all.

"I don't think there's anyone else in the country who has done quite what I've been able to get done here in terms of a collaborative process," he said to me on the phone, matter-of-factly, weary but at peace with himself after another day in the crosshairs. As I listened to him describe how he'd soothed egos, smoothed the path between rocky points, kept contentious moments from exploding into catastrophes and protected the agenda, I thought: this is cutting-edge Beta at work.

■ *Our next Beta thinker is short, bouncy, perky, feisty, fun to be with on the golf course and in the pub after-hours (I realize that may sound stereotypical, but it's true). And she's always deadly serious about her mission. And recently, one of those missions has been to find new ways to help MBA students in a North American country that isn't the USA get the lead and the cobwebs out in a way that few graduate business school faculty members have ever tried.*

The minds of her country's present and future business and organizational leaders are, in her opinion, much too hidebound and conventional. The world, she realizes, has bypassed many of them and they didn't even know to look up. The last time I checked in with her, it was boot camp on the edge of the Pacific Ocean for another 220-odd hopeful MBA degree-holders. Even the Beta thinkers amongst her students—and there were very few—were feeling the steel of her determination and commitment.

She had been deliberately and strategically guileful. There had been no overt talk of Alpha and Beta to her students, who were divided into teams. If inquisitive enough, they could have figured out for themselves that something unusual was going on because they had the information. But they were pressed for time, just as in the real world. Was it possible for the Beta students on a team to be a yeast to their Alpha teammates' dough—help them be better, be more, in the way they think? She'd been watching to see. Even the Betas, she said, "have had challenges with their teams. Some of them are consultants and labor arbitrators—good with conflict as long as it doesn't involve them but if they're involved, they still think they can solve it without outside help and then it all blows up." Sooner or later, it's a common-enough issue for all Beta thinkers: resisting the urge simply to take over and do it by yourself when a team effort is really best.

Did she discern any movement by anyone toward Beta as a result of her interventions? "I ended up with a few [students] who were into cogitation towards the end," she told me. "They were literally vibrating with all the learning and the new self-awareness. I had to reassure some of them that they weren't losing their minds. They were feeling like they were on the edge of a cliff and didn't know when the fall was going to happen." She could hold their hands under such circumstances because she'd once been there herself.

■ *And there's the Beta Thinker Who's Too Tough to Kill. The latter is, of all occupations, a Methodist minister. Retired, ostensibly, to an island off the Carolinas. He's outspoken and forever restless and inquisitive, wanting things to be better, having demonstrated to himself over the years that they often can be.*

I once asked him to rattle off the major indignities his body has suffered. He started with the three bouts of cancer. Then his recovery from near death in the winds of a Deep South tornado. Five back surgeries. And finally a maddeningly debilitating two-year bout with a bacterial infection at the body site of his most recent surgery. To get this under control required an infectious disease specialist at the state medical school and round after round of $800-a-shot antibiotic injections. "The pain of failure, either in health or present circumstances, is a great motivator," he said wryly.

There is much pain and motivation in his family's history, too. I asked him to sketch some of that history for me in an e-mail. His account reached back three centuries.

He wrote:

"Our family includes a signer of the Declaration of Independence. One branch of that 'tree' moved to North Carolina in the 1820s, where he had a large plantation. He had six children, and then his wife died. He remarried and had three more children. He died in his eighties without including these three children in his will. They left in the mid-1840s and went to Mississippi, where they carved out a plantation of over a thousand acres. With the Civil War they lost everything.

"One of the sons of that family was my great grandfather. He was forced to sharecrop on part of the land we once owned. I have seen and walked over that plantation. My grandfather died at about age forty of influenza in 1911, leaving my grandmother to rear three sons. My father, the eldest, was seven. They were forced by poverty to live in a two-room shack where my father was born. I have the fireplace mantle at home. There was no inheritance, so when they started school, my father and his next younger brother alternated working one day and going to school the next to supplement my grandmother's labor, for which they were paid one dollar per day.

"The one thing that they had was a tradition and memory of effectiveness and achievement instilled in my father and his brothers by my grandmother and numerous uncles, and that drove a quest for excellence. It took my father eight years to finish both high school and Mississippi State College in agricultural economics. We lived on a twenty-acre farm where we grew our food while dad worked for the old Farm Security Administration. During those years, my father's youngest brother died of cancer—in 1921. The middle brother was drafted very early in WWII and was killed two weeks after arriving in Belgium.

"In the late 1920s, Dad met Napoleon Hill, the author of the twelve-volume Laws of Success series, and he followed the Hill ideas completely. In 1949, when I was twelve, Dad offered me one dollar per volume to read and discuss Hill's work with him. In 1949, that was a lot of money for a twelve-year-old.

"We did an inventory of our assets to determine how my brother and I would be educated. We decided to cut timber off our farm, paying the sawmill in extra logs, and our great uncle plus some pick-up help built our first broiler house, and our plan was launched. My brother and I fed the chickens and every dime was saved for our college. Additionally, we maintained a grade-point average that generated some scholarships.

"The Farm Security program loaned money to poor farmers who could not get a loan elsewhere, who, in order to qualify, had to place themselves under the supervision of county agents who corrected ineffective conventions (such as routing rows up and down hills instead of around the contours of hills). In thirty-eight years in this job, in the poorest state in the union, dad helped 3,200 farmers to become effective, and he had to repossess only one family.

"I grew up believing that there was nothing that could not be done if you made a plan, committed all your resources and worked hard. For instance, in my second year of college, I decided that as a history major, I needed on-site experience in Europe. I worked out a plan and sold the president of Millsaps College on the idea and together we worked out the details—then I told my dad and mother. The 1957-58 school year at Trinity College, Dublin, was one of my most memorable years. While there I helped organize other students (twelve of us) for a ten-week camping trip all over Europe at a cost of ninety dollars each. We asked farmers if we could stay in their fields or woods and they loved our adventure so much that the fruit, vegetables, bread, wine and milk we consumed were free.

"Why did I decide to be a minister? In the late 1950s, the Methodist Church seemed to be the only institution asking the right questions about the race issue. After seminary at Duke, I chose to return to Mississippi, where I was appointed to the Philadelphia Charge, site of the 'Mississippi Burning' incident. By then I had married Libby and we had a son. We did not last long there. The sheriff was a member of one of those churches, and he did not appreciate my racial views. About a year before the murder of the three civil rights workers, I was kicked out along with twenty-seven other young Methodist pastors in the state of

Mississippi, and we had to deal with the reality that no Methodist church in the thirteen southeastern states would have us. We spent six exciting years in Southern California.

"In 1968, things had quieted down, we thought, and we decided to come to South Carolina—Libby's home state. We've been here ever since."

Next question: how was retirement? That was when he told me about volunteering to be a mentor to eight "limited world-view" African-American second graders at the island school. "Many have never even been to Charleston, and that's just forty miles away," he noted. "This year, for the first time in years, all the second graders were passed on to the third grade. Now, everybody understands that the 'inky cloud' that was limiting these children's growth was not a lack of information but the self-perceptions in their head." When I was last in touch with him, he had already signed up to mentor again the following year.

NOW THAT YOU'VE heard these stories, if you want to insist that some or all of these accounts could just as easily be about thinkers from one of the Alpha levels, you are absolutely right.

Not infrequently, Level 1.6 thinkers do things in ways that are virtually indistinguishable from the way thinkers in Beta might do them. Level 1.5 thinkers also do many Beta-like things. On occasion, even Levels 1.4 and 1.3 thinkers can have their Beta look-alike moments. So a single demonstration of a flare for untying Gordian knots in the affairs of the universe or detecting the underlying giveaway pattern in the chaos that points to a solution does not a Beta thinker indicate or confirm. Nor does staying afloat on a Cortes Bank-like surfer wave of complexity so you can reach a needed goal or evidencing an unusual sensitivity or degree of kindness or courage, inventiveness or self-confidence. But if you are dealing with a Beta thinker, sooner or later you are going to encounter outcomes like these I've been describing.

When I look at users of the Beta mind...

I see good things happening unexpectedly, and when I pull back the curtains to see why, I see individuals skilled and honest at saying "yes" and saying "no," then keeping their promises and commitments, appropriately.

I see people whose influence on events may be out of proportion to the titles they have, the offices they occupy, the way they dress, the way they fail to swing their authority around. Routinely, I wonder how they manage to be so close to the heart of important actions and yet so often appear to be scarcely engaged in the game at all.

I see individuals who are often content simply to bide their time but may, at the first hint of weakness on the part of those whose agenda is too self-serving, narrow or blind, move rapidly to wrest away control and seek to reshape possibilities.

I see personages at work whose vision is nearly always larger than that of anyone who might employ them. In an important sense, their vision *is* their employer.

I see participants with a skill for anticipating how events are likely to turn out that borders on the uncanny. Sometimes, it's a matter of privately forecasting the likelihood of events. Other times, it's their suspicions of how events are going to affect certain people. And sometimes it's their ability to track what goes into the making of an event. When something actually happens, you shouldn't be surprised to learn that they've already been there and gone, leaving their contributions behind them like a vapor trail. And yet at times I see people who are still on the scene long after I would have expected their departure, and I see that there are good things happening because they are still there.

I see a high tolerance for complexity and sorting through seemingly unrelated information to see if they can discern the patterns of a bigger picture (or maybe it's the picture of a bigger pattern). It seems as if they have been inoculated for ambiguities and paradox like the rest of us have for tetanus or the flu.

I see people who shrug off challenges to their ego as if the only thing that matters is what they can do to help you keep yours together—and then, concerning something that would appear to have nothing to do with their ego, counterattack with a fierceness and determinedness that can suspend one's heartbeat. I then realize that somehow they have picked up on a threat to the integrity or longevity or well-being of the whole that others have missed.

I see individuals who mirror the best balance achieved by any level of the mind thus far in integrating the three basic steps of successful problem-solving: (1) understanding that there is a need (2) deciding what might be done and whether it should be attempted and (3) if they think it should be, moving on to attempt and often to complete the task.

I see individuals who on a personal level are utterly indifferent to whether you can see them, and yet, understanding that ideas compete in their own kind of "survival of the fittest" world, think nothing of getting squarely in your face to get themselves seen and listened to. The skills that I've been describing for dealing with a complex world often seem to be a consequence in part of having lived in that world awhile. That is, I never see pre-adults and very seldom see very young adults at the Beta level. On the other hand, the users of these skills may not have begun to use their wide-angle, quick-sort, find-a-clue-in-a-haystack new thinking capabilities until relatively late in life, perhaps even at a time when the people closest to them in age are worried about retirement or senior memory moments. And I'm seeing more and more Beta users in between.

The issue that is begging for an explanation is this: what makes this kind of thinking possible for one person and not for another?

We'll go looking for answers to this critical concern next.

Chapter 3: **Beta Blockers**

*T*HOSE WHO HAVE taken a run at Beta and been repelled have undoubtedly come away with disillusionment in their eyes and their ideals battered. I'm reasonably confident that this includes a sizable percentage of the legendary baby boomer generation, the 76 million persons born in the U.S. between 1946 and 1964.

This would go a long way toward explaining the views of Howard Smead, one of the boomers' historians, and a savvy one. The boomer generation has ended up "gazing at the world we've inherited with a sense of longing, unfulfilled promise, and self-doubt," Smead writes. "We grew by turns more idealistic, less realistic, and, when our dreams didn't pan out quite the way we wanted, more disillusioned with our country and alienated from it than seems possible, given the privileged lives bestowed upon us. We're as immature as Peter Pan."[1]

And, as generations go, as privileged as Cliff and Clair Huxtable.

No generation has been blessed with better odds for getting completely through Alpha's survival training without losing their way or without getting caught in a developmental riptide that would leave them too battered, weary, puzzled or bereft to continue. (Some of the boomers' own children—Gen X'ers and Y'ers—have succeeded as individuals in moving close to Beta, but their generational advantages aren't as uniformly favorable as their parents' advantages were.)

Compared to what their own parents experienced, not to mention what Alpha's pre-modern participants experienced, many boomers virtually boarded a bullet train to the Beta station simply by being born. When you are on a fast track through Alpha, you simply can't beat advantages like growing up as the most affluent generation ever. Or enjoying the safety of suburbs and small towns as you matured. Or being favored with superior health and educational opportunities. Or usually finding adequate if not always exceptional employment as needed. Or being freed of the many fears that countless prior generations have faced as they eyed the future and wondered what kind of lives they would lead—or even if they would have a life to lead. Or stepping outside to find a world that seems to be generally improving itself. (With fluoridation, the boomers were even the first generational cohort ever to enjoy automatic protection for their teeth!)

So why, comparatively speaking, given such a propitious head start and this combination of historically rare, even unprecedented, circumstances for dealing with Alpha, have so few boomers actually succeeded in activating Beta—bringing it on stream, bringing it to full visibility and vitality, bringing it to life? Answer *that*, and stone masons of the mind that we are holding ourselves out to be, we will have inserted the final keystone in the arch that may make it possible for you to get from the Beta train station to Beta itself.

Of course, we already have the answer. Clare Graves supplied it. In the same decade—the idiosyncratic 1960s—that humans first walked on the moon and the earliest boomers were entering high school, Dr. Graves was the first to deduce that each of our brain/minds is capable in the abstract of saddling up and moving past the frontiers of anything it has ever experienced before. Moreover, he provided us with the information we need to explain the mechanisms for doing so.

Brightly beamed then and brightly shines now this epochal Graves-theory-based discovery: if you want to get to Beta, *you get there by coming to terms with the* <u>emotional</u> *enforcers of Alpha. This is what clears the way to your being able to deal successfully with the living conditions of your time. This is what makes it possible for you to respond to circumstances that can cause your brain to "switch on" a new way to think, whether it is Beta or a new level in Alpha.* The map of the emotions—he called them feelings—made possible by Dr. Graves' discoveries accurately tags the progressive stages of Alpha just as surely as the red shift of a photon tells us that galaxies are receding from the Milky Way.

When we go looking for the answer to the monumental failure of so many of the baby boomers to penetrate Beta, we find that the boomers made a singular mistake. As a result, again quoting historian Smead: "Inside every baby boomer is a child wondering what the hell happened."[2] The boomers mistakenly assumed that the rediscovery and recovery of a child-like innocence and energy—*their inner child*, as they themselves often phrased it—would carry them across the boundary that, in finality, has kept so many of them out.

Because they had so much of Alpha's survival training behind them, and so little of Alpha's traditional emotional baggage holding them back, the boomers can be forgiven for such an assumption. For believing that if all of us would simply heal our relationships and our alienations and divisions from each other, we would also heal our institutions. That if we healed our abuses of our environment, we could also heal the planet's spirit. And that this would automatically result in healing for the inner conflicts within ourselves. And that the result of all this new buoyancy would be enough to carry us upward and forward—to Beta or whatever we happened to be calling our new paradigmatic psychological dimensions.

Bob Dylan was making his debut at Gerde's Folk City the same year—1961—that Clare Graves first gave us reason to beware of the deceptive, paralyzing emotions encountered in the final stage of development in the Alpha mind. This was, of course, where most of the emotional work for many of the boomers was left to be done.

Paradoxically, the more people "sacrifice" and go out of their way to avoid hurting other people and their feelings, extrapolations from the Graves theory suggested, the more vulnerable they are to hurting, painfully and irreconcilably, deep within themselves. The killer emotions in the final stages of Alpha are sadness, loneliness and new feelings of powerlessness. In their drive to make themselves and the world a better place, the most advanced of the boomers pushed the Alpha mind to heights that it had never navigated before—and then discovered that these heights require much more to be psychologically functional at a new level than they were willing or able to provide.

And this failure to make it over the mountaintop left many of them more sad, stressed, self-righteous, idiosyncratic or narcissistic than ever. Some of the boomers who reached for Beta— maybe most—then retreated to previous stages of Alpha.

Often, the original Mind 1.6 *Weltanschauung*—world-view— of these individuals keyed on the ideals of the sixties. This produced the New Left and spawned the counterculture. When the worm turned and the most idealistic of the boomers realized that Alpha was not going to be enough to create lasting, sweeping changes, the *Weltanschauung* of many of them changed, too. Key segments of the same passionate population cohort, still as lonely and sad and powerless in their deepest recesses as ever, produced—in the 1990s—a resurrection of the ethos and ideals of the 1950s. This backlash, or regression has, in part, led to the excesses of the New Right and the ultra-religious, ultra-pro-business, anti-pluralistic contraculture that blames the profligacies and excesses of the sixties for many of today's social ills. Strange worm, strange turn, a truly disappointing outcome.

The boomers' experience provides us with a documented example of the mind's tendency to retreat to previous levels in Alpha when it slams up against Beta without being fully ready. Sadness, loneliness and renewed powerlessness are Alpha's final, ultimate emotional enforcers. But there are also all the others. The journey through Alpha is, for each of us, one tussle after another with status-quo-defending emotions, guard dogs of the mind as it is currently constituted. Guided by a psycho-topological map made possible by Dr. Graves' model of the mind, let's look at these signature emotions in more detail. Because, level by level, they provide the hottest tip-sheet going for understanding how we get, or if we'll get, to Beta.

Deadened and numbed emotions. If you are reading this book, we can assume that you are not a victim of Alpha's most vicious and unyielding emotional enforcers. These are emotions so far from Beta as to be analogous at times to cold space detritus orbiting aimlessly far from any warming sun or illuminating star. This is Level 1.1 of the mind.

Think raw survival.

Think barely hanging on.

Think great, potentially fatal vulnerabilities unless there are individuals from other mind levels available to protect you and see to your basic needs.

We need to remember that when we are talking about Level 1.1, we are actually referring to what was cutting-edge thinking in the Stone Age. You won't often encounter this kind of thinking in functioning adults in today's world. Typically, Level 1.1 describes the mental ways of the newborn, the capabilities of senile oldsters or brain-damaged individuals or sometimes those who are homeless and others "on the street."

Their emotions are dulled and numbed to the point of barely responding, if at all. If you attempt to transport people out of the clutches of this most elemental of Alpha's emotional enforcers, you are likely to get nowhere fast. They will cling to what little they have—to what is available and familiar—with a death-like grip.

When users of this level of the Alpha mind are permanently trapped by their primary emotional blockers, I often find myself witness to scenes and circumstances like these:

I see troubled street people, slouched over pilfered grocery store carts often crammed with items that only a deranged or penniless mind would hoard.

I see occupants in human warehouses called nursing homes, most of them aged, some not. But all are lost within the interiority of minds that condemns them to desuetude. They can no longer sort out a cohesive world or connect a meaningful stream of time or anticipate a future that could ever be different.

I see adults who are locked forever in the dark closets of a vegetative state because their brains—through injury, through disease, through tragic bad luck, through neglect or ill-treatment—are not able to dial up normality.

I see infants soon to be dead or whose development is already permanently stunted.

It is tragic, and there is no prayer of activating Beta here.

Vulnerability and abandonment. When found in adults, Level 1.2 of Alpha is easily overlooked in the modern world. One reason is that users of this kind of mind may go out of their way to avoid all other Alpha thinkers. People who think differently don't easily compute here. They may even seem frightening, or mysterious, to the Level 1.2 thinker.

Users of Level 1.2 values are usually loyal only to "their people"—not to any institution or even government. Because they often favor simple, repetitive, low-skilled work, they may be considered unemployable by many businesses. This attitude is particularly hard on those in the inner cities, which can be dominated by ethnic groups whose values are almost completely defined by family, group and a close-knit culture.

In their tribal world, the answer to Level 1.2's emotional enforcers is the blood bond—their inseparable attachment to their own kind, their own people. Rituals weld. Shared superstitions rivet. Incantations empower, curses afflict, magic affirms and spirits protect, all in the name of finding safety and security in the company of their kin.

Level 1.2 thinking saturates the worlds of very young children and the world of modern-day remnants of the once-plentiful and dominant "tribal" societies. That carries over to the kind of thinking that commands the interest of, just to name a few venues, much of anthropology, the Saturday morning TV commercial production industry, toy designers and manufacturers and pediatric psychologists.

When I find people entrapped here, I am witness to scenes and circumstances like these:

I see millions alive on the planet who are unable to cope with the modern world, unable to assert opinions, desires or needs in ways that more contemporary minds would hear and respond to.

I see whole communities often shuffled off to remote corners of society and geography where they can no longer live off the land.

I see people vulnerable to physical deprivation and emotional depression who fall victim again and again to alcoholism and drug abuse, to malnutrition and disease.

I see individuals who have difficulty accepting other "tribes," and whose understanding of people and situations outside their immediate world is tragically limited.

I see both adults and children whose existential issues are simple: Will I be cared for? Can I be with others like myself? Is this acceptable to the gods, elders, clan, family?

I see people—defenseless, hungry, cut off from the ways and means of the industrial or informational ages—attempting to subsist every day of their lives on little or nothing.

And in our great cities, just a stone's throw from abundance and surfeit, I see children undernourished and under-cared-for.

No fertile environment for Beta here.

Rage and shame. At Level 1.3 of Alpha, impulsive emotions can spill over the dam before you can possibly get to the controls for the floodgates. This user of the Alpha mind perceives reality in concrete, black-and-white and physical terms. There's little room for sentiment or metaphysics.

At this stage of Alpha, being shamed means being rendered irrational and diminished by feelings resulting from the fact that you have been entrapped or caught out and left, or so it seems, with no recourse. Societal coping skills are often narrow, minimal or absent. Jails and prisons, not to mention street gangs, day-labor pools and alternative classes for troubled youth, are filled with people trapped deep in this Alpha slough (cemeteries, too!). Add to this list of ordinary Level 1.3 users political dictators and their enforcers who deal out strong-armed control and swashbuckling workers who routinely put life and limb at risk.

Then again, nearly all of us know persons who have managed to have productive, if sometimes idiosyncratic and irregular, lives using this kind of thinking. (Sometimes, they are even members of our immediate or extended families.)

In terms of Beta, we are beginning to see a bit of progress. The Alpha mind is experiencing a new, liberating dash of *habanero*—independence. The individual is, at last, showing signs of emerging. But because the circumstances can be so routinely hostile and relentlessly negative, there's still little to recruit emotionally and immediately that would augment and accelerate a move forward on the spiral development of the mind.

I see school-yard bullies who grow up to be barroom bullies, who never grow up.

I see loners sending out mail bombs or firing sniper rifles or hurling concrete blocks off freeway bridges onto innocent, unsuspecting victims in cars below.

I see out-of-control barely-out-of-their-teens millionaire sports figures or rock music and rapper personalities affecting larger-than-life "heroics" both on stage and off as they ride a drumbeat of extreme impulsiveness, not infrequently to an early grave.

I see convicted murderers trying to attack the juries that have just sentenced them to death or who are headed for supermax lockups, designed to keep them from attacking their keepers and their fellow and sister inmates.

I see arrogant, swaggering, tough-talking vigilantes volunteering where no one has made a request and mercenaries devoted to a blood-filled lifestyle of "dragon-slaying," just for the hell (thrill) of it.

Ashes to ashes.

Beta seems to be—and is—worlds removed.

Guilt and self-righteousness. Because of the emotional enforcers at Level 1.4, the mind is more rigid and absolutist than ever, insisting on one right way only (and shunning many wrong ones) to think about what is moral and good and what is evil and bad. About who is worthy of the ministrations and beneficence of an all-powerful Other that enforces an unassailable order—and who isn't.

At this level of the mind, Alpha proceeds to establish vessel after vessel to contain "the truth once and for all delivered": sometimes a church or a code of conduct, sometimes a culture or a government or government agency or government official, sometimes a charitable organization or a political philosophy or party. And not infrequently, all of these at the same time.

Inject any thoughts of Beta into a user of Alpha's Level 1.4 and, faster than any flick of a Bic, you'll find yourself bringing that individual to their knees with feelings of guilt and self-righteousness.

Level 1.4 thinking goes to church, the synagogue and the mosque regularly and faithfully—and loves bureaucracies, strict hierarchies and other orderly places as much as bees love the hive. The toll this exacts on humanity is profound because of this mind level's slowness to change, its unwillingness to do much if any Monday morning quarterbacking of the decisions of those in

authority and a close-in event horizon that limits its abiliy to envision a future capable of doing something different.

I see millions and millions of pious religious faithful, some bow-
ing to Mecca and some to the Virgin, some with arms uplifted to Jesus
and speaking in tongues, some praying in black clothing and
yarmulkes and refusing to spell out fully the name of their deity.

I see people who insist on handling snakes when they pray and
people who insist they can't handle anything modern or artificial or
they can't pray.

I see patriots waving the colors and massive assemblies of youth
marching in waves, all identically dressed and drilled to lock-step precision.

I see totalitarians and Rotarians. I see Confucius-quoting
Orientals and confusion-proof Occidentals, all convinced that all the
answers they'll ever need are in a book or given to them by a higher
authority or supplied by authoritative, all-knowing powers-that-be.
Each camp believes its truth to be the whole truth and nothing but the
truth, so help them G-d, Chairman Mao or the heavyweight in the cult.

I see True Believers who have not developed a moral compass or
who have lost theirs inducing children to strap explosive charges
under their coat and blow themselves and everyone else within the
range of the flesh-ripping shrapnel to shreds, all in the name of God.
Then I see True Believers who have not developed a moral compass or
who have lost theirs retaliate indiscriminately, blowing up homes, rain-
ing down rockets, smashing with tanks, in all cases destroying the
innocent with no warning while billing their knee-jerk acts of revenge
as warnings to the guilty, all in the name of God.

Beta won't flower here, not now, not soon, not ever.

Fears of being poor or being seen as inadequate. Then
Alpha's emotional enforcers suddenly permit their user to see a
world where multiple options—thinking about more than one
thing at a time—are better than one. Where smart wins over
dumb. Risk taking wins over playing-it-safe. Where the scientific

and the proven triumph over the intuitive and the ideal. And, most of all, where applicators of boot-strapping, win-as-much-as-you-can business principles win over just about everything and everyone else.

At this level on the spiral, the mind assumes that everything in the world is essentially there *for* the winning! And if you don't win it, then someone else will, so you might as well take it for yourself. (Thieves utilize much the same rational, as Charles Dickins' Artful Dodger explains so persuasively to Oliver Twist: "If you don't take pocket-handkechers and watches...some other cove will; so that the coves that lose'em will be all the worse, and you'll be all the worse too, and nobody half a ha'p'orth the better, except the chap wot gets them—and you've just as good a right to them as they have.")

But when you start talking about the need for Earth citizens to give more than lip service to nature's natural needs, patterns and flows, eyes glaze over. When you accentuate the need for people in fast-changing times to be more globally responsible, more ethically sensitive and more personally attuned to the pressing needs of humanity's have-nots, you quickly discover that you have lost any traction you may have gained toward Beta.

Instead you have invited new paroxysms of fear, anxiety and feelings of personal inadequacy and financial vulnerability. Let those who have it fear lest they lose it! At this stage of Alpha—Level 1.5—the feeling is that you can never have enough, so you want to avoid ever losing, and consequently the striving, competing and gamesmanship must never let up. In finality, the focus of this level of the Alpha mind is, as with all the others, still on survival, only this time it's in the corporate jungle, and if not there, in bramble-filled breaks and gullies of bootstrap-enabled entrepreneurship or in the cutthroat gamesmanship casinos otherwise known as the Statehouse, the White House or Parliament.

Level 1.5 thinking reigns from Main Street to Wall Street—and anywhere else there is profit to be made, a competitive edge to be sought or productivity gains to be enjoyed from finding the one best answer from among the many possibilities.

I see people enthralled by John Galt's soliloquy in *Atlas Shrugged*, and I see people appalled at the thought of any dialogue at all on reining in "conspicuous consumption," encouraging "sustainable development" or raising "ecological consciousness."

I see people who think Ronald Reagan and George W. Bush hung the moon and who would not object if Ralph Nader or Al Gore were hung *on* the moon.

I see people who don't mind having lunch with someone of color if they think it will earn them a little green but would do anything necessary to keep the same person from getting to their putting green.

I see fast-moving, hard-talking, unapologetically narcissistic business executives wearing Patek Philippe wristwatches, Prada slacks and Salvatore Ferragamo shoes speeding off in their Dodge Vipers or the occasional Lamborghini Diablo to bid on a Donald Trump apartment.

I see the same fast-moving, hard-talking, unapologetically narcissistic business executives shrug off moral responsibility for exploiting cheap labor, child labor or criminal labor as easy as they shrug off a missed exit on the turnpike; sure, you can have a quote on the record: "Who said life is fair, sports fans?"

I see dissembling thieves running many of our big corporations, lying all the way to their Swiss bank or their mistress's condominium out of both sides of their mouths.

I see ethically bankrupt lawyers who are the CEOs' and so many other crooks' first-middle-and-last lines of defense.

I see the amoral, mercenary wackos who mass-market illegal drugs, tobacco, guns and other unsafe products to a public too addicted, too enamored, too immature or too brain-damaged to just say no.

Human Beta blockers one and all—count on it.

And yet, and yet...with every step, the Alpha mind is drawing ever closer to the jumping off point for Beta. Let's say that you have found adequate psyche-freeing solutions for all the major emotional pockets of entrapment to now.

• Your feelings of abandonment are gone or no longer intense or frequent enough to be debilitating and you're very much your own person, free of the entanglements of family or dependencies on your "people."

• Your rages and shame issues are under control. You are no longer in constant danger of bodily harm, running afoul of the law and the system or seeing your opportunities truncated by abruptly damaged or severed relationships.

• Guilt issues have been defused and contained so they no longer wilt your courage and willingness to seek out what's right and true for you, as an individual.

• The snares of "the achievement complex" have been diminished in your personality. You no longer face the moment by moment dangers and personal emptiness of striving for wealth for wealth's sake, of seeking to placate and feed your fears of being outmaneuvered, of your push to overachieve as a way of not being viewed or caught out as inadequate.

That brings us to...

Sadness, loneliness and reemergent feelings of powerlessness. At this final stop for Alpha, you can expect feelings of déjà vu. Some oldies but goodies are back. Religion, for example. When we last looked, the mind focused on religion as "the truth once and for all delivered." No longer. Now, one religion is usually considered as good as any other, provided that people's needs get met, and love, compassion and sharing are paramount values. At this stop, spirituality is intended to liberate people from dogma and censorship, not encourage the qualities.

Community is back, too. But instead of "Blest be the tie that binds," the anthem of the hour is "We are the world!" This is egalitarian country, with a premium—at least in principle—on looking at many alternatives and points of view, distributing society's resources fairly and widely and taking time to reach consensus and explore the needs of the inner self, all in a spirit of unity and harmony.

Near the end of Alpha, hopes soar. But unfortunately, the behavioral waters of the world still teem with psychological sharks and scorpions. The "turn the other cheek" attitude toward what others do works only as long as the idea is reciprocated. Moreover, in the real world, putting logic in a storage closet for old thinking habits and letting feelings become the primary arbiter and guide to what you decide to do is a recipe for disaster.

In the world where power leads and money votes, justice is not only too often blind but also predictably deaf to most of the entreaties of the needful and deserving. When disaster strikes you and/or those whose causes and needs you champion, you can anticipate that you'll be hit once again with your own righteous anger at your powerlessness and paralyzed once again with sadness and loneliness. If you can mount any objectivity at all (and it may not be possible), you will realize that mostly what you've been doing is talking about the need for change or mounting ineffective protests. You have done little or nothing real to put starch or teeth in your most cherished values.

An ideal kind of place the world isn't and will never be. It continues to churn and grind, blindly, unfeelingly. And if you are an occupant of this level of the mind trapped by the above kinds of feelings, you essentially have three choices:

• You can retreat to a level of Alpha that you think is better suited for dealing with the new realities—or the return of the old realities—that you now confront.

• You can dig in and turn deeply sacrificial in defense of your end-of-Alpha ideals. That may mean accepting hardship conditions and hunkering down to hope for the return of better circumstances, times when your fragile world-view can again find ways to flower. Or it may mean simply putting yourself in danger and following your bliss and your ideals for as long as you can do it and remain alive and whole.

• If your brain is willing, if you can find the energy, if you can recognize that you have the option, if you can make the appropriate choices and if your timing is right, you can move on to Beta.

Level 1.6 thinking presses for true unity and equality for people, along with peace and balance in life. This level of thinker often goes to Starbucks, loves to vacation in Santa Barbara, Monterrey and Seattle and live in Hawaii, Vermont and New Zealand and doesn't surprise us when she or he expresses admiration for the welfare societies of the Scandinavian countries or a strong affinity for the Dutch way of egalitarian living.

I see anti-hunger protesters eating abalone and drinking expensive wines on trendy houseboats in Sausalito.

I see deconstructionists enamored with the postmodern theories of Foucault and Derrida urging everyone to get along with everyone else even as they do everything they can to negate the possibility that hardly anyone can ever get along with anyone.

I see loosey-goosey excitement spring up around such funhouse theories or fakes as The Hundredth Monkey, UFO abductions, Chief Seattle's letter on the environment and the Cherokee boyhood memoir, *The Education of Little Tree* (not to mention tarot cards, clairvoyance, palmistry, astrology, magic crystals, dowsing and divination).

I see noble-savage-minded Woodstock Nation originals who raised their children as born-free, run-free, totally liberated little tykes and ended up producing Gen X "slackers"—irreverent, blasé, irony-sated and completely indifferent to mom and dad's "let's save the world" ideals.

I see minds that don't know how to investigate a murder (JonBenét's), educate our children (pick any school suffering from grade inflation), compete intelligently with the political sharks (the many among California's members of the Green party who refuse to vote), explain reality (those suggesting we pattern ourselves after light bulbs that "self-organize" when wired together with other bulbs) or adjust to global competition (egalitarian Finland's difficulties in dealing with the runaway success of Nokia and its cell phones) or global integration (Sweden's resounding vote against the European single currency).

Basically, I see people who, in numerous ways, are walking sandwich boards for some of the kinds of personal qualities you'd expect to diminish or disappear this close to Beta. I wish them well but often am unable to take them seriously as they promote their "all opposites are equal" messages and lifestyles.

Neither does Beta.

This is where many of the boomers found themselves, and it wasn't enough. So what *is* required if getting to Beta is going to be any more than a will-o'-the-wisp pipe dream or a cheap remake of a Don Quixote potboiler?

In the next two chapters, I'm going to point out the route to Beta that seems to me to get the best gas mileage. And the one most likely to assure a successful departure from Alpha. I'm not saying that there aren't other ways to get there. And I'm not guaranteeing that this one will work. I'm saying simply that, from my perspective, this approach seems to me to be the one most likely to put you squarely and uncompromisingly on the road to a successful transition.

No sooner do we begin the process than we discover ourselves eyeball to eyeball with a neuron-shaking discovery.

Chapter 4: **The Ways of the Will**

*F*OR THE PREPONDERANCE of us, the ride through Alpha to Beta has its moments of emotional upheaval. Some of us are more dry-eyed than others as we make the passage, but it's a safe bet that no one arrives in Beta without having experienced the need somewhere along the way for a fresh box of tissues. That's why I keep returning to how we think with the heart.

Emotions are feedback. They carry information. They are advisors, some of the most important that we have. And, as we have just seen, they can be fierce controllers.

More swiftly than we can possibly forestall, they tell us what's happening in an apparatus for which feedback is in short supply. You don't have to be a neurosurgeon to understand that this well-nigh ineffably wired marvel—the most complex organ in the known universe, with more than two million miles of neurons and a staggering ten times ten one million times (ten to the millionth power) of possible on-off patterns of neuronal firing[1]—doesn't exactly supply us with operational computer readouts or pressure gauges to monitor moment to moment. Nor can we go through life attached to electrodes and EEG machines. Emotions are the fastest way we can learn what's happening below the surface of the Great Gray Eminence in our heads.

In using Clare Graves' discoveries—of Beta and his almost surgical examination of the stages of Alpha—to track the role of emotions, I've grown more and more suspicious that there has been more going on below that surface than readily meets the eye.

Psychology has assumed that as people mature—and as "the people" itself, as a species, has matured—what we have been and are primarily about is the building of a mind. Something to give us logical and symbolic sentience, the ability to introspect, the capacity to innovate and respond. Dr. Graves thought so, too. Viewed this way, the healthy incipient mind gets a few simple problems and learns what to do with them to make them tolerable or go away. Then it gets problems that are more difficult and it learns—develops—mastery of those, usually using new technologies, and grows more. Followed by even more difficult problems, and more and better technologies, and more mastery; then even more difficulty, and more growth. Bringing us to where we are now for more than a few: the threshold of Beta.

But this strikes me as altogether too mechanical. There is something seriously incomplete about this interpretation. Something vital is being overlooked. And I think it is this: that at a deeper, mostly unconscious level or at least with minimum awareness and even less understanding—at a level of the emotions—we've been doing much more than simply building a mind. As we've moved up Clare Grave's "levels of existence" spiral, we've also been providing that periodically reorganizing mind with the time and space—the opportunity—it needs to do something else. Something absolutely necessary. Something utterly instrumental.

What?

Grieve.

And why would I suggest this?

Because of another momentous theory being assembled at almost the same time that Graves was researching and formulating his all-encompassing theory of levels of human existence.

In the 1960s, Dr. Elisabeth Kübler-Ross was doing the spadework for her famous treatise, *On Death and Dying.* In this internationally acclaimed book, she outlined a way—a path—along which the emotions of loss are processed. More specifically, she sketched a trough of deep-seated feelings that terminally ill people tend to experience after being told of the inevitability of their demise. Kübler-Ross's model is, like Dr. Graves', a stage-bound model. And when we look closely at these two road maps to human realities, we are suddenly privy to a bombshell realization: their "nodal points" are virtually identical. That is, when you look closely at the stages described by Dr. Kübler-Ross for dealing with profound, inescapable grief, you see that they share remarkable similarities with the psychological growth stages that Graves mapped in Alpha and Beta![2]

Let me show you what I mean. In the first column below are the Kübler-Ross stages. In the second column are Dr. Graves' levels of existence. I invite you to compare them.

DR. ELISABETH KÜBLER-ROSS' GRIEF STAGES	THE EMOTIONS CONNECTED CLOSELY WITH DR. CLARE W. GRAVES' LEVELS OF EXISTENCE
Shock.	**Level 1.1.** *Deadened and numbed emotions.* With these most elemental of Alpha's emotional enforcers, feelings are dulled and desensitized to the point that a person barely responds, and sometimes not at all.
Denial.	**Level 1.2.** *Emotions of vulnerability and abandonment.* Such feelings drive one to seek solace, safety and security in the company of their kin, spirits, magic and sacred customs.
Outward focus to anger.	**Level 1.3.** *Rage and shame.* The emotions here drive one to all-or-nothing responses, cause him/her to lash out, ignite feelings of threat and make one determined to defend the self against criticism and avoid shame at all costs.

Inward focus to anger.	**Level 1.4.** *Guilt and self-righteousness.* Stay-in-place, punitive emotions at this level leave people rigid, deferential, resigned to one's fate, filled with judgmental oughts and shoulds and seeing no alternatives to the obvious.
Bargaining.	**Level 1.5.** *Fear of being poor and feelings of inadequacy.* Emotions here are seldom turned to "off" and constantly motivate the individual to try and improve, progress and compete, win and reach for "the good life." Virtually anything is negotiable if it reduces the stresses that come from one's ongoing concern about being out-bargained.
Depression.	**Level 1.6.** *Sadness, loneliness and recycled feelings of power-lessness.* At this point, the brain/mind's abilities for thinking in relative, context-guided ways and in situational terms leaves an individual open in priniciple to many choices and alternatives. But, alas, few are likely to do much that genuinely helps in reducing the dogma, greed, selfishness, lack of empathy and the other tragic qualities in others that works against the have-nots of the planet. This can rekindle feelings of angst and regret that the world is not a more loving, supportive kind of place and feelings of powerlessness are rekindled. When we are seriously depressed, all of us are have-nots.
Acceptance and moving on.	**Mind 2.0. (Beta)**

Is this not a riveting possibility: that almost to this very moment, the mind has been as consumed with finding a way to deal with its grief as it has been with developing a way to deal with its ongoing problems? But then, you should ask: what has the mind been grieving about?

How about this irrefutable fact and inescapable reality that confronts all of us all our days: the fact that this mind—and the container that houses it—exists.

We exist.

One day my career-minded, fashion-conscious, Gen-Xish daughter Mendy stuck her head around my office door and dropped this thought on me: "Daddy, isn't it possible that we've been grieving all this time over the fact that we were created?" She paused a moment, then added, "Life is hard."

I agree: despite all the self-protective brave fronts, brave faces and brave words we generate to try to persuade ourselves and others that it is otherwise, basically, life *is* hard.

For that reason alone, I have a soft spot in my heart for just about anything that is alive, especially when things take a turn for the worse. Even for creatures that could, if they have a chance, do me harm. The deadliest of bacteria being attacked by antibiotics. A cornered rat that is about to get its skull crushed. Captured and doomed rattlesnakes so ugly they look like warmed-over death. A rampaging grizzly bear or a spooked elephant or out-of-its-element alligator that is about to be shot...right up the chain of sentience to the meanest tattoo-festooned occupant incarcerated in the nearest supermax prison for hideous crimes committed.

Each of these entities shares something in common with each of us: none asked to be alive.

Life was thrust on us, at us, into us, without any consultation *with* us. In cosmic terms, we have all been plopped down with certain self-organizing, self-recreating and sometimes (as in the case of most humans) self-reflexive qualities and, in essence, have been dared to make something of where we find ourselves. Make something *of* ourselves. And do it in a finite amount of time and do it under what always—*always!*—ends up being arduous, less-than-optimum conditions. Regardless of our IQ. Regardless of our income. Regardless of our beginning stakes or later breaks in life.

I realize that many others have called attention to our "existential" nakedness. But I like the way Mendy put it. Thanks to my daughter, I now have a compact reason to explain countless millennia of human grieving: the irrefutable fact and the inescapable reality that we exist. Can you think of a better way to explain why the innate pattern and progression of our mental development is a virtual carbon copy of the innate pattern and progression of our grieving process in the most difficult of times? Largely unbeknownst to our conscious awareness, it would appear that we've been grieving from the get-go at the deepest levels. If so, that's another reason why Clare Graves' exploration of Alpha and discovery of Beta are so important. Grief is a way of dealing with radically changed realities. Grieving is a critical way of letting go. Of working things out. Of preparing for what comes next.

The argument being made in this book is that, from the beginning of life, the whole of this creation has been laboriously caught up, knowingly or not, in the monumental task of getting us to within striking distance of Beta. Getting us to a point where we can say "yes, but there is more" to whatever entity, force, process, circumstance or accident—you choose—that put us here. And declaring to that "first cause" or "insatiable organizing principle" or utterly indifferent but ongoing "total accident"—you choose—that we intend to act as free of it as possible! To the point where we can say: I may have allowed my freedom to be taken away in the past, and I may find my freedom foreclosed again in the future. But in the here and now, I am free to choose. *And the first choices I am going to make are what I will be responsible for!*

If this philosophic stance cops an attitude, so be it, for this is where we find ourselves at the end of Alpha. You cannot know if this is true until you choose, of course; the noted American psychiatrist Dr. Rollo May said you can't know what is true until you take a stand for it. If and when you choose to take that stand, you will see that nothing is more important to your destiny than your willingness to be responsible for what you will be responsible for.

In Beta, it can be a lengthy list. I'll start it and depend on you to keep it updated. This is one of those inventories that is never really completed or exhausted:

Your character.

Your integrity.

Your dignity.

Your anxiety.

Your use of language.

Your anger.

For saying yes and meaning it.

For saying no and meaning it.

For recognizing the critical gray areas in between and allowing them their say.

For making the decisions that need to be made.

For discovering your purpose in life.

For happiness.

For finding your own meaning.

For how much risk you will take and how you will take it.

For determining when you are to do the acting and when you are to be acted on.

For deciding how much you are going to allow the frustrations and limitations of life to upset you, knock you off course and keep you from living the kind of life you'd like to lead.

For your money. And for your debts.

For your emotions, understanding—as existential philosopher Jean-Paul Sartre and Gestalt therapist Frederick (Fritz) Perls, among others, have emphasized and as I have been emphasizing in this chapter—that emotions are a way of apprehending the world. They can show us things, teach us something.

For how much evil you are willing to tolerate, especially if you define evil, as does philosopher Peter Koestenbaum, as "the destruction of civilized values."

For not doing things simply because everyone else is doing them (like Heidegger's *Das Man*, who follows the crowd).

For learning how to cope, long before trouble arrives. And for using those coping skills effectively when it does.

For being willing to observe and learn from other people's experiences and outcomes as well as your own.

For being willing to honestly evaluate the effectiveness of your own efforts to handle situations.

For being open to many kinds of solutions—and intolerant of those that need to be interdicted or terminated.

For keeping your mind where your body is, the here and now, where you are in a much better position to be responsible for your actions.

And for understanding that, no matter what the factual balance between nature and nurture, gene and scene, turns out to be in your instance, the possibility that you may now be in a position to make the leap to Beta successfully is inseparably tied to the choices you have made. Nothing has changed nor will it ever change the reality that each and every major step that you have made along the path to increased maturity has not only been felt coming on but, of equal importance, has also been encouraged and allowed to flourish because you in no small measure chose it.

There may be many reasons—choices—why you didn't get to the threshold of Beta sooner. And now that you are finally here, even if all your other ducks are aligned propitiously, there is still one remaining hurdle: you simply cannot get to Beta without choosing it. (As one anonymous author has couched it, "Growing old is inevitable; growing up is optional.")

And, as we are about to see, there are choices, and then there are definitely Beta choices.

Chapter 5: **Accepting the Power**

THERE'S NO FREE lunch when it comes to fundamental personal change. Or, since we are discussing the move to Beta, maybe I should say there's no free launch when it comes to making the leap. When you change, a lot of other changes ensue, whether you intended for them to or not.

This is so because in changing, you have pushed away from one position in life in order to arrive at another, and it is the "pushing away" that sets so much elsewhere in motion. The inevitability of this counter-response didn't escape Sir Isaac Newton's eagle eye. He made it his third law of motion: for every action, there is an equal and opposite reaction. This is as true in the psychological world as it is in the physical world.

Your first real inkling of Beta making a difference elsewhere may come when you notice that some of the occupants of your personal world are withdrawing from you. Probably, this will not be something that you will have engineered, at least not consciously. But it is an expected, necessary consequence of your move to Beta.

Because you have moved on in such a singularly progressive fashion, the glues that have kept certain people close to you, or at least closer, may begin to lose their adhesiveness. Particular friendships or professional relationships begin to cool. Drift sets in, and you recognize it.

In your Alpha life, under such circumstances, you might have sought to make amends and reestablish the status quo. But your Beta mind will immediately help you to see that old contexts and many of the old attractions are gone, and once mutual interests and once shared appreciations are, like ice floes, moving apart.

Your world has already begun to present signals and sensations that are unrecognizable to others, and their psychological immune systems have gone to work to shut down channels to you, to keep you at bay. Eventually, if not sooner, some of them may shut you out entirely. The rejection of individuals seen or sensed as "the other" is a primordial tendency in human nature—in nature, period. In Beta, you will enjoy new skills and energies for resisting this destructive habit, but you'll not elude its consequences in others. Likely, in response, your mind will do a reverse of the Venus Flytrap. You will probably set these individuals free without guilt, resentment or thoughts of accusation or recrimination.

Because of this wholesale shakeup of the interior workings of your mind, there are crucial adjustments in your own inner mental dynamics to be worked out, too. This is why, in the previous chapter and again in this one, I've placed so much emphasis on the importance of choosing. And not just on making choices for the sake of making choices. But on making the kind of choices that can lead to Beta.

The debt that we owe Clare Graves is all the more profound because he jump-started the inquiry that has stripped the secrecy from what to choose if you are confronted with the opportunity to choose Beta.

Here are some of the more significant choices available:

■ *You can choose to be something that most others are not, and will never be.*

There have been approximately 105,472,380,169 (give or take a few billion) people who have lived on the earth.[1] Of those billions upon billions, how many of them do you think have been Beta thinkers? The percentage is so small that it is virtually negligible. Scarcely the equivalent, in my own mind's eye, to a few grains of sand in a loaded railroad hopper car. As a Beta practitioner, you'll be a rarity, no matter how many individuals manage to activate a new kind of mind for themselves in today's sometimes Beta-advantageous atmosphere.

So classes in activating Beta aren't likely to be crowded, and at times you may find yourself altogether alone. (That's no big deal, for in Beta, one is still good company.)

You are alive for no other reason than to nurture life, which you've been given, and see that it endures, and in Beta, you'll see that this is more than reason enough. This makes you a steward of life quality for every living thing now, and all living things to come. A pretty awesome responsibility. For all its achievements to now, Alpha appears increasingly unable to handle the complexities of safeguarding and maximizing the conditions for living. Tragically, it is bungling its responsibility to billions now alive and even more so, to those still to live. Your choice is to feel significant, to *be* significant and to use that significance creatively, courageously and accountably. And in every moment that you are alive, to live for life, knowing that your "personal life is absolutely unimportant, but because it is part of life, there is nothing more important in the world."[2]

To say it another way, it can be your choice to believe that while your life is insignificant in the overall scheme of things, nothing is more important to the overall scheme of things than how you live. This provides us with one more item to add to your list of responsibility issues, and it's a big one: your responsibility for life itself.

With that responsibility comes accountability, of course. For what, specifically?

Well, for a number of things.

For being effective at dealing with people from all the levels of the Alpha mind and from Beta—so as to make the whole of the mind's developmental spiral a more fair, responsive and productive place.

For using your Beta thinking skills to routinely cut to the heart of the critical issues and point to the soul of a suitable solution when you are focusing on a development or need. (On most occasions, I would expect to see such thinking appear as swiftly as an instinct, and I would expect to see it often.)

For dropping nearly all cant, jargon and argot in favor of accessible language and time-saving information transmittal as a way of moving things forward economically and expeditiously.

For subtracting the extraneous and not adding to hokum and the feel-good, the posing and the politics-as-usual.

For being able to deliver routine proof of your creativity, innovative spirit and new ideas convincingly at work.

For developing new success at the demanding art of balancing your own best self-interest with the needs and best interests of other living things.

For displaying confidence in your adroit people insights and showing that you can use them to move skillfully through the mine fields of human interactions.

For bringing forth a certain elegance and consistency in the delivery and performance of your actions and results.

What I've been describing is, of course, a full-blown litmus test for fully developed Beta thinking. I'm quite sure that you will be able to deliver on some of this now, and on much of this before too long, and on virtually all of this when your Beta mind reaches cruising attitude and speed. (And if you aren't seeing these kinds of thinking outcomes demonstrated consistently by individuals who claim to have made the leap to—and in some cases, beyond—Beta, then it is probably wise to be cautious of both their claims and their capabilities.)

■ *You can choose to give up your belief in magic.*
    This will free up your skills for using the power of the paradoxical.

In simpler times, people conjured up the magic of deified ancestors and multifarious spirits, using dreams, trances and rituals (and in less worldly cultures, they still do). Later came the magic of a transcendent First Cause, summoned to the supplicant's aid through prayer or contemplation. Then followed the magical powers of "positive thinking" and finding and applying again and again "the one best answer," with their success-summoning incantations for manipulating Earth's resources and conjuring up prosperity and the good life. After that came the New Age's metaphysical and spiritual magic—its psychic readings, crystals, tantra, Wicca, guardian angels, UFOs, aromatherapy, chakras and such and postmodernism's deconstructionist abracadabras for defanging any "facts" or "realities" that don't suit its devotees. All magic, all the time. All around you.

And we're still at it!

Listen to Hattie Bryant, the producer and host of PBC's "Small Business School": "Personal magic is unexplainable power and is seen by some as supernatural power. You have to find it for yourself. When you apply your magic to your work, you see miracles happen."

In place of these beliefs in magic as a way of solving problems, the Beta mindset puts its focus and its efforts elsewhere: on the authority of knowledge and necessity, on the guidance of reality, on personal competence, on acting responsibly in one's self interest *and* in the interest of others. And on being cautious with what we don't know and what we suspect that we may not even know that we don't know.

The late Richard Feynman, the Nobel Prize winning physicist, once confided to the audience of the BBC television program "Horizon": "I can live with doubt and uncertainty and not knowing. I think it's much more interesting to live not knowing than to have answers which might be wrong. I have approximate answers and possible beliefs and different degrees of certainty about different things, but I'm not absolutely sure of anything and there are many things I don't know anything about, such as whether it means anything to ask why we're here, and what the question might mean. I might think about it a little bit and if I can't figure it out, then I go on to something else, but I don't have to know an answer. I don't feel frightened by not knowing things...."[3]

In my opinion, that's a thoroughly Beta point of view: *Whereof we cannot speak, thereof we should remain silent.*

Life's inherent contradictions are everywhere. One of the things that makes Alpha so deadly and destructive for so many is that their skills for handling paradox and uncertainty are so poor. That includes ambiguities, conflicting feelings, clashing opinions, contradictory ideas, possibilities that are opposites and possibilities for not ever knowing. Instead of embracing Richard Feynman's agree-not-to-need-to-know approach, the Alpha thinker can be faulted more times than not for relegating to the realm of magic those things that lack square corners and clear-cut answers. Or any answers at all.

AN EXPANDING SPACE

With each step "up the rung" in Alpha, the mind grows more spacious. It is capable of admitting more and more paradox, harboring more and more polarities or conflicts, simultaneously. And this inner tension is, as the philosopher Kierkegaard, pointed out, the source of our passion. "The thinker without a paradox is like a lover without feeling," he concluded. "A paltry mediocrity."

Choose Beta and you'll find that suddenly your brain—and your appetite for paradox, and passion—is becoming very spacious indeed.

More than one of the existentialist philosophers has argued that the biggest paradox that confronts us is one that we face almost every moment of our lives: do we choose for the future (with all its uncertainties and unknowns) or do we choose the status quo (where we may feel and even be safer but may also miss one opportunity after another)? Beta says you need to keep both options open, simultaneously. And, choosing the future with all its unknowns introduces a paradoxical outcome of its own: the more we permit the future to call in question the reality of who we are, the more authentic our being in the present tends to become.

Harnessing the power of polarities is the wellspring of nearly all creativity, growth and improvement. It is a specialty and staple of the Beta mind and thinker, and it is free to flower in the absence of that old bugbear of false hopes and distraction: magic.

■ *You can choose to live a life much freer of inner compulsiveness and anxiety than most others.*

Normally I am not one to remember much about my dreams. But one night not long ago, upon awakening in the morning, I remembered three dreams vividly and in detail because each had been profoundly disturbing. I could not recall having awakened and announced a nightmare more than once or twice since I was a child. Now, I had a trio of them to talk about, all from one night's phantasmagoric and troubled passage.

The first dream had been a Dick and Jane kind of thing. Nothing elaborate. Just me seeing myself awake in my bed and hearing this terrible, soulless scream. Even now, as I relive it, once again goose bumps are popping up all over my body. That night, I awoke immediately, walked to the bathroom and drank a glass of water as I searched for an explanation. I wondered if my dad, who was in a nursing home close by, had just died, and I had somehow tuned instantly into his absence. (Not the case, thankfully.) I sat up in bed for a while, my shoulders twitching involuntarily several times as I replayed that unearthly scream.

Later in the night, the second all-surreal, all-in-my-head video spooled by: I'm perched high in a gallows, looking down. One person is already dangling lifelessly to my left. Immediately below me, looking up as if he's unaware of mortal danger he's in, is one of America's most well-known political figures, a noose around his neck. Coming awake again, I find my incredulity growing. I remember quizzing myself about any medications I might have taken before retiring that could be causing this. And realizing there had been none.

No sooner, or so it seemed, was I asleep again than my private Stephen King was back on the job. This time, I found myself pushing against a door on the second floor of our family residence only to encounter resistance. Pushing harder, I gained a space wide enough to get my head through and peered into the semi-darkness. Dimly, I could see a body, a dismembered body. Hurrying away, I summoned the police. Soon after, law officers were telling me they had found eight more bodies in our house and were still searching.

It is good—and this is why I am subjecting you to this account of my night of morbidity—for us to be reminded in undiluted fashion that we are never more than a hair's breath removed from anxiety, and for good reason. Experienced from Alpha or Beta, life is no cakewalk. It is full of surprises. Many times we can feel helpless, out of control. All around us all the time, there are people who aren't doing well even when we are. At any given moment, people in the next town or city, the next subdivision, the next block, the next house, sometimes the next room, are being permanently affected: injured, ruined, perhaps annihilated. Death is omnipresent, sometimes coming at the end of a long, fruitful life but also too often, snatching away the young, the good, the gifted who have not yet fulfilled any or much of their promise. Often, reliable justice seems a mockery. Life is too complicated, power too unevenly distributed, and it's all too easy to be too blinded by one's own cares and fears to be that concerned about the injustices and shortfalls that others are suffering.

Against such a Hieronymus Bosch-like tapestry, is it possible to choose to live a life largely free of inner compulsiveness and anxiety?

Obviously, I believe that it is.

ACCEPTING ACCEPTANCE

I'm reminded of the comforting, encouraging words of the German-born, American-adopted theologian-philosopher Paul Tillich. In the 1950s, he wrote a book, *The Courage to Be*, that electrified many. It was an international bestseller, and a half-century later a new edition has recently been released. We might say that his views on how anyone might respond to "the profound disquietude provoked by modernity's confrontation with death and meaninglessness"[4] placed him, along with his contemporary Clare Graves, in the forefront of the search for a way to exit Alpha.

Being a theologian, Tillich thought—and talked—in theological terms. That explains why he would describe the courage to be as "the courage to accept oneself as accepted in spite of being unacceptable." In one of his most famous sermons, he suggested that if you can evoke the courage to be even in a time of despair over the lost of meaning, it can be as if you hear a voice saying, "You are accepted. You are accepted, accepted by that which is greater than you, and the name of which you do not know. Do not ask for the name now. Perhaps you will find it later. Do not try to do anything now; perhaps later you will do much. Do not seek for anything; do not perform anything; do not intend anything. Simply accept the fact that you are accepted! If that happens to us, we experience grace."[5]

Most existentialist commentators will suggest that we have finally run out of gods and that it's time we accepted that and courageously reached within ourselves and dealt with the circumstances. Umberto Eco, the novelist and semiotician, said it this way in *Foucault's Pendulum*: "I have come to believe that the whole world is an enigma, a harmless enigma that is made terrible by our own mad attempt to interpret it as though it had an underlying truth."[6]

But I don't think this is quite the discovery that awaits us at the end of Alpha or if it is, that Dr. Eco says it quite the way I'd prefer. I much prefer that quote from Dr. Tillich's "You Are Accepted" sermon and all that it implies.

Don't worry about all the "God" talk or the "there is no God" talk, counsels Tillich. Don't try to explain it or use it to explain something else. Don't try to act on it, or do anything with it. Just accept the fact that you are accepted. End of sentence. End of grieving. End of disenfranchisement. End of worrying about being half animal (body)/half god (mind and spirit), or (in the unforgettable words of the late psychotherapist-polymath Ernest Becker) "a god who shits." End of Alpha. Bring on Beta!

So in the end, I vote with Dr. Tillich, not with Dr. Eco, even if the reason may be merely—largely—a stylistic difference.

Since grace presupposes that you are part of something bigger than you (however you wish to define that), it feeds the courage of confidence, Tillich said.

With the courage to be—the will to *will* courageously, the will to *choose* courageously—comes the self-affirmation of being, even in the face of death, which is the ultimate experience of meaninglessness.

CALL TO RESPONSIBILITY

With the courage to be and the courage to choose, you can put the old anathemas of Alpha behind you. All those fears, all that guilt, all those insecurities, all that bone-chilling loneliness— all that always-just-beneath-the-surface-of-things doubt-filled *anxiety*! You may be able to find good in the face of evil. You may be able to believe in love even in the demonstration of hatred. You may be able to perform competently, reliably, functionally and naturally, with an energy that revivifies, moment by moment, time and again, because you've moved past the fear of nonbeing into a new kind of existence, one where you truly feel free to be.

(I would be remiss if I didn't include one important asterisk here. Researchers have made it clear that there is a valuable, even critical, role to be played by feelings of anxiety in responsible forward-looking decision-making. "The capacity to experience anxiety and the capacity to plan are two sides of the same coin," says psychologist David Barlow.[7] Experts like Barlow suggest that we aren't likely to make forward-looking decisions unless thinking about the delayed consequences of such decisions immediately evokes emotions like anxiety within us at the moment we are contemplating making such decisions. What changes in Beta, in my opinion, is that "less is more" as far as anxiety goes. We not only experience less anxiety than in the levels of Alpha but we also have more opportunities cognitively to channel how we respond to anxiety—in short, to experience less contaminating and paralyzing fear as we think about the future.)

Again, let's call in Dr. Graves, the discoverer of Beta. He felt so profoundly about his conclusions that, as you listen to his descriptions of Beta, it almost sounds like you are listening to a reading in a great cathedral. Here's a paraphrase of what he said he found after studying individuals he believed had achieved this quality of human mind and maturity:

"People in Beta do not fear death, nor God, nor their fellow humans. Magic and superstition hold no sway over them. Beta man and woman are not mystically minded though they live in the most mysterious of 'mystic' universes.

"Beta man and woman require little, compared to their Alpha ancestor, and get more pleasure from simple things than the Alpha man and woman think they get. Beta people know how to get what is necessary to their existence and do not want to waste time getting what is superfluous. They will get satisfaction out of doing well but will get no satisfaction from praise for having done so.

"Beta people know what power is, how to create and use it, but they also know how limited is its usefulness. In living their lives, they constantly take into account their personal qualities, social situation, body and power, but these are of no great concern to them. They seek to do better but are not ambitious. They will strive to achieve—but through submission, not domination.

"They enjoy the best of life, of sex, of friends, and comfort that is provided, but they are not dependent on them. They are no longer living in a world of unbridled self-expression and self-indulgence, or in a world of reverence for the individual, but in one whose rule is: Express self, but only so that all life can continue. What commands their unswerving loyalty, and in whose cause they are *ruthless*, is the continuance of life on this earth [italics his]."[8]

I doubt that you'll ever find a better prescription for living a life less affected by inner compulsiveness and anxiety than most lives. Or a greater call to be personally responsible.

■ *You can choose to devote yourself at every opportunity to helping the young—your children, grandchildren, anyone else's children, children you may teach, children you may coach, any child you love and have the capacity to influence and, most importantly, the child in you—move along the mind's highway toward Beta.*

And how might you do this? Here are ideas:

• Make sure they grow up with at least one loving adult always close at hand, with schools capable of challenging and educating them and with at least one teacher at all times who thinks they are special and allows them to share in her or his own idealism.

• Help instill and encourage an innate curiosity in them that refuses to take "no" or "go away" as acceptable answers on issues and in circumstances that offer them the opportunity to discover something valuable for themselves. Teach them how to distinguish adults who will let them operate outside the box—and better still, expand the box—from all the others. Strengthen their skills for handling the naysayers who can be counted on to dump cold water on their fledgling efforts to take a road less traveled and pursue ideas not yet recognized or accepted as the norm.

• Help them learn to recognize El Toro Poo-Poo when they step in it, no matter how many camouflaging fragrances have been added or what it is being called. As soon as they are old enough to handle it, encourage them to develop a continuous, low-boiling impatience with any explanation they are given by someone who professes to know things they should never question or is trying to provide them with explanations they should consider incontestable.

• Assure them that if and when they are mistreated, lied to, ignored without good reason or otherwise abused, they have a right to be angry—and when the opportunity arises, the right to retaliate. Teach them how to be good at it and how to protect themselves when they do.

• As soon as is practicable, make sure they understand the value of learning how to do something to support themselves other than hiring out to someone else and ending up in an employer's straitjacket. This way, their job can never be used to control them or diminish their passion for discovering what might work and then seeing how it plays out.

• Show them how to learn new things every step of the way—right to their final breaths.

• Help them understand the danger of adopting without examination and introspection the beliefs of those whom they befriend or affiliate with. The sooner they can see that running with a crowd doesn't automatically mean they have to run with the beliefs of others, the less likely group-think will stymie the maturing of their own mind and judgment. It's critical for Beta-thinkers-in-training to be comfortable and skilled at asking big questions and working out their own answers.

• Introduce them as quickly and skillfully as possible to the innately deceptive nature of their own brain. Let them know that it's okay to make that brain defend and explain itself. Encourage them to solicit outside opinions when they sniff their own inner duplicity in avoiding hard choices or acknowledging unpleasant truths. Embolden their willingness to intervene in their own thought processes and say no, yes or whatever needs to be said to the parts of their thinking apparatus that need to be reigned in, checkmated or reexamined. And, as soon as possible, help them to understand that even with the Beta thinker's skills, it can still be difficult as the devil to always know what they are up to. Sometimes, they just won't have the foggiest idea.

THE INATTENTION FACTOR

The issue—and the reality—is that, at least prior to Beta, this most complex of biological machines stuffed into our economy studio of a cranial vacuity was not fabricated to explain itself well but to keep its user alive long enough to have as many offspring as possible.

When it has paid any attention at all, the brain has chopped the world into bits and pieces mostly based on their survival utility. Even today, unless assisted by good, objective science and Beta's additional level of close introspection of its own workings and output, the brain is likely to talk about both itself and the world in terms of fairy tales, tribal rituals, grand mythologies, folk psychologies, Iron Age religious beliefs—and magic. It usually has no idea just how inobservant and inattentive it can be.

Do I really expect you to choose to have these kinds of conversations and interactions and reactions with—and influences on—children?

Yes. Where the opportunity arises and where it is appropriate and where there is a mind that can be influenced by such actions and interventions on your part, I do.

And, in reality, is there an ulterior motive in drawing your attention to this list of adventurous, free-thinking, free-spirited admonitions at this particular moment?

Yes, there is.

These are attitudes, qualities and actions that never lose their efficacy or importance in paving the way for the arrival of the Beta mind. In you, in anyone. Choose to take them seriously, and you've added to Beta's launch capacity, however close or distant you may be from actually moving into the orbit of this new way of thinking.

■ *You can choose to deal courageously with what is coming.*
Can you feel it? I'm betting that you can. Sometimes, I compare it to cruising along a well-tended stretch of asphalt, one clearly routed with signposts and mile markers, when without warning a feral environment brutishly asserts itself. The smoothness in the road gives way to teeth-shaking, safety-threatening granularity and much worse. Pot holes. Uneven surfaces. Obstacles sud-

denly in the right-of-away. Boulders hurdling past. High cross winds that whip potentially lethal debris dangerously across your path as you struggle to avoid a calamitous ejection from the roadway.

The times seem to resemble those that writer John Clute has described: "The planet is buzzing with human activity, and with stress. The human race itself is more active than ever before, more numerous, more powerful, more dangerous, more happy, more desolate, more alive, more dead."[9]

I don't think very many in Alpha, even among supposedly well-educated and well-read folks, understand just how much the rules for developing and sustaining the fitness of the species are changing as we speak—or how important it is in the gambles we are taking in behalf of our human nature that we play the limited chips we hold as smartly and intelligently and intuitively as possible. I don't think it is inaccurate or unfair to suggest that too few realize how crucial it is to think these days at a premium, to think through, around and over the cheap answers and seek, instead, the steeper, more challenging payoffs.

And that only a still quite small minority, maybe enough for the long haul but then maybe not, understand that the best off-road vehicle in sight for ramping up human thinking capabilities to compete with changes arriving exponentially with each new round of challenges is the mindset to be found in Beta.

At this stage, Beta is hardly ever operational in the power centers—in top-level leaders in business, politics, sports, professional government ranks, religion, medicine, science, the law, the media, education, the military or hardly any other of our customary, workaday institutions—in those individuals who are so well known that their names are virtually household words.

NOT AUTOMATIC

Hopefully, some day Beta will be operational in many such minds. But for the moment, the processes needed to produce Beta are alien to and largely unnoticed by most people at the top. This leaves their Beta thinking skills just as dormant and undeveloped as those in billions of other, less powerful and influential mortals. This is, I think, a danger for many who see themselves as responsible, forward-thinking business people or political leaders or educational pacesetters or any of a couple of hundred other critical categories of influence and accountability. If they fail to discern the need for Beta, and fail to involve themselves instrumentally in all that is necessary to activate it in themselves, then these power-wielders could easily discover themselves one day soon stuffed in with the laundry, bleached white and hung out to dry.

And then there are the character-building times we have been going through!

Not only in America but throughout the world, we all have had to deal with the new millennium's heavy diet of toil and trouble: the unspeakable 9/11 tragedy, the ongoing terrorist threat, the wars in Afghanistan and Iraq, the battered geopolitical comity between nations and the tensions between opposing policy camps, the seemingly unsolvable Israeli-Palestinian conflict, the implosion of the stock market, the telecommunications industry's epic downturn and bubble-bursting depression, the relentless spread of AIDS in Africa, the Columbia space shuffle disaster, the worldwide SARS illness outbreak, the massive power blackouts in the Northeastern U.S. and Canada and in Italy and a disheartening number of disruptive, depressing spin-offs from these and other misfortunes. All this against life as usual, in which in so many locations the gains of the haves grow more pronounced in comparison to the meager and disappearing resources of the have-nots.

It may be true that some things in life will never change. And for certain, some things in life come automatically.

Your first tooth. Your first word. Your first step. Puberty and all its hormones. Your first job. Your first visitor from a neighborhood religious institution proselytizing at your front door. Your first high-blood pressure warning. The first time you experience a "senior moment"—and someone brazenly points it out. Your first real thoughts about retiring. Your last breath. But Beta isn't like that. Beta doesn't come automatically. I hope by now, one revolutionary idea has come through loud and clear: that activating Beta in yourself, for your own private, self-guided uses and applications as well as broader applications, will come about only if, when you sense the opportunity, you choose for it to come about. Quoting the Danish philosopher again, it was Kierkegaard who noted that you can understand life looking backward but you must live it going forward. And you shape the quality of the living by making good, sometimes courageous, choices.

I know people who have wanted it badly and searched for some means of entering Beta for much of their adult lives—and could never make it happen. In simple terms, there were aspects of Alpha they couldn't let go of. More often than not, it has been an "aloneness" issue. There was something compelling about their hunger for the company and approval of others that kept them from standing and proceeding alone when it was needed or advantageous. And so they remained conjoined—in Alpha—with their beloved friends and companions and their friends' and companions' cherished beliefs and values...to their obvious periodic grief and disappointment at not getting to where they wanted to go. At other times, it has been a competency issue. They simply could not find ways to keeping from repeatedly shooting themselves in the foot, not infrequently precisely on those occasions when it counted most.

CHOOSING YOUR LEVERAGE

As Clare Graves' brilliant discoveries constantly remind us, improving the mind is a dominion reserved exclusively for the psychologically aware, ambitious and responsive. *Getting to Beta requires that you be pro-active with your personal opportunities and choices!* Mother Nature can supply you with the genetic wherewithal to put a healthy, striving Beta brain together. Uncle Culture can follow along with hale and hearty living conditions and opportunities: loving parents, supportive teachers, suitable economic conditions for producing an adequate or better-than-adequate living, a democratic society, a thriving, vital marketplace of ideas and other brain stimuli. And Father Time can put you on the scene at the right place and the right moment—when there is a need to counter stagnation in the general ethos of the culture and a looming want for whole societies to think differently to keep this calculated gamble called life going.

But in the end, *you* must choose Beta.

This is your freedom. This is your leverage. This is your methodology and, in the end, your release.

This is the route up, out and forward; it's the only way.

I recommend the Beta choice in no uncertain terms.

Quoting Dr. Graves again: "After being hobbled by the more narrow animal-like needs, by the imperative need for sustenance, the fear of spirits and other predatory persons, by the fear of trespass upon the ordained order, by the fear of people's greediness and the fear of social disapproval"—in other words, by Alpha— "*suddenly* human cognition is free [italics his]."[10]

If there are still courageous decisions to be made, I am encouraging you to muster all the resources at your disposal to help you make them. If you need to second-guess yourself, please do. If you need to reread this chapter again, do that, too. If you need the help of a professional therapist or counselor or mentor or just a supportive friend who will listen as you seek to deal with lingering issues from Alpha, please find one. From this point forward in this work, we will assume that you are ready to explore what a liberated human cognition can provide you, and you in turn—from Beta—can offer the world.

But I must warn you: Not a single human who successfully makes the transition finds the advance to Beta an easy stroll up the mountain and a trouble-free leap across the great divide. There are many different kinds of stories about how people have gotten to Beta. But I know one best of all, and I'd like to share it with you.

Chapter 6: **The Story of One**

*I*NEVER DELIBERATELY** set out for Beta. That doesn't seem to be the way things work. But in retrospect, it would appear that I set out for somewhere fairly early. You probably did, too.

In telling you about my travels, I have only one purpose in mind: providing you with the most authentic, close-up, first-hand view of these things happening to a real person that I'm likely to come across.

As I look back at my own experiences, perhaps the most succinct thing I can tell you about the brain/mind of a Beta-user-in-training is this: somewhere along the way you develop a knack for, and learn to be comfortable with, putting yourself squarely in the widest available path of advancing life. If you are able to remain there, you may eventually find yourself with a shot at the optimal psychology of your times. Maybe even gain an opportunity to morph to the most audacious world-view of the species then up and running. It so happens that the optimal psychology and most audacious world-view of our era is Beta. And that for those who have the opportunity and make the effort, the switchover is always a highly customized experience.

For me, activating Beta has been a stop-and-go, raucous, fly-by-the-seat-of-my-pants undertaking. Along the way, there has been much pleasure, joy and satisfaction. Occasionally, I'll allude to some of those lighter, brighter moments. But for the most part, the color of this account will be gun-metal gray because getting to

Beta, or so my memory of the passage tells me, has required that I keep an eye peeled for the serious side and its consequences.

I happened to have been born severely hearing impaired—the general level of loss approaches 60 to 70 percent in both ears—and did not acquire my first hearing aids until I was 14.

Not only do I not communicate normally in the world of the hearing but neither was I taught the sign language of the deaf. Nature then did what it had to do: acutely sharpen my powers of concentration, observation and interpretation. I was in the eighth grade by the time anyone tried to teach me how to read lips. But it wasn't necessary. I'd taught myself.

Reading lips is an iffy art at best. You may still miss one-third to a half of what is being said in the good times—and too often, you miss just about everything. If a person's back is turned toward you, if an individual talks too rapidly or doesn't move their lips appreciably as they speak or if they cover their lips at any time while speaking, then during those times you "hear" nothing. At such times, the troubleshooting manual for people like me advises, "Fake it 'til you blow your cover, then cover your tracks while back-pedaling like crazy!" Thus any conversational encounter is actually a success if you have been able to avoid sounding at some point in the dialogue like the village idiot.

You may wonder why my parents didn't see that I was outfitted sooner with hearing aids. I've wondered, too. After I was grown, we talked about it. They, too, were mystified at why they waited so long. As best I can tell, these were their reasons: (1) The expense (in those days, hearing aids were costly). (2) I never ask for them. (3) I was so convincing in faking it.

Consigned by genetic fiat to a loner's world, not surprisingly, as a child, I quickly took on a loner's outlook: controlling, sensitive to intrusion, jealous of prerogatives, blunt-spoken, saddled by much anger and shame, prone to lash out and retaliate, retreat and sabotage, especially if overlooked, ignored or excluded.

Barred from ordinary, satisfactory participation in other people's worlds because I couldn't communicate dependably with them, I did the next best thing: create my own unique personal world and where there was incongruence or a conflict in desires or judgment insist that the worlds of others yield to my own.

Consequently, during childhood and for a long time afterwards, my entering an occupied room or getting involved in an activity or process with two or more people had a way of immediately and abruptly altering interpersonal rhythms and agendas. Not infrequently, it signaled a processional train wreck not too far ahead. It was just the way I coped, the way I survived.

Fortunately, the coins that are people come with two sides. On the other side of me was tenacity, curiosity, a gift for innovating and pushing against limits, a knack for describing and naming things and, as the "physically challenged" often acquire, more than a little street-smartness, toughness and determination. Paradoxical combo, this. Sometimes it caused doors to be slammed in my face. But it opened them, too. On the whole, if you think about it, such a regimen is not all that bad a preparation for much of life.

GOSPEL PREACHER'S SON

That I was also born the son of a fundamentalist, Southern-styled preacher who bounced around back-country pulpits in five states—15 pulpits in all during his 52 years in the Christian ministry—contributed in both positive and negative ways.

One of the pluses in this equation was that my father was far brighter and better informed than most fundamentalist ministers. He had three years of college. He competed in university debate from the Texas Hill Country to West Point—and excelled. He was quick on his feet and a far better orator than most of his peers, who were often little more than self-anointed, self-taught "cowboy camp meeting"-styled pulpit-thumpers and Bible page-flippers. Many of those who heard him preach thought my father might just be one of the smartest persons they'd ever met, and that was probably so.

He was intensely curious about how at least some parts of the world worked and was well-read, albeit in a narrow-cast way.

His personal library contained somewhere between 5,000 and 10,000 books, journals and magazines, I'd guess, though I must admit that most of them pertained to dense, obscure religious themes and were, to me, stultifyingly boring in spite of my best efforts to profess an interest in them. Nevertheless, I plowed doggedly through the basics. To this day, I can still rattle off the names of the sons of Jacob, starting with Reuben and ending with Benjamin—12 in all—-in a fusillade, like my ABCs. My father insisted that I memorize some such Bible-based list or scripture text every Saturday morning before he'd yield pocket change for Johnny Mack Brown, Roy Rogers or Hopalong Cassidy at the Rex or the State or the Majestic cinema that afternoon.

His father had plowed much more modest ground, figuratively and literally. My paternal grandfather, a small, tentative man born in Georgia, had raised cotton (when there was rain) and a family of four on the nematode-infested, nitrogen-depleted red dirt of a small farm near Sweetwater, Texas. My grandmother had stayed at home to raise two boys, though much of the time she faked one variety of illness or another and just stayed in bed. For much of his life, after walking several miles home from school, rain or shine, my father had played nursemaid to a pseudo-invalid mother before turning to the hard chores assigned by an often abusive, poor-spirited father.

By the time I knew them, both of my father's parents had mellowed into sweeter, more caring people. But it was easy to see that being raised by them had left my dad permanently scarred. And though he was ambitious in his way and gave it his best shot more times than not, he was never able to move all that much beyond either the psychological or geographical confines of his upbringing.

Even when he was there for his nearly deaf son, he often managed to queer the outcome. He repeatedly got his instructions wrong. He sometimes let a bad temper spoil good moments. He could turn unreasonably sanctimonious or unnecessarily unctuous on a dime. He often failed to do the commonsensical thing. Or he simply acted stupid when he obviously knew what it was that he *should* be doing.

During my third year, he backed his dun-colored '41 Pontiac coup over my Radio Flyer—smashed it almost in two. I don't recall doing so, but family legend has it that not long after, during a family drive, I leaned over from the backseat and gravely spoke my mind. "Daddy," I told him, "if you had been watching where you were going, you wouldn't have run over my red wagon." I was to learn that watching where he was going was not one of my father's strong suits.

But all that, of course, focuses on the darker side of a two-part equation. Back on the sunny side, there were many, many hours of pleasurable, bond-creating father-and-son conversation and activity. For all our perceptual differences and frequent interpersonal conflicts, ours was an unusually deep communion for a father and a son—in those times, for those places.

ON THE ROAD

As any minister's daughter or son can attest, while growing up, you must share your parent with the community to a degree probably not exceeded by any of the children in town other than, perhaps, the town doctors' or the town drunk's. But you also often have extraordinary access. Usually, the parsonage is next door to the church, across the street or down the block. When I wanted to see my dad, I just ambled across the lawn, moseyed up the stairs and shoved open his office door. Usually, I didn't even bother to knock. Didn't even think about knocking. Around-the-clock access to your daddy's study was a given, a preacher's kid's prerogative.

During those formative years, my dad and I talked about nearly everything. Politics (he was a Truman-loving Democrat until he met Ike). Finances (it was clear that he and my mother had more high-drama encounters over money than Gary Cooper had with outlaws). God (he usually preferred to let his well-thumbed American Standard version of the scriptures speak for itself on this subject, and it always did). Cars (he loved Pontiacs and

Cadillacs, thought less of Fords and Studibakers). Texas (it was the mother's milk of statehood). Building things (no sooner did he cross paths in *Popular Science* or *Mechanics Illustrated* with a set of plans for a weaving loom, airboat, canoe, slingshot or nutcracker than we were out in the garage constructing one). Snakes (we both hated rattlers most, he because he'd been bitten by one as a child). Floods (Noah's was our favorite, but Wewoka Creek, in central Oklahoma, could mount a nasty one, too, we both agreed). Food (having once worked in a slaughterhouse, he wouldn't eat frank-furters while I could scarf a plateful without a thought to their ori-gins or contents). Eternity (we both agreed it was a hell of a long time to suffer from untreated burns and were pretty much content to leave it at that).

During the summers, I often had my father's uninterrupted attention for hours at a time. That was because the distances between towns in Texas and Oklahoma can be long and vacant.

With little to look at when we were en route to gospel meet-ings or other places where he was to speak, he and I talked. And talked. Usually, we drove the family Pontiac, though sometimes we took the train. Once we boarded the Texas & Pacific and trav-eled all the way from West Texas to Tennessee, where I was born. (Going down, we ate the cheapest thing on the dining car menu—"Boston Baked Beans and Brown Bread"—for three meals in suc-cession because, as usual, my dad was nearly broke. Coming home, he'd been paid for a week of preaching twice a day, and we luxuriated on tuna fish and beef stew.)

Once we drove all night so he could speak at chapel the next morning at a Christian college in Arkansas on one of his favorite topics: "The Hydrogen Bomb and Our Best Defense Against It." (God, of course.) The one thing I never remembered him mention-ing—not a single time—as I was growing up was sex, as in "how to." *However*...in clear view on his office shelves there were sever-al fully illustrated "sex manuals." In addition, there were fifty-plus years of bound back issues of *National Geographic*. It took me several years to puzzle out the purpose of a male erection, but I was something of an expert on external female anatomy by my eighth birthday (all those full-color *au naturel* photos of tribal women and girls in the *Geographic*). Dad said the sex manuals were for his pre-marital counseling sessions. But he liked the *Geographic* himself. I'll never know if we were both attracted to the same pictures. Or for the same reasons.

For all his faults and failings, my father was still basically good to go in my eyes because at his core he was a good-hearted, scrupulously honest, altogether righteous man. He'd have been a natural for joining Lot as a second reason for removing Sodom and Gomorrah from God's cooking griddle. And I was his little man. I loved him deeply, flaws and all. Right up to and beyond his passing at age eighty-eight, not so very long ago.

GUILT TALK

I'll speak of my mother—a sweet, dear woman—momentarily, but there is no understanding my advance toward Beta without accounting for my father. He frequently administered corporal punishments for my ample misdeeds—probably more often and more punishing than was necessary. Usually, this involved a good, stiff belting while I was bent over an aging commode in some barely rain-proof church parsonage in one nondescript Texas or Oklahoma farm town or another. Because of what sometimes stopped just short of child-abuse, I had little trouble moving from Alpha's tribal-and-family-oriented Level 1.2 to its expressionistic Level 1.3: using rage and shame to stoke a desire to be my own individual in this war-is-hell, where-only-the-fit-survive world. To this day, those who know me well will have little trouble recognizing the lasting influences of having so much pious, upright, holier-than-thou, belt-swinging authoritarianism to rebel against.

On the other hand, developing guilt wasn't that much of a strain, either.

Guilt-encouraging talk was plentiful at our household as I was growing up. This included frequent warnings of Judgment Day, the fires of hell and the horrors of being damned for eternity and, on the other hand, the bail-out benefits of what the God of our fathers had done to provide a worm like me with a second chance. In addition, there was mandatory attendance at well-argued thrice weekly sermons from the paterfamilias. Somehow, he always seemed to be looking squarely at me as he closed his sermon and said, "The Lord bids you come."

One summery Sunday when I was nine, it was impossible to stand being numbered among the damned any longer. Within minutes of walking forward to the front of the congregation—what the Methodists termed the altar call but the Churches of Christ called the invitation—I suddenly realized to my horror that I had just been baptized by full-body immersion in my only pair of long dress pants (even though it was standard fare for my father to advertise as part of his closing sermon spiel that "garments are provided for both men and woman"; that Sunday, they weren't available for a little squirt like me). This meant that I would be wearing a pair of short pants to my first communion service that evening. Only seconds into being saved, I was mortified. So guilt, and shame, I had a'plenty. At the time, I had no way of knowing, but another stage of Alpha—Level 1.4—had been nailed, and Beta was a little closer.

The next step in Alpha is developing the part of yourself that is willing to compete. This is the part that will motivate you to step out ahead of less intrepid, ambitious souls and hunt for a way to make good things happen, especially for your personal benefit. Again for me—and please again bear in mind that my experience is not to be taken as any general template—development of this step toward Beta started early and moved strongly forward as the years passed.

THE FREE-ENTERPRISING ROUTE

My parents were never really hardscrabble poor, but as I've already hinted, they were usually in debt and constantly bemoaning their financial circumstances, especially to their children. The solution seemed clear to me: make more money.

So at age seven, I peddled vegetables in the neighborhood out of my (new) Radio Flyer. At age ten, I was searching the barrow ditches along highways in far West Texas for discarded pop bottles because each one was worth the return of a three-cent deposit at grocery stores in Pecos, Texas.

At age eleven, I was baby-sitting the daughters of the infamous Texas swindler Billy Sol Estes (a surprisingly nice, genuinely agreeable guy when not faking mortgages and fleecing investors). One Saturday night he paid me in silver dollars. Just stood there dropping them one at a time into my outstretched palm until I said stop. I was so startled I didn't say anything at all for the longest time. (As you might expect, my dad insisted that I return most of my windfall to Mr. Estes at Sunday School the following morning.) At one time I had hopes that Estes might commit to providing the funding I thought would make me the world's youngest and biggest parakeet-breeding tycoon, but he never answered my letters. At age thirteen, I acquired a printing press and sold business cards. In high school, I was the church janitor. In college, my family was still as broke as ever, so I sold frozen steaks to help pay my expenses. (Later, supported by a loyal young wife, I went on to get a graduate degree at The University of Texas at Austin.)

In my early and mid thirties, I did something that few journalists, and, as best I could tell, not a single one in my sizable city, thought could be done: year after year, I made a six-figure income selling magazine articles and other kinds of writing as a freelance. It helped that I was a stringer (part-time, non-staff correspondent) for *Business Week* (for which I actually wrote a couple of cover stories and turned down more than one job offer), *Newsweek*, *The Economist* and other publications in my city, state or region. In a stretch of a few years, I also wrote several stories for *Reader's Digest* and did a couple of special sections for *Fortune* and otherwise published in about 225 other journals and newspapers around the world. *Writer's Digest*, the industry's trade journal, once ran a cover piece I wrote coaching others how to earn an impressive income year after year—and we both got called liars.

My peers in my trade simply didn't have the faith in their earning capacity that I had in mine.

Remaining in my preferred mode of employment—that is, self-employed—I did something else that many attempt but fail to achieve: write a best-selling book.

By the early nineties, *Strategy of the Dolphin®: Scoring a Win in a Chaotic World*, written with a bright young self-development theorist Paul L. Kordis, had built a near-fanatical following among late-stage Alpha readers interested in enhancing their personal change and performance skills. In translations, the book topped out at No. 3 on an important French-language business book best-seller list, and was fifth on *Capital* magazine's list in Germany. Self-help bookstores in Germany, Switzerland and Austria rated it No. 1. In the U.S., it was a Literary Guild alternate selection. A speaker before England's House of Lords quoted from the book. One smitten small press owner went so far on his Web site to name *Strategy* as "one of 17 books in the English language you absolutely must read." So, handling the personal achievement aspects of Alpha, while not always a snap, usually wasn't all that much of a sweat either. Consider the ticket for that stage of Alpha—Level 1.5—punched. Onward and upward.

ADVENTURER'S STREAK

That left two more challenges. One was triggering the wrap-up stage for Alpha, the one where you take stock of the toll and damage you've done to yourself and others as you swashbuckled your way up by your bootstraps. Do personal penance and, more importantly, personal healing. Of yourself, relationships, inner sorrows and outward connections. And after that comes the big one: finding the desire, resolve, fortitude and requisite insight needed to break free of Alpha and move on to Mind 2.0, to Beta, provided that the opportunity, the energy, the good fortune and the right choices materialize.

Looking back, I can see that the trenching for my exit from Alpha, like so much else in my unexpected-outcome-filled life, began to be put in place early. Some of it came from the father who never came close to delivering on his promise as an exceedingly bright (valedictorian of his high school class), handsome, articulate farm lad. And some of it came from the pretty, musically talented (gifted pianist, professional-quality singing voice) mother who never professed to be anything but proud of her first-born son's ambitions but harbored no real aspirations of her own other than being First Lady for her wayfaring husband's out-of-the-way congregations. Both of these sometimes problematic parents passed along a number of crucial qualities to me having to do with people.

They both believed in the importance of the family—and of community. Of being responsible for others. My dad had an especially soft spot for those who were down and out, and he reached out countless times to help them, even when he suspected they were deadbeats hitting every church in town and every town along the road.

My mother loved to make people happy, loved to make them laugh, loved to spark joy in their hearts—and did so almost effortlessly. She cooked for them, she sang, she joked and she smiled, always the smile. And most people in the communities where we lived loved both of my parents in return. (My dad used to say, "People respect me. But they love Miss Mabel.") As a young journalist, I often wrote about the downtrodden and the underdog—sometimes to find my stories trashed by my editors who didn't want their communities portrayed as running roughshod over the have-nots or their papers seen as too bleeding hearted. But when it was people pitted against the entrenched powers, it was clear to me that I'd arrived at adulthood clearly biased in favor of the people and that my parents' predilections had much to do with the reasons why.

Strange as it may seem, given their modest achievements, both of my parents also possessed an adventurer's streak.

That went a long way, I think, to explain all the moving. The never-ending parade of new churches, new communities, new friends, new problems, new debts. They liked the novelty and variety that a change of address brought, especially if you changed cities or states, while largely ignoring the costs. And they passed that love for the habitually new on to me.

Which equipped me better than I could possibly have imagined early on to keep moving along. Toward Beta.

Chapter 7: **Free to Be**

*T*HE DECADE OF MY twenties was the 1960s for the world at large, and as for so many others, it again put me in motion. My young wife, Sherry, and I moved from New Mexico to Texas to New Mexico to Texas to Washington state to Texas to Arizona during that tumultuous decade.

In the 1970s, I went into therapy and learned much about the impact of my hearing loss on my behavior, about my fears and anxieties, about intimacy issues—more adventure.

I started to do workshops and then a monthly newsletter on creativity and created something called The BrainMap to market through our little family company, called Brain Technologies. I also found California attractive, and in my writer's role, I traveled there frequently to interview people like Stanislav Grof, the psychological expert on the hallucinogen LSD; Stanley Krippner, the dream expert; Thomas Harris and Muriel James, the inventors of Transactional Analysis, the down-to-earth therapy approach known colloquially as "TA," and Willis Harman and James Ogilvey, the futurists at SRI International. After all, what are writers if not professional adventurers?

In the early 1980s, we moved again: to Colorado. Then in the mid-nineties back to Texas. Hundreds of human resource professionals from more than twenty countries came to be trained in Brain Technologies' personal and organizational development methods. When they weren't coming to the States, I was going there. Eventually, the only continent where I'd not presented a seminar or made a speech was Antarctica (no invitations from personal-growth-oriented penguins!). All very simpatico with the kind of content that, in late Alpha, my current psychological container should be interested in.

As I look back at it, this two decades' long sojourn at the edge of Alpha could have, and probably should have, ended much sooner. Remember that during this final stage of the species' first great mind's construction, we are trying to put to rest a growth-limiting compulsion to belong. To get beyond this stage, we need the ability to go away, stand on our own, call hard shots and let the chips fall where they may—that is, cut the umbilical cord to the all-consuming need for the group—without succumbing to intense feelings of sadness, loneliness, powerlessness and of ultimate defeat.

During this lengthy stay in Alpha's final stage, I was caught, or so I now conclude in my own self-analysis, between Scylla and Charybdis, the rock and the whirlpool.

FORECLOSED OPTIONS

Because of my severe hearing difficulties, it was impossible for me to function well in a group—*any* group. If you had been watching me, you'd probably have concluded that most of the time I did just fine. I was in front of audiences, speaking. I led seminars and workshops by the dozens. You'd have seen me at parties and conferences, in restaurants having dinner with clients and friends, going anywhere, doing almost anything that hearing people did. But it was nearly all an act. Forever an act. Almost every moment of every public appearance, I was faking it. Where two or three or more were gathered together, they were quickly filling the air with so much sound that I couldn't possibly participate meaningfully in the conversation. And reading lips, as I noted earlier, only gets you so far (about eight to ten feet) and in today's fast-forward conversational world, that is almost never far enough.

Eventually, I began to drop out.

Forget a comfortable after-work drink with friends or colleagues in a bar: too noisy. Forget accepting invitations to formal dinner parties or even dinner in a restaurant with people: too noisy. Forget chatting with people in a moving car or on an airplane: too noisy. Forget schmoozing with people at a convention, in the lobby of a symphony hall at intermission or even at the annual neighborhood picnic: too noisy. And even if I were present physically, often I wasn't emotionally. So painful was the experience of appearing to interact competently despite my deafness that in almost any public, people-surrounded eventuality where I was called on to participate in the conversation, I was counting the minutes and seconds until I could make a reasonably graceful exit.

One by one, virtually all my options for being with groups of people in a meaningful way were foreclosed. And yet here remained this compelling need, desire, hunger to be a full-fledged, fully participating part of the scene, *any* scene. I can now see that, unable to discern any viable alternative, I put in place the Groucho Marx Defense: I eventually refused any longer to consider being a member of a group, especially one that might have me. It made for years and years of profound isolation despite all my visibility and notoriety, and the final stage of Alpha began to stretch out, its basic existential conditions remained unresolved and clinging.

I became vaguely aware, though at the time nothing seemed all that clear, that I could conceivably end up becoming a devastating train wreck of one. A life lived this way was taking its toll.

For once, my prized entrepreneurial instincts and creative energies were not coming through. They were simply...absent. Increasingly, I felt will-less, soulless. Everywhere I looked, the future seemed to be seamlessly mirroring the past, and because of what I knew from having already been there once, I didn't want to go there again. But where else was there to go? It wasn't that I had reached bottom; the issue was that no matter how far down I reached, I could no longer feel any bottom. I no longer had any wish to be with people, no more than I wished to be by myself. I thought of seeking out a therapist again, but the one thing my

imagination seemed capable of was creating a make-believe conversation in my head between a therapist and me. I listened in
briefly and rejected the idea. Even if it was an irrational thought, I
felt I needed to go beyond where any therapist could take me.

Was this one of Elliott Jaques' mid-life crises? I considered
this and didn't think so.

Things got worse. In the midst of all this, my mother chose to
die rather than go on dialysis, and thirty days later, on a blistering
August day in western Oklahoma, we laid her to rest at age
seventy-nine. My eighty-year-old father immediately withdrew
into an emotional shell from which he'd never reemerge. Now, I
was his primary caretaker.

The world had turned into a hauntingly lonely place. A loving, increasingly concerned family didn't seem to be able to help.
An insightful and supportive wife couldn't find any way to ease
the angst. In torment one day, I blurted out to my frightened, baf-
fled spouse: "I don't want to be here."

And there were other problems.

More than I had realized, our life as a family had gotten in
considerable disarray. Debts had mounted. We'd bought a house
twice as large as we really needed, even if we housed the company there, as I'd always preferred to do. In the hot Texas summers,
the utility bill alone was twice as big as our first house payment
had been! Clearly, we needed to downsize, but what, I agonized,
was I going to do with my own 10,000-volume library? Where
would we store our inventory of printed products? What would
our clients think of having to traipse through the family room to
get to our offices?

I had assumed that one of the answers to a lengthy slump in
our business would be a tried-and-true solution I'd turned to more
than once: write a new book on a subject that deeply interested me
or invent a marketable new learning or assessment product. And
I'd been trying for two years now, but this time, no matter how
often or deeply I seined my imagination, there was no book, no
new viable product there.

As I look back on it, what happened next still seems as improbable to me now as it did then.

HEADQUARTERS SHOWDOWN

Suddenly, after more than twenty years of becoming increasingly becalmed in this late stage of Alpha, after months and months of literally fearing that I'd never again see a lighthouse beacon in my stygian night, I discerned a slight movement outside the porthole. Was the good ship S.O.S. Dudley moving again? I was almost afraid to consider the possibility.

On an impulse, I abandoned the book effort, picked up the phone, made some calls. Essentially, the message I put out was one I'd used before in what I sometimes have called a career of "intellectual entrepreneuring": "Thinking skills for hire."

Soon there was a bite.

A very well-known American company was in deep trouble. Because of legal considerations, I can't tell you the name of the company or much about the details. But the big firm had been accused of mishandling some of its materials. Neighbors to its plant claimed to have been affected. Whether they had or not, serious illnesses had arisen. People had died. Understandably, lawyers had gotten involved. Some of the families whose members had been affected by these illnesses had been led to expect a court victory and a huge financial settlement. But because of convoluted happenings in court, neither the victory nor the big payoff had materialized. Now, massive publicity was about to descend on the company because journalists and others refused to let the story go. At minimum, it was a surefire public relations disaster in the making. And because the company was publicly held and sold a variety of products, a black eye in the media could exact another kind of penalty: it could put them out of business. But because it additionally faced hundreds of millions of dollars in potential legal judgments from other claims against it, the firm was reluctant to do what nearly everyone but its legal team said it needed to do to put itself in a more favorable and morally respectable light: apologize.

Someone needed to stand before the CEO of this beleaguered company and explain in uncompromising terms that although his firm had won in a court of law, it was about to lose disastrously in the court of public opinion. And because the media viewed it as such a compelling story of David versus Goliath-like conflict and larger-than-life pathos and was covering it like a perfect storm, the whole world was going to be watching when it happened.

So on an overcast November day in the late nineties, in a second-floor East Coast boardroom packed with high-priced lawyers and public relations people, surrounded by audio-visual equipment and open brief cases, that's what I did. Turned both hearing aids up and argued throughout the morning, and argued throughout the afternoon, much of the time one on one with the CEO.

It is an all-too-common occurrence in corporate America: cut off from the person in the street, surrounded by sycophantic "yes, sir" subordinates and stonewall-minded lawyers, CEOs find it extraordinarily difficult to believe that their company can literally be hated for its actions, no matter how solid the evidence.

In this high-profile, high-level crisis management situation, I lost the decision. (And, within a few months, the company filed for bankruptcy. Whether a different decision on the CEO's part during the session I spent with him would have made any difference, none of us will ever know.)

VIEW FROM THE INTERIOR

But the consequence that mattered for me in all this was not the CEO and his almost predictable reaction. It was the fact that somewhere in the midst of this demanding, months-long assignment, I believe that I began to take the serious steps necessary to move on to Beta. If I'd lost the (corporate political) battle, I ended up winning the (personal) peace.

My first recognition that perhaps there had been a significant shift in my thinking came as I lay in bed one night. At one moment, my world was one way. The next moment, it was something very different. In the briefest of instances, I became aware of a shift, a leap! To be honest with you, I can't tell you that it actual-

ly happened at that moment or whether I simply became aware of
it then. But as I lay there marinating in the experience, the awareness took hold and grew that I no longer felt any of the paralyzing
loneliness and estrangement and sense of personal powerlessness
I had experienced for so long.

The feeling was almost impossible to explain. I still felt
alone—but I also felt *connected*. New connections without and
within. The deeper part of me—the self?—now suddenly went
deeper than ever, or so I was experiencing the feeling. The connections between the core that was me and myself at the periph-
ery also seemed altered. I somehow felt more porous, more per-
meable, more accessible. Whatever you had to say, I would no
longer seemed obligated to the core of my own being to work so
assiduously and vigilantly to maintain my perimeter defenses. As
if it would be easier now for me to hear you and find you acceptable, whether you were speaking to me from the heart or simply
passing the time of day.

I felt like I had been subjected to some kind of fitness or wor-
thiness test, and that I had passed with strong marks. In other
words, that I had, as every aspirant for Beta must do, faced the bar
of choices and made the right ones in sufficient combination and
numbers. At long last, I had decided with considerable specificity
and firm feelings of surety—I could indisputably feel that—what
I would and would not be responsible for.

I can't say that my whole life passed before my eyes that
night. But as I lay there, it did seem as if my personal history had
been instantly recruited as an agent of my own resolve to make a
difference. This time I seemed resolute about doing so with real
effect. This time with a minimum of the baggage of what I have
come to call Alpha. This time, if necessary, as alone as alone can be,
while not feeling the least diminished or impeded by such a reality.

As I engaged in an unexpected instant retrospective, I felt
like I'd spent my entire life laying the foundations for this. I felt
that I was confidently out in front of events as I never had been

before. At the same time, I was experiencing the strongest kind of attachment to what I saw when I looked back.

Within days of that night when I first consciously detected the signs of a new "lightening of existence," we arranged for a real estate for-sale sign in our yard. I started going through that library of books, deciding to keep only those I couldn't bear to part with. Seven thousand books went into one of the biggest garage-patio-yard sales our city had ever seen. Along with enough furniture to fill an ordinary-sized house for a family of four. Plus years and years of accumulation of never-to-be-used office supplies that only a publishing and seminar-production firm would have ever thought they needed: reams and reams of paper, felt-tipped pens, flip chart refills, audio cassettes, calendars, brochures, stationery, carbon paper—you name it, we had it, and didn't really need it all. We were leaving a house that was once considered the biggest executive home in our still-upscale Texas bedroom suburb for a very ordinary place that was half the size.

"Downsizing?" people asked.

Right.

"Retiring early?"

No.

I could have added but didn't: *Finally moving on in ways that you probably wouldn't find interesting or begin to understand.*

From that moment, I have trusted my observations and my judgments, my hunches and my instincts, and acted on them, in ways that are often new to me. Everything about *me* and everything *about* me seems to have been jostled.

There have been many adjustments in attitude and perspective, in levels of acceptance and expectation. With respect to people living and dead, with respect to histories prized or detested, with respect to events planned and unplanned, with respect to outcomes satisfying or having fallen short. Coincidentally or not, that outsized (by our needs) house was soon sold, and at a profit, defying the predictions of more than a few that we were about to take a financial soaking in a weak housing market. Our debts were soon erased. And the book that refused to arrive? You're reading it now.

If you were to shadow my new Beta thinking life, watchful for indications of obvious changes, you'd be more likely to notice differences if you already had a longstanding acquaintance with my thinking habits. (No doubt those *with* such knowledge would have preferred that Beta's arrival for me not been so tardy!) Many of the changes are subtle, and more than a few of the most profound ones may be shielded to any view but the one from within, since this is the only one capable of judging the influences of *both* Alpha and Beta.

Alpha never disappears. In fact, as I'll note more than once in the pages ahead, it is always the chassis on which Beta runs. This bestows an importance on Alpha that we cannot and should not ever overlook.

POST-BETA POSTMORTEMS

My own authentication affirms that Beta isn't so much an installer of highly original new thinking gear as it is a repairer, strengthener and orchestrator of thinking apparatus that is already up and running. Staying with the auto mechanic's mise-en-scène for a moment, my own experience of the Beta mind has been that it takes a few billion years of natural selection's cagey if blind-eyed mutational handiwork, several thousands of years of the ape/human-to-be's groundwork preparations for symbolic thought, my own unique half-century-plus stop-and-start assemblage of the species' hard-earned Alpha stages and engages in one hell of an overhaul. It isn't, or so I have concluced, that you ramp up from eight cylinders to a V-10 or a Ferrari 12-cylinder flat engine in moving to Beta. Staying with the reliable V-8 that got you this far, you get pistons, connecting rods, valves, condenser, coil, alternator, distributor, spark plugs and all else under the hood, cleaned up, tuned up, shined up and revved up. As a result, to again use that telling description from the gifted discoverer of Beta, "*Suddenly*, human cognition is free!"

Free, more than ever, that is, to be what it is!

If it is true, as Martin Seligman, author of *Authentic Happiness* alleges, that about half of us human folks are born genetically calibrated to be happy come what may and the other half has to apply ourselves even to acknowledge that the sun is out, then I now realize that fate has assigned me to the latter group. Color us naturally endowed crepe-wearers as being a tad too realistic, too much of the time. Pre-Beta, whether woolgathering between the action, sizing up implications in real time or lying in bed critiquing the day just ended, I customarily focused—in unblinking, no-phooey concentration—on the part of the glass half empty. What my mind recycled most easily was where things went wrong, and why, and how it felt and how it affected things and how it affected me. I silently debriefed life—my life, your life, all lives within my purview—endlessly, ruthlessly, with few exemptions. As a full-time assignment, it can get to be pretty heavy.

Post-Beta, I still do this. I do it as predictably as fries go with burgers.

The difference, though, between then and now is that as soon as my Alpha machinery starts churning out brutal postmortems of the day's performance, Beta often grabs the output and tacks on an instantly transformative and playing-field-evening, and very commonsensical, *AND!* As in, "Yes, you took a real risk that got pounced on in that meeting this afternoon *AND* don't assume that you didn't put something worthwhile in motion!" Or, "Sure, you allowed yourself to use your outrage as a cudgel *AND* remember, outrage often greases needed action when you can't get people to commit or decide." The most powerful of my new Beta automatic self-correctives is one that reverberates through my cranium sometimes a half-dozen times a hour as I am confronted with yet more instances of being barred from normal conversational pleasures or formal participation because of my congenital inability to hear well. Pre-Beta, the emotional spin-offs of the consequences of this physical imposition were often inwardly searing. Post-Beta, my new mind tells me at the slightest arousal of the old feelings of isolation and diminishment..."*AND*, be that as it may, you *are* accepted and included!" My view of this is subjective, of course, but I don't sense that my learning and analytical abilities have been at all diminished by Beta's ability to neutralize many of the "viruses" and "worms" of my old affective programming. My post-Beta style of postmortem review still encourages close scrutiny to what just happened but seeks quickly to examine it in a more reasonable framework. The main exception seems to be when a situation is genuinely perilous or an outcome unquestionably tragic. On those occasions, the Beta-generated *AND!* seems to tactfully recede, if only for a time.

KEEP IT SIMPLE...ENOUGH

My world is now so different from the world of many of our long-term acquaintances that I can often feel my place in their worlds peeling away. Some of them are buying retirement places in Arizona, Colorado, Oregon, South Carolina or Florida and settling in. They e-mail us photos of driftwood logjams on the beach, hummingbirds buzzing around the feeders on the back porch, fellow Harley riders on the Albertan blacktop. And bully for them! As Clare Graves said so many times, people have a right to be.

But I can't imagine this kind of personal disengagement from more intense slipstreams of the world ever being right for me. I don't think very many Beta users would unless and until, to cite the only obvious reason that comes to mind, their health requires it. There's still too much to life, too much yet to be lived.

For all its easy, automatic, confident insistence now on being true to itself, my mind is clearly no longer wholly its own. In opening itself to Beta, it has become acutely aware of the massive need for new thinking involvement, wherever it comes from, in every culture and economy and slice of life, developed or developing, in every corner of our more and more complex existence. Personally, if I ever could have envisioned voluntarily reining in the fullest possible engagement of my mind with the world, however modest that may turn out to be, I can no longer do so. Any such retreat back across the mind's great divide will have to come on its own time, on its own terms (which, should I continue to live long enough, will probably occur). I will not consciously aid and abet it.

Another appealing feature of this new kind of mind is its gift for unearthing simplicity in the complexity—or the chaos—and talking about it in straightforward ways. The Beta mind is going to prove to be, or so I'm experiencing, remarkably jargon-averse. Whether it ends up being adopted by lawyers or scholars, consultants or regulators, theologians or politicians, the Beta mind is going to view using specialized vocabularies to keep people out or protect your monopoly on a corner of knowledge or show off your academic pedigree or spotlight your personal brilliance as little better than Boss-Tweed-style sleaze or out-and-out Mafia extortion. It's more than being pragmatically sloppy. It's more like being morally indifferent to the costs of using your professional or technical argot to drive a wedge between you and others or causing others to drive a wedge between themselves.

I've always liked the way that Kevin Kelly, the technocultural pioneer who helped birth and guide such trend-shaping institutions as *Whole Earth Catalog*, the Well on-line service and *Wired Magazine*, said it: "The only way to make a complex system that works is to begin with a simple system that works."[1] Or, as the nonpareil Albert Einstein observed, perhaps looking at the same issue from the opposite end, "Everything should be made as simple as possible, but no simpler."

I hope you are seeing evidence—and value—on these pages of a plain vanilla, Beta-style approach to ideating and commenting even on complex topics. I think the absence of specialized jargon in a work that frequently alludes to the hard sciences, philosophy, religion, psychology, economics and much else of a specialized character is a net plus. Even if you encounter a word on these pages that is unknown to you, I think all you need do is listen for the cadence of the story being told or the idea being advanced. If you do that, then I think you'll find most of the time that the word encourages the drumbeat, reinforces the heartbeat, expands the box—and fits the occasion. At least, this is my intent and my hope.

A story that matters should choose and field its words like a good recipe chooses and fields its condiments, good surgery its scalpels and good love-making or decision-making its moments.

PERMANENT ENGAGEMENT

If you ask me what finally brought Beta within my grasp, I can do little more in the aggregate than I did at the beginning of this personal screed. I can only say once more that somewhere along the way you develop a knack for, and learn to be comfortable with, putting yourself squarely in the widest available path of advancing life. First at one level and then at others, and more at some times than at other times, I think I've always been committed to this posture. But only since Beta's arrival can I say that I've been committed more deeply than ever, for most of the time. For the longest time, I now see that there was a duality of me. One part utterly implacable for life, and another part often repulsed and frustrated that it was necessary to invest such energy and vigilance to pull a life off. This duality is now substantially gone. The negativity about life seems to have metamorphosed into an even more acute sense of realism, something that showed up early on my personal radarscope. Even less than before am I willing to make time for fools or buffoons or waste time over a notion that seems patently fatuous to me.

So for me, this is the way it has been: the good, the bad, the difficult, the scary, the eye-opening, the redesigning and the reaffirming.

This is how Level 1.6 of Alpha came to a close. And how Beta—Mind 2.0—came to be a reality.

Your own story, and every other person's story, is going to be as unique as mine—and just as instructional. And yet we can expect important commonalities. This is true because, to say it again, each of our minds is built on the same great chassis. And each of us, for all our uniquenesses, has worked through similar emotions and has surmounted a similar slate of existential realities and requirements to get to where we are.

Understanding this, it is more than time, I think, for us to take a closer look at Alpha. At all those mini-leaps from level to level. We won't spend as much time with the earlier levels because we spend relatively less time with them in our everyday lives. (And as far as our own psychological development, the influences of the earliest levels are hazy and hardened, largely beyond our conscious grasp and intervention.) But the later stages of Alpha loom in our faces so frequently because this is where we find so many people. They are the ones that we must interact with with increasing skill and perspicacity in our ever-more-complex surroundings and our efforts to be the best mind we can be. So we'll look at these levels more closely.

Chapter 8: **Alpha's Chassis**

NO MATTER WHAT mind level we are targeting—whether it's one of the Alpha levels or Beta itself—probably the most crucial question the mind ever asks itself is this one: "If I behave or think or feel in a particular way, what can I expect from the world and how do I explain it?"

The importance of such a question isn't difficult to illustrate.

Consider the original users of Alpha's Level 1.2 mind. It is obvious that these early practitioners of the thinking art puzzled over questions like these:

- Can spirits mediate between gods and men?
- Does the heart of a person in love beat faster?
- Does a drink made from the juice from toasted lentils bring down a fever?
- Should I, a mother of young children but without a husband, slay my newborn child or should I marry the brother of my late husband?

Compared to the knowledge and explanations available to us today, the fit between what the mind of this early-day thinker understood and could predict and what its user experienced was often very poor. But it was better than no fit at all. At least the early users of the Level 1.2 mind had a way to try to anticipate events and to improve their powers of prediction, explanation and control.

As more and more behaviors based on these kinds of questions were tried on for size more and more times by the mind, wider, more dependable patterns of predictability began to be noticed. An overarching system of meanings gradually emerged, available for fitting over the realities of the world.

Over time, through six unfolding levels of the Alpha mind, the repertory of predictions and behaviors available to us humans has become sizable. In many ways, the thinking skills within the Alpha mind have become quite good at predicting a fit between how we believe the world works and how the world actually responds when we act, think and feel within it. Despite the fact that our brain is so often duplicious and cryptic, we have become much better than perhaps we give ourselves credit for at predicting the consequences and outcomes of at least some of our behaviors.

In Beta, our sense of control and prediction has never felt better, and for good reason: we have never been better at charting a course of behavior and anticipating the results. We have a palpable, approachable, applicable process for, on the one hand, identifying the elements of ourselves best calculated to help us make sense of the world as it now exists. And, on the other, for helping us identify those elements of ourselves that are rickety, outmoded and perhaps hazardous, that still need to be defused, encased or abandoned, and to do something about it. And the means exists to be better still.

Let's again put this process to good use by dispatching our Beta mind on a speleologist-like assignment—beginning with Level 1.1 of the Alpha mind:

1.1

THE PRIMAL PROGRAMMING and fledgling emotional footprints of Level 1.1 within each of us are, and always have been, largely beyond our conscious reach. If anything of consequence is missing or flawed there, it will likely remain so, and as grown-ups, there is little we can do about it in ourselves.

But anyone who has been around a new infant in recent memory has occupied a ringside seat for observing a mint-fresh Level 1.1 mind at work. Consequently, you will understand exactly what I mean when I observe that there is much that can be done to impact this callow new mind that can be influential for a lifetime.

As this is written, I've had just such a privilege—and adventure—for nearly a year now.

That's because our son-in-law's high-paying job disappeared during the telecommunications depression of the early 2000s and didn't come back. Sherry and I invited the economically strapped soon-to-be-parents to move into our spare bedroom. And that's how we happened to be just down the hall from ground zero at the hospital when our first grandchild was born and how we found him just down the hall at our home for many nights to come.

In hardly any time, it was clear that our tiny grandson's nimble mind was busily interrogating itself and the world. There were questions—behaviors—being spread about. Inquiries were going out, and answers were being taken in. In his alert little mind, callow as it was, replication and learning were quickly afoot.

As any alert mother intuitively recognizes, and the rest of us were swift to learn, distinctive signatures appeared in his cries almost from the start.

The "bleating goat" cry signaled hunger. If a bottle of warm formula didn't appear promptly, this plaintive entreaty increased in decibel levels. On those occasions when the big people in his life were undependably slow in the kitchen, the bleating goat's cry became the raging bull's bellow. This always speeded up the food delivery. The sanitation summons had a different quality. An irritated, intermittent cry, coming from a squirming, quick-to-kick little body. Boredom triggered an indecisive, wanna-be whine—did he or didn't he? Sleepiness was signaled by progressive crankiness and unreasonable protest. And then there were the sudden, unrelenting, Four Alarm screams brought on by severe gas pains. We big people seem to be evolving rapidly right along with the little guy.

It took but a couple of accidental sideswipes of a wiggly figure attached to his mobile, and thereafter, when he was awake, our grandson's little arms were seldom still. Within a few days, they were making the figure on the mobile dance like a puppet. Granddad and all the others smiled at this. We cooed and giggled. In short order, our favorite Level 1.1 mind was smiling back, then cooing, then giggling itself. A feel-good, oft-repeated routine was born in which the mannerisms of the youngest were often the most adult of the lot. Not a bad achievement for a mind so new to the scene. Not bad at all.

All totaled, there were five adults in the household who, at one time or another, throughout the day and night, were at our new arrival's beck and call. His aunt was a medical assistant in a pediatric office. She put a wealth of professional medical knowledge and experience on the scene. There was a loving, attentive mother, and a doting, experienced grandmother, who sent many private whispers into those tiny ears. And a daddy and granddaddy who both value a challenged mind and who spoke to the new brain in their midst from the first as if they were already preparing it for college admissions exams.

Yet there were moments during our grandchild's first weeks when I would occasionally skip a breath. The cause was the thought of the large number of infants born the same week whose minds would get little positive feedback at all to the questions they put to the world. It would be mostly negative answers for them, most of the time. Negative answers from crack house mothers too stoned to notice the subtle signals in their newborn's cries. From abysmally poor mothers too ignorant to know about, and too destitute to afford, Zantac for their baby's gastric distress or Simethicone drops to relieve the symptoms of gas. Babies born to mothers with AIDS, soon to be too ill to care about, or care for, a child that probably has the dread virus, too. Infants born to alcoholics. Infants born to mothers too young. Infants not wanted born into a world not caring.

I strongly, strongly doubt that many of my readers were born into such circumstances. Thankfully, I wasn't. But this mustn't blind us to just how serious the damage has been to the nascent minds of individuals of all ages who, as little people, first put their questions to the world and found an abysmal response to their needs and expectations.

Because of what has already happened at the 1.1 level of the mind, the hope of the world for getting great numbers of people to Beta is dashed at the outset. The Level 1.1 mind has been irreversibly damaged in millions of the planet's citizens. Doing something different for the generations of newborns ahead is one of the planet's gravest, and greatest, challenge.

1.2

LEVEL 1.2 OF THE mind seems to be about 80 per cent imagination. It can conjure—and appreciate—a fearful story, fierce god, vivid superstition or fanciful item of artistry out of little or nothing. No wonder, then, that we see the Level 1.2 mind assigning a premium to natural harmony and balance, to safety and security.

Not bad choices, given the world this mind sees and often experiences.

Level 1.2 develops at a time and place for bridging and for commingling. It has to be confusing much of the time.

To begin with, Level 1.2 environs are the headwaters for all that is made possible when you start to appreciate "the other"—your mate, children, family, elders, clan, tribe...your people. But it's more than merely matching lonely organism with communal comfort and security. At the same time, old brain is bridging with new brain. Skills of the hand with skills of the head. Artifacts of the eye with rhythms of the heart. Sacred places, rituals, items and roles with wisdom and content in the collective memory. An identifiably human consciousness is, at last, introducing a degree of behavioral variety and sophistication amid the animal instincts and thinking processes so long used to calling the shots. The Level 1.2 mind is, in many ways, a perfervidly busy, larger-than-life kind of place.

In examining Level 1.2, your Beta mind will find the origins of much that it will hope to see preserved and encouraged in any functioning brain, no matter what its primary mind level is. Positives like these:

• *The life-long value of nurturing your "inner child."* We really do have a component of our personality and thinking processes that can accurately be thought of as "the little gal" or "the little guy" within us.

This is because, when time was that we were callow and new, our Level 1.2 mind was being assembled behind a pre-literate curtain of secrecy. Words and logic are often powerless to penetrate it. But not sounds, symbols, rituals or the "lightness of being" that comes with liberating play.

It's a mesmerizing thing to let halting or pounding or soul-probing music pierce the veil of our own personal antiquity and engage and renew something arresting there. Or to realize that a symbolic artwork, dance or customary observance is speaking movingly to us we know not where. Or to surrender to a role (or role play) that takes on a life of its own. There's much that is valuable in our deepest, darkest, least modern available rhythms of the mind, and it pays to find ways to spend quality time with them long after they've been put in place.

• *The dividends of the loving family's investment in the infant and child pay off both early and late.* Why? Because absent this early positive bonding, a void materializes that invites bonding later in life for all the wrong reasons. That may include entering into bad marriages and other corrosive relationships to assuage paralyzing loneliness. Joining cults to fill the emptiness. Or pledging gangs to compensate for the lost esteem and sense of belonging. Likely, there are no calibrations quite as vital to the subsequent healthy development of our persons as the dial settings established once and for all early on—in the hungry-to-be-included recesses of the Level 1.2 mind.

• *The understanding that true buddies are literally priceless.* For all its impediments and limitations, this level of the mind is quick to recognize that the strongest attachments between humans happen when no one is keeping score or taking names.

All this stems from real-time brain development at a time, literally, when the Level 1.2 mind was the cutting edge. When people never met more than fifty or so other humans in their lifetime. When for children, the extended family/tribe was more than family and tribe, it was everything. When there was nothing beyond the blood bonds except the animistic spirits in the rocks and trees and stars and winds. When there was no concept of a self, only a concept of the group: the family first, then eventually the clan and finally the tribe.

What a powerful spawning ground for the concept of a buddy, be it a grandparent, a sibling or a non-blood-related individual who has slotted herself or himself into a *Clan of the Cave Bear*-type role and connection almost as old and storied as the beginning of consciousness itself!

Buddies are multipliers. They are the eyes you need in the back of your head. The power of oneness that you feel when you are together can be the feedstock of courage as well as contentment. With buddies around, you can become more than you are. And the knot that ties buddies together is forged in the smithy of the Level 1.2 mind.

• *The realization that becoming one with what you are tracking is the key to almost any kind of successful search in life.* From time immemorial, from the sere sands of Namibia to the desiccated expansions of the Australian interior to the dense foliages of the Amazon rain forest, the best Level 1.2 trackers have realized that understanding the living habits of what you are tracking is a much more productive approach than seeking to locate the next track that was left behind.

Even if we comprehend that, we may overlook another equally important insight: the biggest step toward knowledgeable mastery of your quarry's or objective's world is thoroughly knowing your own. It's an eye-opening discovery to realize that in every crucial and successful search for the other, you eventually end up tracking yourself.

Our Level 1.2 mind intuitively understands this. Why else would it presume a spirit for nearly every aspect of its world, animate and inanimate?

As you can see, we get plenty of positive benefits for life from Level 1.2. And the potential negative carryovers aren't that hard for our Beta mind to identify either.

Playing stupid is one. There was a time when comprehending causes was beyond us, but that was then. Sometimes believing we aren't smart enough is tied to believing that we really can't control anything. Surely, this explains most of our superstitions, our fears of abandonment, the need to stay in relationships that are destructive and the tendency to continue family customs and traditions when they serve no purpose.

Now, looking on from beyond Alpha, we know there is much that comes with being alive that we can influence, shape, guide and anticipate. No powerful spirits, human sacrifices or ritualistic ceremonies are needed, just awareness, learning, practice and courage. If your Beta mind identifies such lingering Level 1.2 influences in you, you will want to act on the caution flag it raises.

So, when *does* it make sense to call upon what we learned and mastered back when consciousness was little more than a cavernous gateway to mystery and the future?

When your children are so very small, and again when the grandkids come along. When it's time to observe family holidays or mark a rite of passage in a child's life. When you are faced with throwing out or keeping family heirlooms or childhood mementos. When you are very sick or someone whom you are close to is, or when death is near in someone who is dear. When the person you are dealing with seems frightened or alone or confused. When your pets are wounded or ill or simply wanting attention. When the community needs to be reminded that a slight to one is a blow to all. When the team needs to revisit its essential human character and needs. When someone you care about needs a buddy.

1.3

PEOPLE CAN DO terrible things when in the clutches of the Level 1.3 mind.

If you live, as do I, in a metropolitan community of several millions, it happens around you nearly every night. Home invasions where blameless people get shot dead. Drive-by shootings, carjackings or road rage incidents in which innocents are slaughtered. Thugs firing bullets without reason or mercy into convenience store clerks or taxi drivers even as they are handing them the money. Pitched gun battles between territorial drug-dealing rivals or ethnic gangs. Infant children beaten lifeless by guilt-oblivious fathers or boyfriends of the babies' mother.

And these are the amateurs.

You want professionals, go and audition a Saddam Hussein or a Kim Jong Il. Drop in on a Sudanese or a Columbian warlord. Do lunch with the next Pol Pot. And while you're at it, take a moment to remember Joseph Stalin, Countess Elizabeth Báthory, Ivar the Boneless, Attila the Hun and Caligula.

The negatives of Level 1.3 scream for the mind's close scrutiny and, where at all possible, steadfast attenuation. Users of this level of the mind are perpetually on the edge of anger. When pushed over the edge by some perceived unfairness or slight to their sense of machismo and dominance, the Level 1.3 user characteristically has but one interpersonal strategy: strike back. Retaliate. Conquer. Search and destroy. Since guilt is lacking, punishment not only doesn't work, it often becomes a trophy ("how many times *you* been in the joint?"). The ability to be introspective about dying is absent, and this tends to put both the Level 1.3 user and those around him (or, more and more often, her) in harm's way. The focus is never far removed from immediate gratification of personal desire. There simply is no easy handle for reining in the brash self-assertiveness, the rampant ego, the assumptions of immortality and invincibility or the thinly veiled, testosterone-fueled tendency to rage ever present in the person whose mind is centered here.

Moreover, because guilt is not yet a part of an individual's neurochemical repertoire, whatever the issue or the outcome, the Level 1.3 mind doesn't see or feel itself at fault. Any purported evidence suggesting that users of Level 1.3 should volunteer to step up to the bar of accountability is always, to them, a bad rap.

So why is it that when we take a closer look at the Level 1.3 mind, we find positives we didn't expect?

Because Level 1.3 marks the birth of the individual!

What you often find here is a person who is spontaneous, creative, courageous and exploratory-minded. Level 1.3 users have persistently led the way in discovering new worlds, scouting the frontiers and taking risks in doing things that no one else dares to try. More often than not, this is where heroes come from. There is daring and bravado available in Level 1.3 the likes of which are found nowhere else. And as they live their lives to the fullest, individuals here often do so with great charm—not infrequently accompanied by the power of an intense sexual drive.

Above all, Level 1.3 is a laboratory of energy for the emerging self. Energy for making things happen. Energy to escape with. Sometimes, energy without which you may be about to die.

I find the thinking and experimentation done by Dr. Robert Kegan of the Harvard Graduate School of Education's Institute for Management and Leadership in Education to be of importance on this point.

Kegan, author of *In Over Our Heads*, points out a dark side to something that, since the 1960s, has been touted by life-style counselors and commentators as a cure-all for everything from burnout to existential angst: a personal sense of balance and harmony. Kegan says the condition is much less rare than we may think. Each time we attempt to change ourselves, he argues, we set in motion a powerful counteracting force that seeks to keep things largely the same. "Balance," says Kegan, "is continuously manufacturing non-change...It's almost like a reverse engineering of the Buddhist idea of each moment we're creating anew."[1] Kegan calls this change-defusing force negentropy—negative entropy (entropy being a measure of the disorder and randomness in the universe). You and I can say it differently: when we seek to change ourselves, something within us seeks to negate the influence of a more forward-looking mind. Something soaks up energy we otherwise could be using to promote change and channels it into maintaining, restoring and protecting—balancing and harmonizing—the status quo.

As we move from level to level in Alpha, the power of the mind-negating force of negentropy grows. And why not? We can appreciate the positive uses of such an equilibrium-defending force. It is there, after all, to remind us of just how much our brain and mind have invested in a time-honored way of understanding how the world works. What has proven useful time and again shouldn't be tossed away on a whim. So it's easy for us to view maintaining the status quo as a form of self-protection, of fending off personal disaster. As the mind becomes more complex, more sophisticated, more outgoing and, yes, more energetic, so does the anti-change negentropic force guarding the home hearth. Each new release from one level of Alpha to the next requires greater and greater applications of energy to overcome that level's equilibrium-producing instincts and machinations than the one before. By the time Beta looms on the scene, a truly massive investment of psychological energy, adroitly focused and applied with unremitting determination, is required to escape Alpha. This, more than anything else, explains the need for a momentous leap to get us over the gap.

Where is such energy to be found? There's only one dependable supply: Level 1.3. It is as though this sometimes problem-beset, peace-disturbing mind level has an often-missed, sub rosa message for us more "civilized" moderns. The one from the battery commercial: "You can pay me now, or you can pay me later."

Thus when your Beta mind returns from reconnoitering Level 1.3, I predict that it will have much of unexpected importance to report:

• *Sooner or later, you will need to call up raw Level 1.3 energy—call it ruthlessness, implacableness, irascibility or most any other indelicate term you wish to use—to make a difference in the world.* Playwright George Bernard Shaw called it unreasonableness. The complete quote, as you probably remember, goes like this: "Reasonable people adapt themselves to the world. Unreasonable people attempt to adapt the world to themselves. All progress, therefore, depends on unreasonable people."

• *You'll probably find it difficult to do "highly original" thinking if Level 1.3 energy isn't available or you aren't comfortable with it.* Much has been made of the idea of "the flow," of entering into a highly productive and satisfying personal zone of creativity and total involvement. What usually gets ignored is the role that Level 1.3's energy often plays in setting up the flow state. Nothing quite clears the sinuses of the imagination like getting thoroughly frustrated at the mind's seeming unwillingness or inability to help you resolve an issue, solve a problem or innovate on the edge even though you've done the research, thought about it long and hard and tried one approach after another. When you call on Level 1.3's creative energies, frustration can lead to perturbation. Perturbation can lead to incubation. Incubation can lead to the bank. Often, the only way to solve a knotty problem is to get mad at it!

• *When none of the other levels of your mind are being listened to, Level 1.3 can usually penetrate the hubbub, indifference or confusion.* Let's just say that this level of the mind has a way with words and activity that gets people's attention. That's nothing to sneeze at if you have an emergency, are tired of wasting time, need immediate respect for your authority or require an instant response from others to your instructions.

• *If you are going to bite a shark, route your thinking through Level 1.3.* Of course, other actions may come better recommended. Like getting out of the pool altogether or seeing if you can negotiate a trade-off. But if your back is against the wall and you have no choice but to fight, this is no time to place limits on your Level 1.3 furies. You need to demonstrate that you intend to win whatever the cost. You should think nothing of fighting dirty. You may be surprised at who backs off or thinks twice about challenging or assaulting you when it's clear that "the wounded tiger" in you will offer no quarter. Even if they don't retreat, you still may triumph with an unrestrained Level 1.3 response.

• *When all other levels of the mind have decided that there is no hope, Level 1.3 may be the only one willing to say, "Let's saddle up and ride!"* Sometimes, this is the only available answer to the question, "So what do we do now?" Motion in the world is a normal thing. Something is always going on. Something may always turn up. "In fact, that is the way the universe exists; it exists by happening," says one insightful observer.[2] Basically, then, the universe *is* an event. With the universe constantly eventful, always changing from one moment to the next in comparsion to its former self, you should never be surprised what comes out of a mind that is doing the same. No other level of your mind does this with more valuable gusto and dispatch than this level.

The thing always to remember about Level 1.3 is that its instigative value and its roundhouse punch tend to have a short shelf life. Call it shower power. While we're under the influence of this level of the mind, our mind tells us, we need quickly to get in touch with the power, apply it, and then, once we're finished, head immediately for the shower.

1.4

I THINK ONE USEFUL way to look at Level 1.4 is to picture it as the mind's equivalent to an oil well blowout preventor.

I learned about blowout preventors early in life. Long before condoms. Or how to steer into a skid when the road is icy and your car wheels lose traction. Because where I grew up, oil well drilling rigs were a common sight, and so were blowout preventors.

These massive devices look like something out of science fiction. Think of giant metal vertebrae, a stack of them, towering higher than your head—defensive, ponderous, unyielding. They do sentinel duty atop the holes that oil well drillers are poking into high-pressure below-ground reservoirs of oil and gas. Their job: to contain the pressures downhole if all else (mostly meaning the drilling mud packed around the pipe stem doing the drilling) fails. If a well blows out, it's an expensive, dangerous mess. A disaster.

It took a long time for the mind to figure out how to craft a blowout preventor for itself. An even longer time was required to understand how to maneuver it over the drill pipe. And yet more time to learn how to bolt it in place and keep it there. That explains the numerous millennia between Moses and Michelangelo that were devoted to the task.

The blowout preventor analogy also serves us well when it comes to understanding the negatives that our Beta mind turns up here. In its most functional aspects, Level 1.4 is also defensive, ponderous, unyielding.

No surprises there.

If progress toward Beta was to continue, something had to be done about Level 1.3's outsized ego, impulsiveness and self-originated destructiveness.

Level 1.4 pronunciamentos about what is true and good typically offer few exclusions, variances or exceptions. That's because Level 1.4 tends to polarize things. Good versus evil. Right versus wrong. The saved versus the doomed. The accepted way versus the prohibited ways. The rules usually exist in a sacred or revered book (a holy scripture, the collected sayings of an authoritarian leader, the employers handbook, the law books of the land), and they are to be taken literally. From start to finish, the Level 1.4 mind floods its user with the neurochemicals of guilt as it seeks to displace a frightening, threatening world of evil with a world of discipline, regimentation and hard work. "I'm a man who believes that right is right and wrong is wrong," said the late Johnny Paycheck, the country singer. "Treat me right, and I will give you my all. Treat me wrong and I will give you nothing. They don't like me for that, but that's the way I am."[3]

Level 1.4's either/or thinking patterns can be costly, especially when applied to people. Making others "foreign devils," "the great Satan," "goyem" or "gaijin"—outsiders—has a way of coming home to roost for the separators. They can easily become vulnerable to their own self-initiated isolation, blindness and arrogance. (But then, as James Michener's character says in *The Source*, "If he had a different God, he would be a different man.")

Are we having fun yet?

Well, possibly. If you are carefully minding your P's and Q's.

Level 1.4 may approve of a hay *ride* (but never a romp *in the hay*). A *gamble* in bidding at dominoes or bridge (but no *gambling* at the casino). Getting high on *Jesus* (but never high on *drugs*). Music that *edifies* the soul (but no beat that *excites* the libido). *Barnyard* humor, possibly, (but hardly ever *schoolyard* humor, especially if it involves four-letter references to genitalia or procreative activities). For the user of the Level 1.4 mind, life is seldom a laughing matter for more than brief stretches.

And yet, and yet...

You can see how there might be strong contradictions or countercurrents emerging in all this. A judgmental mind is a busy mind. And when you feel strongly about knowing what the right-eous thing is and doing it right, about avoiding idleness, about being charitable toward the needy, about sacrificing for the good of the whole, this also makes for busy hands. Busyness means movement, and movement may open up cracks in what people see, what they think, where they go, who they meet, what they talk about.

Then, too, Level 1.4 involves itself in a constant review of what the best of yesterday was and how it can be revived. This assures constant ferment and discussion about how not to have the wrong ideas and how to get back to the right ideas. And while Level 1.4 produces a strong respect for authority, it also has strong expectations of authority. When the powers that be fail egregious-ly enough and often enough, then challenges to orthodoxy won't be far behind. This creates turmoil and ferment, and at the edge of the chaos, as we've learned from our sciences of complexity, you can expect yeasty, unexpected things to happen. (The American Civil Rights and the women's suffrage/feminist movements, for example, were products of dissatisfied, boundary-challenging Level 1.4 minds.) This is why I argue that while it took the longest time, when Level 1.4 finally got its act together, it didn't take long to produce all kinds of restless personalities and inquisitive intel-lects intent on exploring the world from a different kind of think-ing platform.

We'll look at what that restlessness turned into in the next chapter. But with regard to Level 1.4, when your Beta mind returns from checking it out, you can expect to hear that it found a plethora of mental dictums intended to help you keep your life orderly, purposeful and patient. Expect your Beta mind to return from Level 1.4 touting distillations of hard-earned wisdom and no-nonsense rules that took the brain the better part of three mil-lennia to turn up and discover how to make stick and that are still worthy, even essential, for healthy living today.

Courtesy of Level 1.4, we know that it pays to remember that:

• *High-minded, salt-of-the-earth, steady-as-you-go virtues can have a durable practicality.* Pay attention to Level 1.4's call for thriftiness, and you'll have a valuable inoculation against runaway credit card debt and compulsive spending.

Heed this mind level's call for keeping your promises, and you'll soon have a persuasive balance in your "integrity" account—along with many spending possibilities.

Make telling the truth a personal 24/7 commitment seldom broken (occasionally, there are legitimate, even compassionate, reasons to lie), and you'll automatically eliminate a lot of unnecessary drama with others and inner tension for yourself.

Be personally responsible and accountable, and you'll be practicing one of the best time-management programs around.

Use patience, prudence, good preparation and attention to detail, and you may end up a survivor when those who are hot-dogging and hero-ing have long since crashed and burned. (There is a reason why the Navy tells its aircraft-carrier-based fliers that "there are no old, bold pilots.")

• *Sometimes evil is a label we can't avoid.* Some behaviors, some outcomes, some objects, some people are so anti-good—so wicked and cruel—that they are diabolical. They deserve special handling all out of proportion to our usual treatment of deviance. Without piling cruelty upon cruelty, in such cases, we need to do what we can to cocoon the devil's handiwork. Neutralize it, isolate it, sometimes destroy it. At such times, our Level 1.4 mind may need to be heard, and heeded, at the least as an early-warning signal.

(The issue of evil is, however, like gasoline vapor: so dangerous you'd prefer not to have to handle it at all. And the dangers of both are much the same. You may not realize how vulnerable and close to disaster you are until it is too late. As former New York University religion professor James Carse noted in *Finite and Infinite Games*, "Evil is never intended as evil. Indeed, the contradiction inherent in all evil is that it originates in the desire to eliminate evil. 'The only good Indian is a dead Indian.'...Evil arises in the honored belief that history can be tidied up, brought to a sensible conclusion....It is evil for a nation to believe it is 'the last, best hope on earth.' It is evil to think history is to end with a return to Zion, or with the classless society, or with the Islamization of all living infidels."[4] Alas, all of these conclusions originate with the Level 1.4 mind. Therefore, like gasoline, they should never be poured into, stored in or transported in glass containers.)

• *Though you'll most likely want your children to center themselves elsewhere, they need to put down roots here.* The higher on the spiral of mental development we are at the time we begin our families, the less likely we are to pay attention to our children's needs at the levels below us. But as I hope my reader is seeing with a new appreciation and clarity, insufficient development at any of the mind's levels has a damaging cost. Fail to encourage and assist the development of Level 1.4 in a child, and you are almost guaranteeing the world a cynical, unnecessarily rootless and ultimately unhappy adult down the road. Each of us needs the capacity to believe. In ourselves. In something greater than we are. In a good reason for being alive and, ultimately, for having lived. Level 1.4 is where we get important tools for healthy, long-term self-validation and where we first learn how to use these tools to keep our feet on the ground.

• *If you ever feel totally lost, you may need to go home temporarily to Level 1.4.* This is "born again" country. Not that you'll necessarily need to join a fundamentalist faith to partake of the fresh-beginnings feelings available here. More than likely, you'll find other ways to get in touch with the back-to-the-basics reassurances you're looking for. A reconciliation with estranged family members. A visit or a move back to where you came from. Getting clear on your purpose for being alive. Finding ways to contribute to the community. Leaving the future to a higher power and proceeding one step at a time, armed with a belief that things work out okay for those who keep the faith and live responsibly.

Among the admirers of Dr. Clare Graves and his biopsychosocial theory of human maturation, there is disagreement on exactly when this level of the mind emerged as a potent, full-blown historical force, and I'm definitely in the minority on this question.

This would put me in opposition, for example, to those who would point to the start-up dates for the great monotheistic religions like Islam, Judaism and Christianity as convincing proof of a firm arrival date for Level 1.4 strongly moralistic brand of thinking.

My observation would be that spirituality is a notoriously shifty subject in terms of Dr. Graves' biopsychosocial model. That's probably because it is best envisioned as operating primarily in another dimension altogether. The safest thing you can say about the great religions is that they have this uncanny ability to float their way from one level of the mind to the next and become whatever they need to become to have a chance of gaining entry and acceptance by the mind's newest configuration. The strategy doesn't always work, or work very well. But, it seems, the effort is nearly always made. (That's probably why we call them "great religions" in the first place.) In addition, in so many ways, most of the great religions of the world, the ones just named and others, have never been entirely successful at severing themselves from what appears—at least to me—to be strong Level 1.2 influences and beginnings.

That noted, I can see why it is tempting for those who want to argue for long-ago beginnings for Level 1.4 to point, for example, to Moses, the Israelite prophet who lived in the twelfth and thirteenth centuries, B.C., and suggest that the Level 1.4 mind was solidly in view and on the move from that moment on. The "Thou shalts" and "Thou shalt nots" that Moses—and, in the movie, Charlton Heston—carted down from Mt. Sinai certainly have the no-phooey law-and-order, shape-up-or-else, eye-for-an-eye qualities that characterize so much of Level 1.4 thinking.

But here's a problem.

After Moses tripped over his stern new monotheistic god's rules and ended up buried in the valley of Moab instead of the

Promised Land, a real hiatus followed. About twenty-eight centuries' worth of hiatus. Twenty-eight centuries of continual backsliding, flip-flopping and lollygagging by the brain as it seemed to take two steps backwards for every one forward. For every Roman republic and Greek city-state, there were a thousand going-nowhere-fast nomadic kingdoms or marauding, civilization-thwarting warlords still around. For each tradition-founding Jesus of Nazareth, there were legions of fly-by-night soothsayers, evil spirits managers and demigod wanna-bes on the prowl. One new century of recycled Level 1.2- and-1.3-thinking-styled behaviors after another kept tumbling over the heels of the old ones. Magic and animism continued to permeate the pastoral life. "Closet" pantheism and out-of-the-cloister venality and power-grubbing stalemated and degraded the religious life. And anarchy or feudalism dominated the social and political order.

To my eye, if you want a firm date for the onset of real, lasting influence for Level 1.4, peg it around 1450 A.D., give or take a half-century. Before that, what we don't see in retrospect is a long, long period of hegemony for a strong Level 1.4-oriented civilization or major society not badly contaminated by Levels 1.2 and/or 1.3 thinking.

Even then, no sooner did Level 1.4-anchored thought processes seem to find a compelling groove for themselves than some of their lead horses began to jump their traces.

Suddenly, Level 1.4 seemed aflame with a desire for new ways to synthesize its most sacred cows. Almost immediately, its best, brightest and most comprehensive, correction-minded intellects were at work putting in place the foundations for revolutionizing religion (the Reformation and birth of Protestantism), the study of nature (the Scientific Revolution), manufacturing (the Industrial Revolution), the intellectual and economic scene (the Renaissance), politics (the rise of the constitutional state) and communications (Johann Gutenberg's invention of printing and all that followed). A more enterprising, expressive level of the mind would take up the quest and harvest the greater gains from these reformulations, especially in the nineteenth and twentieth centuries, but, make no mistake, it was the pioneering greats of Level 1.4 who first sowed the seeds of modern civilization.

Copernicus, Galileo Galilei and Ibn Battuta. Zwingli, Erasmus and Melancthon. Boccaccio, Petrarch and Colet. Giotto, Leonardo and the Medicis. Even if it didn't really manage to plant its flag solidly on the beach until much later than some have supposed, there is a lot to ponder and celebrate as we reflect on the legacy and role of Level 1.4.

In my pondering mind, I recall a title that R.F. Delderfield gave to one of his novels in the early 1970s: *To Serve Them All My Days*. That's an appropriate notion for Level 1.4, too. The blowout protector that doesn't quit is intended to serve each of us all our days, even when Beta has become the permanent home for our mind. And in terms of putting our modern civilization in place, as we've just seen, it has also paid its dues well there, too.

Chapter 9: **Alpha's Chassis, Con't**

WHEN DID THE FIRST faint glimmers of Beta appear? And from where—or whom? You would expect the earliest signs to show up as stranger-than-strange intimations in the mind of an intellect that was both acutely prescient and totally out of step with the establishment thinking of his or her time. That's why, when I go looking for evidence that a very modern mind is struggling to define its birth form—that is, when I go searching for glimmers of a thinking platform that seems to foreshadow Beta in significant ways—I think we might have what we're looking for in the brilliant, passionate, acutely insightful, yet agonized and tortured ideas of Friedrich Nietzsche.

In the late nineteenth century, Nietzsche offered a vision of the *Übermensch*, the Superman. He hypothesized that this new type of mind goes beyond all established values, beyond all previous codes, all rules and restraints of civilization, literally beyond good and evil—and shouts, "I will!" In doing so, this perfervid individual creates his or her own values—or, as Nietzsche once put it, undertakes "the revaluation of all values." Life is given to a person without meaning, but so what? The *Übermensch* wills his or her own meaning to life, living confidently, creatively, instinctively, completely—even dangerously—as he or she strives, desires, exerts and prevails.

By no means am I about to argue that Neitzsche's *Übermensch* is any guide to what you can expect your mind to be like in

Beta. But I do believe that Nietzsche caught one of the earliest glimpses of the possibility of a radically new style of thinking. In particular, there was a future for Nietzsche's ideas about the importance of will. These ideas were to do yeoman's work in the development of a new philosophy soon to flower in the twentieth century. It was called existentialism.

Very Neitzsche-like, existential philosophers have argued that "existence precedes essence." Before you can have something, you must first make the determination that you will be there to choose something. Meaning—essence—comes from within, not without. *You find meaning when you choose meaning!* The key is always to be caught thinking like a player, not like a spectator. To quote another great philosopher, Yoda, from Episode V of *Star Wars*, "Do, or do not. There is no 'try.'" Not until you have the *will* (there it is again!) to act do you know what your nature is and whether there is any meaning for you at all.

But before the mind could get its head out of the burrow of its own hoary beginnings far enough to begin to think expansively along these lines, it had to work its way substantially through the next of the mind levels we are about to discuss—and well into the one that follows that.

1.5

OF ALL THE VARIETIES of minds that we humans experience in Alpha, Level 1.5 is straightforwardly the most self-aware *and* self-absorbed. No real mystery here. This is a consequence of what its user sees as the best route for gaining in influence and in affluence, the twin megaliths of Level 1.5's ambition. The first sentence in the satirical *The Sweet Potato Queens' Big-Ass Cookbook (And Financial Planner)* hits the Level 1.5 nail pretty much squarely on its big-a** head: "In life, it's vitally important that you buy your own crown and declare yourself Queen."[1]

Level 1.5's self-help philosophy begins with the assumption that the way to get ahead in the world is to reach for your bootstraps and pull yourself up. Faith in greater external powers is out, faith in yourself is in. What you have going for you are your innate skills and competencies. Your guiles and your wiles. Your savvy use of what you've learned in the "school of hard knocks" as well as the schoolbooks and your abilities to make choices that will give you an edge. You realize you are competing in a world with many possibilities. But it is your mind's firm conviction that, if you can but only figure out what it is, there's likely to be but one best answer at any given time to any given need. Coming up with that right answer is, of course, something you need to do before someone else—someone who's after the same thing you're after—does it first.

So it is usually the assumption of the Level 1.5 mind that whatever you need to know, do or become an expert on, you need to act quickly. The competitive clock is always ticking. And it may even be that there's no need actually to learn the part or the ropes. You may be able to get by merely by looking the part, by looking like you're competent and in the know. After all, when you see life as mostly a game to be won, you see the world as mostly a stage intended for people who look like winners. For a time and on the surface, the Level 1.5 mind can often fake it even though it'll never even try to make it—becoming, for the moment, a close-enough approximation of whatever is needed to land the prize. Dressing for success, learning the language of winners, looking and sounding like the employee your boss wants you to be.

I once paid a high-powered marketing consultant from out of state to spend a day with me critiquing my sales efforts for my assessment products. When he arrived, it was obvious that he was distraught. He explained that his Rolex watch had disappeared en route. Throughout the day, I periodically overheard snatches of his phone conversations as he tried to locate it. At some point, it became clear to me that he hadn't lost a *real* Rolex. He had lost a *knock-off* of a Rolex.

No matter. It was part of his Level 1.5 persona, and he was in pain.

If you are dealing with a Level 1.5 mind, you need to exercise caution. The inner circle to which you have been invited by the user of this mind level can just as quickly become a hole in the floor. Should the circumstances change, what looks like personal warmth or friendship can disappear in a heartbeat. "Nothing personal," goes that most notorious of Level 1.5 brush-offs, "but business is business" (or "politics is politics"). Or as Robert Greene, author of *The 48 Laws of Power*, sums it up, "Everybody is replaceable. There's no sympathy and no pity. It's a cold world . . . so we all must establish and demonstrate our power."[2] In the Level 1.5 thinker's view of reality, winners make it to the top and, one way or another, the losers make dinner. As the mother of govWorks.com co-founder Tom Herman, who was forced out in a company power shift, says in the documentary film, "Startup.com," "Caring for people and how they feel is not part of this new world."[3] Or, it can be added, any world where Level 1.5 values are pushed to the hilt.

If it is true that the greatest achievement of the Level 1.5 mind has been to inject a free-market-energizing, free-enterprise-practicing middle-class between the very rich and the very poor, it is also true that the model has never worked as trickle-down economics predicts. For vast parts of the world's population, having a healthy, growing, stabilizing middle-class is a mirage. For most societies, there is little sign of the functioning work engine of a wealth-widening midsection between the wealthiest and the near wealth-less. In most societies, nothing much ever changes: it's a rule of nature—those who have take and those who have-not get taken. Even the American middle class, perhaps the greatest in history in terms of its size and wealth, is being threatened by declining wage levels, runaway health care costs, mounting debts, a deficiency of decent jobs and a seeming inability of society's leaders to frame the discussion in anything but Level 1.5 terms and self-interests. Yet voters keep returning politicians to office who promptly vote against the best interests of most of those who put them there.

The Level 1.5 mind has the formula for winning in public influence and governmental control down pat.

If you say the right thing, you don't necessarily have to do the right thing—and if you obfuscate, delay or dilute things enough, you may have to do nothing at all. In the "medium is the massage" world of TV sound-bite news, you can paint the right ideological picture, and you, as a politician or special interest decision-maker, can do almost anything you wish behind the scenes. You can offer repeated tax cuts mostly for the wealthiest and claim they are benefiting everyone. Pledge to help society's gravest problems but then refuse to provide funding for programs. Say one thing on the evening news and the Sunday morning talk shows and do something diametrically different when you craft the regulations and the legislation—or appoint the people who will actually call the shots.

ABUNDANT NEGATIVES

On those occasions where reality calls you out and exposes you for the calculating, self-serving Level 1.5 mind that you are, well, there's an effective tried-and-true Level 1.5 formula for dealing with that, too. Intimidate your critics every chance you get with accusations of lying, unfairness, disloyalty or appeasement. Claim that up is actually down, and offer contrived justifications and explanations if you must. Weave complex cover stories that provide you with the fig leaf of plausible deniability as needed.

Time and again, such smoke screens work because nearly everyone who might be in a position to call a spade a spade, assign accountability and enforce it or actually insist that public moneys be devoted to meeting needs caused by blinds spots in the market or other worthy public activities is, herself or himself, operating from Level 1.5 of the mind. In calculating their own best self-interest, they leave uncalculated the needs of those with no calculator or the best interests of the whole. They ignore the reality that there are numerous places in society where the Level 1.5 free-market model doesn't work. Places where there are needs so serious that they kill, maim and impoverish people when ignored. And places where leaving these needs unaddressed is morally reprehensible—evil!—no matter how often those in power show up at the door of the church, the synagogue or the mosque and profess piety and devotion to a deity that surely must approve of all this. Else, why would they have been placed in charge?

Seek to make this point to a typical user of the Level 1.5 mind and you can usually expect the standard spiel: the poor should lift themselves up. They should try harder. Giving them a hand or a handout is a waste of resources. The refrain will sound cocky, smug, superior and self-righteous, which it is. And no amount of anecdotal evidence or hard data, no appeal to fairness or human kindness, is likely to change this mind.

So there is much in a negative way for your Beta mind to label as unwanted or in need of remedy at Level 1.5. Likely to make the list are this level's tendency to:

• Discount anything it can't control or cite proven indications for or that arrives after it has reached a conclusion. Maddeningly, the Level 1.5 mind usually shuts down forever once it makes a decision and adamantly refuses to consider new evidence. We see this again and again in law officers, prosecutors and judges; in executives and managers; in journalists and in university presidents and school superintendents—anywhere the Level 1.5 mind holds sway.

• Close its eyes to the needs of have-nots in society, refusing to acknowledge that the boot-strap theory of self-betterment is overly simplified, severely limited in its application and often inhumane.

• Put so much emphasis on winning that the result is a one-dimensional person for whom life is seldom any more than a competitive game, whether the issue is child-raising, seeking charity donations or fighting for the next available promotion.

• Ignore long-range needs and opportunities in favor of quick fixes and temporary adjustments that will curry its own image, grease its own agenda and flow to its own private benefit.

• Lack healthy perspectives on what the good life really is, how complex the world is, how much is enough, how to lose graciously (on occasion) or how to deal intelligently with real limits.

• Treat people as pawns, coldly and calculatedly viewing them as expendable and interchangeable even while professing to care about them personally and pretending to see to their needs and best interests.

• Waste resources with little real philosophical sense of personal perspective or responsibility as it uses all that its money can buy to buttress its feelings of self-importance. Or compete in the "keep up with the Joneses" games. Or enhance its image as a superior player or person.

• Wound people with its indifferent attitude, bossiness, tacky comments and insensitivity to the feelings of others.

That said, it is now time for the "on the other hand" part of the picture. As I'm sure you were expecting and surprising as it may be, I also have strong positives to point out about Level 1.5 thinking. Very important positives.

For all its self-serving drawbacks and potential damage to the individual, the family and the rest of society, Level 1.5 offers too many heretofore unavailable gains in the mind's march through Alpha to be ignored. Let's look at some of them:

• *Don't expect to do well in contemporary life without some of Level 1.5's skill, confidence and chutzpah for dealing with authority and power.* This is especially true if you don't have the personal resolve and ability to ask for what you want, argue for what you need, push for what you deserve—and do it effectively. And those are cardinal Level 1.5 thinking qualities.

Another important Level 1.5-arbitrated skill is the ability to win under pressure. Often, because of the way the world works, you will be surrounded by game-faced-bearing competitors dedicated to seeing you lose. Professional football coach Bill Parcells has faced such straits many times. His results speak well of his ability to tap into Level 1.5's strategic and tactical skills when the going gets tough. After all, his teams have won two Super Bowls and played in a third. His secret? "Your team has to understand that the opportunity to win a game is always going to present itself sometime during the course of a game," he once told a banquet audience in Grand Prairie, Tex. "What separates the teams that know how to win from the ones that don't is the ability to recognize that opportunity."[4]

It's hardly the whole story, but one of the secrets of winning big, or so say high-profile Level 1.5 thinkers who have won big, is having an enemy to compare yourself with, to bedevil you, to light your fire. For Apple Computer, it was IBM. For the Manhattan Project, it was the Axis Powers (literally). For Coca-Cola, it is Pepsi...and vice versa. Former Coca-Cola chairman Roberto Goizueta was dialoguing with former General Electric CEO Jack Welch in a session recorded by *Fortune* Magazine when he said that any organization that doesn't have an enemy should create one. Asked why, Goizueta replied, "That's the only way you can have a war."[5] Warren Bennis and Patricia Biederman probably gave a better justification for defining an enemy in their book on creating great groups. "More often," they said, "the chief function of the enemy is to solidify and define the group itself, showing it what it is by mocking what it is not."[6] It's a common focus of the Level 1.5 mind: pulling out all the stops to augment your chances for winning.

• *There is a pure joy and excitement in awakening to new facets of yourself that become available for the first time at Level 1.5.* It's a feeling and willingness to commit, explore and grow that will come in handy ever after. This phenomenon hasn't been overlooked by Level 1.5-styled self-improvement authors. Listen to some of the book titles they've authored: *Awaken the Giant Within*, *Awaken the Diet Within*, *Awakening the Wisdom Within You*, *Awakening the Heroes Within*, *Awaken the Olympian Within*, *Awakening the Talents Within* and on and on. The last time I looked at the Web site of bookseller Barnes & Noble, it was reporting that the word "awakening" appears in 1,302 of its current book titles.

Self-calculated possibility thinking begins at Level 1.5. How high can you climb? What else can you achieve? How do you become all that you want to be? This level of the mind is not without an important kinship with the Beta mind. After all, the Beta mind itself is nothing if not a mind devoted to the discovery of new ways to be. If this kind of thinking doesn't begin here at Level 1.5, it is unlikely to begin at all.

• *Level 1.5 is where we first fully recognize that our mind can do and think more than one thing—and in more than one way—at a time.* Call the quality multiplistic thinking. Or multi-tasking. Or pluralistic thinking. It's a feature of the mind that is never more noticeable than when it is absent.

Consider the remodeling contractor who has just let my daughter's beloved Pug, Bogie, escape through an open gate. He explains, "I just turned my back to get something out of my truck." Implication: You can't expect me to do more than one thing at a time.

Or listen between the lines to the explanation from the nursing home duty nurse who has come close to letting my father die of pneumonia while laboriously proceeding line by line down a checklist for summoning outside vendors like the mobile x-ray clinician. "We have to follow the procedure in the book. Exactly," she said. Implication: Don't expect me to think or act outside the rules. Ever.

At Level 1.5, we cross an important threshold. Now, we're open to thinking in alternative ways. With our new "muddling through" willingness to look at the world from more than one perspective, we begin to come alert to the reality that our mind is a parallel processor. One part of it can work on one issue while another part of it is working on another. Our real genius at using this simultaneous thinking capability comes later, but this is where it starts. As the explosive wealth-building capacity of so many users of the Level 1.5 mind has demonstrated, a little multiplistic thinking can go a long way.

• *Level 1.5 has provided us with our first great progressive laboratory for testing how to grow a huge economy affecting substantial portions of a society—and our first qualified successes.* In 1902, economist Alfred Marshall spoke of "the springs of vigor" that are the hallmark of the Level 1.5 approach to economics. During the past century, those springs of vigor led to marked increases in goods and services. And increases in goods and services have led to the unquestionable gains that we Americans, among others, have enjoyed since 1900 in medicine and health, travel and communication, food production and labor-saving devices. In short, in the reduction of the dangers from being alive.

Wall Street Journal writers Jane Spencer and Cynthia Crossen summed it up this way: "Armed with scientific and technological breakthroughs, Americans have dramatically reduced their risk in virtually every area of life, resulting in life spans 60% longer in 2000 than in 1900. Many deadly infectious diseases were tamed, food and water were purified, drugs and surgery helped forestall heart attacks, and thousands of safety devices—window guards, smoke detectors, circuit breakers, air bags—protected against everyday mishaps. Even the risk of financial disaster was reduced by insurance, pensions and Social Security."[7]

Ever heard of Blue Monday? Your mother or grandmother probably knew the term intimately. It was wash day. But by the 1920s, the electric iron, washing machine and hot water heater were eliminating the need to limit the washing of clothes to just one long, laborious weekday.

By the 1930s, the American standard for bathrooms had been established: the recessed tub, a single-unit toilet, an enameled sink, tiled floors and walls, brass plumbing and a medicine chest. At the same time, public health gains were eliminating rat-associated outbreaks of plague and much else.

After the Second Great War, antibiotics began to do for civilians what they had done for so many soldiers: salvage their lives. Such gains were only the beginning.

Granted, it's true that the Level 1.5 mind still produces a huge amount of retched excess, waste and unfairness. We need to save space in that category for what has been called "the alpha male,"* for example. He's hell-bent to acquire more wealth than others at whatever cost. Why? To cite one important goal, so he can attract a trophy mate (or more likely, a series of them). And so he can raise his offspring in a way that will allow the kids to repeat the cycle and up the ante. The alpha female also stands equally ready to neuter many of her better instincts as a person with her own special variety of Level 1.5-generated competitive testosterone.

But, for all its self-serving drawbacks and potential damage to the individual, the family and the rest of society, we mustn't forget that Level 1.5 offers the many heretofore unobtainable gains we reviewed a moment ago. Awakening to new facets of yourself. Wondering how you can become all that you want to become. Also, the skill of doing more than one thing at a time genuinely flowers here. So does learning how to get want you want—and managing to do it consistently and repeatedly.

Using these skills, Level 1.5 has provided the fuel for an engine of discovery, productivity and personal beneficence, and it deserves credit. I think we should come right out and say it: if not for Level 1.5's gains and contributions, it's difficult to imagine that Beta would ever have emerged. And for certain, there would never have been a Level 1.6 of the mind, because, as we are about to see, it doesn't stretch our model or our credibility at all to suggest that almost everything the user of this next level of the mind holds sacred and unnegotiable has been elevated to such a lofty status as a result of the egregious abuses and failures of the level we've just been discussing. We last witnessed a counter-reaction of this strength and nature in Level 1.4's "blowout preventor" response to Level 1.3. This time, instead of getting its mouth washed out with soap, the mind is about to be sent to therapy.

---

*When used in this way, the term "alpha" has a different meaning than when it is used in this work to speak of "the Alpha mind."

1.6

*T*O TRULY LEARN what Level 1.6 is about, you need the time to observe its user closely. Level 1.6 is a complicated, variegated representation of the mind and deserves to be treated as such.

In place of hard-and-fast rules, it believes that responding to each situation exclusively—situationally—is the stance least likely to damage the fabric of people's lives, needs and hopes. At this level, truth and moral values are not seen as absolute but as molten and relative to the persons or groups holding them. Firmly at home with diverse information and the by-play of alternatives, the Level 1.6 mind is no shrinking violet in the lively outlook department, and yet it harbors a natural suspicion of logic and a linear intelligence. This, above all, gives rise to an operating sphere hospitable to feelings. Users of the Level 1.6 mind theorize that feelings go deeper than other mental messengers. This quality, it is believed, makes them more authentic and dependable for evaluating underlying realities of elemental importance than, for example, the mental activities attached to verbal characterizations. Feelings, it is felt, are more sensitive, more indicative, purer, holier than just about anything else the mind utilizes.

When they are at the top of their game, users of the Level 1.6 mind have one overriding concern: *don't harm others.* No physical or economic violence. No torture, murder, death sentences or executions, wars or war crimes, sweatshops or other health-destroying business practices. No setting out literally to destroy someone. No knocking on anyone's door with a gun or a baseball bat.

Sounds like a totally humane, totally desirable, totally admirable human spirit—and for much of the way, it is.

How about hurting someone else's feelings?

Oh, sure, you'll find this happening when the Level 1.6 mind gets its hackles up over a perceived injustice or feels an affront to its values or simply gets into an our-ideas-are-superior-to-yours snit. Then, you should expect Level 1.6 to be strong and assertive as it serves the group and its valued interests. But it would be a rare occasion if blood were to be shed. Honoring this pacifistic ideal takes lots of time. Not to mention patience, awareness and caring. An astute onlooker, like your Beta mind, there to expand its understanding of what is happening at Level 1.6, is simply going to have to get comfortable and be willing to go with the flow to absorb the full picture.

EGREGIOUS EXCESS

The desire of the Level 1.6 mind—indeed, this ability of that mind—to put itself so completely and acceptingly in the shoes of another has proven irresistible in places where an automatic reticence to treat others unfairly or disrespectfully already exists. Like the Scandinavian societies, known for their inbred cultural gentleness and all-around egalitarian outlooks. Like New Age-flavored communities and other devotees of the Age of Aquarius, conditioned to be sensitive and caring and sharing. And like college and university campuses, where the sheltered humus of academic potting soils can join almost overnight with the shortened growing season of young minds to breed arcane new ideologies and movements based on an ideal of non-intervention and non-aggression.

The core of Level 1.6's understanding of the world is that all people deserve to be treated fairly, equably and equally as much of the time as possible.

In no time at all, this admirable belief was fed—like so much firewood—by empathetic educators in the social sciences and the liberal arts into a raging cook stove of a philosophical movement called postmodernism. The extreme versions of postmodernism soon produced an omelet of egregious excess that ultimately was as indigestible as it was irresistible to many Level 1.6 thinkers. Postmodernism's equality-for-all-now fervor was especially appealing to those predisposed to attack what they viewed as the hegemonic forces of cold rationalism, runaway "scientism" and naked materialistic self-interest in Western society. Soon, critical thinking and facts-backed reasoning were under sustained attack on practically every state-supported college and many private ones in America.

The six most damaging words in postmodernism's pillaging of the campus's thinking sensibilities came from French philosopher Jacques Derrida: *there is nothing outside the text.*

Meaning what?

Meaning that, or so postmodernism's cook stove tenders argued, that we humans live in only one dimension: a verbal one. Our reality is of a singular nature only: verbal interpretations. Only language is real, and since language by its very nature is so illusive and subjective, so susceptible to lopsided bias and manipulation by power structures, there are no facts—no objectively true claims—to be had at all.

Well, who ever said that there were?

Why, those male, racist, imperialist, Western ideologues with names like Voltaire, Kant, Bacon, Hegel and Jefferson who framed the rational ideas of the Enlightenment.

Viola, let's attack the Enlightenment thinkers.

And so, ignoring the fact that postmodernism's vaulted egalitarian-minded "politics of difference" owes its heart and soul to the Enlightenment's concept of collective self-respect, that's what happened. A "crit-lit" firestorm of vituperation and bile was tossed at anyone audacious or unwary enough to claim that there are genuine, ongoing foundations of order to the world. And that this order is worthy of rational, Enlightenment-like examination and—yes—interpretation through experiment, reflection, dialogue and the utilitarian discovery of (often hierarchical) moral and practical fruits within. The anti-reason, anti-hierarchical, trash-the-Enlightenment movement of Level 1.6-actualized postmodernism has been nasty, time-consuming and, in the end, incapable of demonstrating much lasting gain at all for the greater good.

Just one amazing example of postmodernism's often out-of-control absurdities, and we'll move smartly on to some much finer moments to be enjoyed in Level 1.6's ambit.

THE DANGERS IN FEELINGS

Disability studies. It is a new academic sub-discipline, one that has tirelessly undertaken the task of rooting out—in post-modernism's all-or-nothing "cultural studies" fashion—the social construction of disability. You can get Ph.D.s in the subject, from very fine universities. There is a Society for Disability Studies, which meets every year. Go to SDS's annual conventions, and you'll soon be up to your chin in explanations of how the concept of being disabled is another of those unfair, Enlightenment-like false realities foisted on undeserving groups and individuals by the verbal constructions of a larger society.

At a recent SDS conference, these assertions were made by straight-faced academicians whose salaries are paid, for the most part, with your tax dollars and mine: USA actually stands for "the United States of Ability," which happens to be filled with "body-fascists, who, if given the chance, would happily exterminate their disabled population." Case in point: all of "Dr. Death" Jack Kevorkian's patients were severely disabled. "It's not suicide," said the speaker, "it's genocide." The disabled body, said another speaker, is actually "the norm" for humans. After all, he argued, life starts disabled in the womb. And it ends disabled by old age. So life is just a brief window of ability between natural states of disability. This scholar's upside-down conclusion: *disability is normal, and non-disability is abnormal!*

And then there was the professor of German who claimed that being able-bodied "is the precondition for being a tool of the ruling class." Therefore, she concluded, being disabled is preferable to abled-bodied.[8]

And so it goes.

What a place, Level 1.6 of the mind in its more outrageous costumes!

Your Beta mind is going to understand that postmodernism has actually been a sideshow, though a high-kicking, garish one, in Level 1.6's overall development and influence. The most important consequences of this level's approach to thinking about how to improve the human condition have happened elsewhere. Moreover, more than a few of the most outspoken and vituperative voices in postmodernism's camp have probably not been users of this level of the mind at all. Not infrequently, they have been infiltrators and opportunists from other levels, notably Level 1.5 or even Level 1.4, who have recognized a good prospect for boosting their academic careers when they saw it or have just used postmodernism's quick-to-emerge superciliousness and self-righteousness to cloak their natural tendencies toward snobbishness, exclusionist behaviors and absolutism.

Nevertheless, you can expect your mind to present a lengthy list of no-no's for Level 1.6. The new respect for feelings is healthy and a genuine step forward, but the flight from rational thinking is a dangerous thing. Feelings have this positive feedback, roll-over-on-themselves quality. They can start small and keep reinforcing themselves, until suddenly they are overwhelming. High suicides rates are an all-too-real concern for Level 1.6 users. It's easy to despair about how unfair life can be, and how little impact your ameliorations can have for those who suffer the most, yourself included.

REASONS FOR CAUTION

The gullibility factor at Level 1.6 is also something to guard against. Sometimes, all you need to do is to step away from the group-think so prevalent when you are with your like-minded Level 1.6 thinkers. When you do, what was credible and inviting only moments before can now be seen as little more likely than one of Stephen King's nutty fear-inducing fantasies. Crystals don't channel good vibes. Feng Shui furniture arrangements don't bring "chi" bubbling into your living spaces with harmony and prosperity. The I-Ching doesn't divine the future any better than a table of random numbers. Homeopathic medicine is a one-way ticket for a hearse if you are deathly sick. Even Level 1.6-enabled offshoots that may have sensible uses—like the Neuro-Linguistic Programming (NLP) approach to restructuring mental processes, any number of wellness and fitness regimens, the split-brain studies as applied to decision-making and developmental issues or, heaven help us, the play-your-baby-some-Mozart phenomenon—can quickly see their plausibility go south in the hands of uncritical, overeager users of this kind of mind. Like all the levels of the mind previously to it, what the Level 1.6 mind wants to believe and do, it usually believes and does, regardless of the evidence (or lack of it).

Meanwhile, it's easy—too easy—for Level 1.6 to miss its deadline or not pay attention to the budget. (Credit card marketers positively, absolutely love this mind level.) Far too many Level 1.6 projects and enterprises get started simply because somebody had a dream and pursued it with no market research. And, of course, they fail at about the same rate for the same reason. And when immersing yourself in a community of Level 1.6 users becomes your crutch and your excuse for not taking a hard look at yourself, making tough, needed choices or getting on with your development and your life, you haven't joined a salutary group. Instead, you have checked yourself into a feel-good hospital that, rather than help you get well or get real, is designed to keep you from ever walking out the door, especially the one leading to Beta.

So why not just work around Level 1.6? Why not do your best to avoid it altogether?

Believe it or not, there are those hard-chargers in the developmental-theorist ranks who say this is what they have done. They maintain that their route to Beta unfolded this way: (1) They developed Level 1.5 nicely, learning how to compete, achieve, handle themselves calculatedly and handle others without raising undue ire. Looking around for greener, greater pastures, they spotted Level 1.6—and promptly pronounced it a terminal turnoff. They adjudged that there wasn't a communal bone in their body, much less any affinity for political correct thinking, and consequently made a beeline for Beta like they had been shot from a cannon. You'll have to judge for yourself, but I'm not persuaded. When I'm around one of these folks with such extreme "inner self" avoidance, I feel like I'm walking around with a muscle builder. Their mental/emotional bulk is all out of proportion to the psychological image they are trying to project. I sense that they've tried to do something on the cheap, and to me, it shows.

My technical take—and my personal experience, as you've already seen—is that it is not possible to skip Level 1.6 and travel any further on the mind's odyssey. Personally, I'd not want to miss this stage. What I expect your Beta mind to conclude, after a long, close look at Level 1.6, is that the gains to be had there are, no less so and arguably more than the gains at all other levels of the mind, indispensable to moving on. Let's take a look.

• *At Level 1.6, your neural apparatus begins to demonstrate a genuinely maturing capacity for dealing effectively with the world's astounding diversity.* If you are watching for it, you can sense this new, expansive, empathetic interest in the wide, wide world of life immediately upon entering the lair of almost any Level 1.6 thinker. At this level, the mind tends to be very spatial, visual and kinesthetic. It tends to keep nearly everything out in the open. Visitors can expect to find the kind of tools and toys that are appealing to someone who enjoys the search for new ideas and insights. For experiences that will help them connect and interact with others. And that are likely to produce new, ever-changing feelings!

Reflecting on Level 1.6 environments I have known and loved, I recall the doctor's office with the numerous aquariums and plants, the big windows and natural lighting, the photos and highly personal, hand-crafted bio's of each employee on the walls, the perking coffee pot, the friendliness and responsiveness.

I remember any number of restaurants throughout the world free of both tawdriness and glitz but jam-packed with warm, pleasant colors, (invariably) fresh flowers, bright paintings, tactile-friendly objects and other idiosyncratic touches that spoke to the owners' personal fantasy of a life-enhancing environment.

I'm reminded of the difference between, say, a New Age bookstore and one specializing in books for evangelical and other conservative Christians. (It strikes me as the difference between a let-it-all-hang-out domain and a take-great-care-what-you-let-in domain.) In exploring new worlds and developing new senses of yourself, an important need is for you to be able to share with others. You feel most at home and most stimulated when you are in the company of people who are equally attracted to your new Level 1.6 world of change, novelty and variety.

• *Level 1.6 helps make you at home in an environment that requires constantly scanning for new possibilities.* Some experts have suggested that time seems to run from the future to the present for Level 1.6-thinking individuals. Perhaps what they are saying about you when you are using this level of the mind is that what could happen is often more real than what is happening. And, of course, what is past is past. Level 1.6's almost obsessive curiosity and ceaseless reaching out for newness means you are very much at home with change and variety. You tend to be a source of good, and often novel, ideas anytime anyone is willing to take the time to ask you and listen to what you have to say. With Level 1.6, you don't tend to experience life as sequential. Your schedules, your scenarios and your opinions are in constant flux. As a matter of course, you should not be expected to provide many straight-line solutions to issues and challenges. Conversely, the payoff is that you can be an excellent ally when there's a need to tackle the unknown or the unanticipated.

• *Level 1.6 offers you great strides in understanding what it's like to be a responsible interdependent member of a larger good or community.* At Level 1.6, you want to assume that the world is basically good, a beneficial place overall. Your big-picture view makes you aware that, even in mundane manners, we are highly interdependent on this planet. This we're-all-in-it-together view drives your belief that it is important for everyone to care for and support everyone else. In a sense, you see yourself as a defender or safeguarder of just causes and important relationships that enhance people's lives and the survival of humanity as a whole. Your desire is to see benefits appear quickly for as many people as possible, so you're likely to be willing to sacrifice some results and options if you're convinced that doing so will create life-enhancing benefits for yourself and others now and in times to come.

• *Level 1.6 equips you to shift more easily than ever from a "what is" mode of thinking to a "what might be" mode.* Critics may call it blue-sky thinking as your Level 1.6 ideas tumble about with little more coherence than this week's laundry being tossed to and fro in a clothes dryer. Bewildering as this can be to occupants of other mind levels, the Level 1.6 mind is perfectly at home making life seem like jazz.

Discussions where users of this level of the mind are gathered together can quickly elude the agenda...if there ever was one. Trains of thought get truncated and pierced and hoisted abruptly, leapfrogging over seemingly indispensable logic and set down in another time, space or emotional dimension—with nobody seeming to notice the displacement or the incongruity. When the whole affair runs smack into the brick wall of absurdity, this simply stokes the companionship-loving Level 1.6 user's appreciation for such compatible company. At an all-Level 1.6 confab, shared laughter is the lubricant of choice, and camaraderie flows as easy as water.

Get the picture?

It really takes a Level 1.6 mind to truly understand and enjoy another Level 1.6 mind for very long. Most of the other levels of Alpha will have difficulties with the user of this mind level. Some will see this flavor of thinker as irrational, some will see her or him as threatening or disruptive and others will see the Level 1.6 user as impractical. This general prejudice tends to magnify the natural inclination to live as exclusively as possible in a Level 1.6 world—move to San Francisco, Boulder, Vermont, Hawaii, British Columbia or New Zealand. For the 1.6 thinker, this means that if you want to improve the chances that your presence and ideas will have influence in the world, you must be prepared to do the homework required to demonstrate your relevance and usefulness. The key is letting individuals from various mind levels tell you or show you what is important to them and then mapping your innovative insights onto their interests in ways they appreciate and value.

Or so your mind can be expected to report before putting in for a well-deserved, hard-earned, Level 1.6-designed vacation.

• *Level 1.6 is potential "cap and gown" time for the Alpha mind.* Looking back on your final moments in Alpha, whether they were relatively swift or hypnotically slow in passing, you'll probably recall that at times your emotions seemed strapped into the front car of a world-class roller coaster. It was back and forth, up and down, and precipitous for the entire ride. When on top of the world, you blazed confidently into the future. Then, back in the trough of despair, you recycled old hurts or replayed emotions that you had thought—and hoped—were history.

I believe what is happening here is a case of "ontogeny recapitulating phylogeny" that is actually real.[9]

At Level 1.6, as our mind feels the tug of Beta, it seems to revisit all the previous stages of Alpha. At times we simply want to retreat to infancy, get in touch with, become and remain our "inner child." Other times, we experience fierce anger, raging against both the light and the darkness. We have our moments of extreme humility, feeling one with a great authority and thinking this is enough, this I can hold to, *here* I will remain. But we don't because there are also "highs" that trigger concentrated enterprise and initiative to move on in behalf of a "wholeness" that sometimes feels centered in us alone and other times in a greater "all." And then, mixed in with all the others, there are powerful reoccurring periods of intense sadness and loneliness, feelings of being helpless to discover and enact what it is that we yearn for— solutions to the ills that society is committing against the innocent. Answers to all the unfairness. Correctives for all the unnecessary pain and waste produced by selfish ambition and thoughtless actions. Level 1.6 users grieve for what they feel should be possible but they know isn't so. For what would be so edifying and fair, so rewarding and permanently desirable, if only a way could be found to make their visions come to pass.

Sometimes, people give up and retreat, as I have been pointing out for years with regards to many in the so-called baby boomer generation.

Sometimes, people stay on the treadmill, coming close to, or perhaps actually, destroying any hope of peace of mind or accommodation with reality, until they do themselves lasting damage. Tragically, they may literally destroy themselves.

Sometimes, persons do make Level 1.6 work for the long haul, finding a happy circumstance of a good-enough personal inner equilibrium, adequate resources, safe-enough surroundings and a stable, companionable, supportive community (if only the have-nots of the world could be so lucky).

And sometimes, as your Beta mind attests, people do graduate. If our mere, substantially animal-oriented survival skills were to have ended up as the final plateau for our human development, we would have demonstrated only that we had been able to exist for longer and longer life spans—at least thus far—despite being constantly victimized by the hard realities of our long developmental trail, often hard-wired within us. And that, at least for those of us in Beta, is not enough. We would never have demonstrated any real powers, in ways that are meaningful and enduring, for effectively challenging the blind forces of evolution and entropy. For molding, you might say, our humanity into a genuinely inquisitive, creative, redemptive force.

Such a realization is a powerful inducement for building on the remarkable chassis we've been examining in the past two chapters and moving on. And for assisting, as I now need you to help me do, in sparking a Beta revolt!

Chapter 10: **Neinja**

*I*T JUST DOESN'T COMPUTE for me that the workings of my brain—the nitty-gritty chemical-and-electrical environment where my thinking is produced—closely resemble a Wild, Wild West, shoot-'em-up kind of place. I simply don't experience my brain this way. I doubt that you'll find it easy to imagine your brain as a Darwinian-type, survival-of-the-fittest, witch's brew ambiance, either. (Honestly, from the inside looking out, it seems more like Campbell's Tomato Soup territory to me.)

But such a claim is being made. In most instances, its originators are thoughtful observers of the mind—from philosophers to evolutionary psychologists to cultural anthropologists to biologists.

Proponents of this view contend that the reigning processes of the brain successfully *muscle* their way into influence—into consciousness. In doing so, these experts believe our neural processes bend to the rules and the rhymes of their own interior, hyper-competitive world, and little else. Because this is the way the brain seems to work, or so these authorities argue, there is no evidence for, no explanation for, *no place for* a centralized operator with a unique sense of being. Nothing at all of the kind of independent, in-charge entity that we have traditionally called the self.

Seen from this perspective, the brain houses gazillions of "processes competing for ongoing control." Each of them, you might say, wants to be famous—be conscious. When these processes go mano-a-mano with each other, the one "with the greatest clout dominates the scene until a process with even greater clout displaces it." The processes lacking the requisite clout get no fame and "evaporate into oblivion"; those remaining are elevated as conscious events, hanging around, "monopolizing time 'in the limelight,'" as cerebral celebrities.[1]

One of novelist Don DeLillo's characters in *White Noise*, winner of the 1985 National Book Award, expresses a similar idea:

> Who knows what I want to do? Who knows what anyone wants to do? How can you be sure about something like that? Isn't it all a question of brain chemistry, signals going back and forth, electrical energy in the cortex? How do you know whether something is really what you want to do or just some kind of nerve impulse in the brain. Some minor little activity takes place somewhere in this unimportant place in one of the brain hemispheres and suddenly I want to go to Montana or I don't want to go to Montana.

The researchers who hold to this view admit that, even for themselves, it certainly feels like a self is in there somewhere. But in finality, since they haven't found any proof they find convincing, they are referring more and more to the self as *an illusion*, a shadow thrown by an exceedingly artful projector—no less than the brain itself. Their conclusion: when all is said and done, we are reduced to the sums of the operations of our parts. There is really no real "you." And no real "me." We are simply flesh-and-blood receptacles playing host to warring chemicals and electrical impulses.

TALE OF TWO REPLICATORS

To get to this point in their explanations, two monstrously important and seemingly improbable developments had to fall into place, and it appears that both did. One has been convincingly documented, and claims about the other are not theories or assumptions that I have any quarrel with.

Neither development telegraphed any advance warning of its impending emergence or eventual importance.

One advance had to do with genes. Genes—apparently about 30,000 of them—are embedded in the structure of our DNA. This is the endlessly repetitive dual-sided data string that contains the "code of life" and is found in the nucleus of every cell in our body. Genes are self-copying instructions that transmit the design and construction information for numerous characteristics from parent to offspring, throughout living things in nature.

Genes, of course, are all about Darwinism.

Nineteenth Century English biologist Charles Darwin launched the ideas that grew into a theory that now dominates scientific explanations of how life came to be: the idea that it is the fittest among living creatures that survive to procreate in the largest numbers and thus gain an outsized influence on the nature of current and future generations of living things. This happens by a test-and-generate process. Genes are skilled at finding ways to help their hosts reproduce themselves whatever the odds or the obstacles. Genes are the quintessential replicator.

Today, people attracted to Darwin's ideas are often called neo-Darwinians. Dr. Richard Dawkins, a British biologist, is one. (And so, up to a point, is your author.) In fact, Dawkins is one of the most creative and outspoken neo-Darwinians. Dawkins' first book about all this, published in 1975, was named *The Selfish Gene*. But even before he finished it, he decided his book was more about selfish *replicators* than selfish genes.

"Darwinism," explains Dr. Dawkins, "is a much more general idea than the particular version of Darwinism which happens to explain life on this planet. Darwinism in this more general universal sense refers to the differential survival of any kind of self-replicating coded information which has some sort of power or influence over its probability of being replicated."[2]

Genes are certainly the best known of the Darwinian-type replicators.

In the vast sweep of their history, genes didn't have to group themselves together into organisms (like us) as they have done. Conceivably, they could have remained in their own separate, private little worlds. But group themselves they did. With a vengeance.

The result, among other organisms, is our magnificently complicated, multi-system human body, with thinking, oxygen-disseminating, visualizing, nutrient-converting and a myriad of other biological tissue, gene-designed-and-assembled inventions too splendid and extraordinary for engineers in most cases to come close to replicating elegantly if at all.

The other outlandish development that was needed to buttress the idea that the self is an illusion involved another type of replicator: the meme. This name came, once again, from the imaginative Dawkins. In the final chapter of *The Selfish Gene*, he proposed the name and the concept: infectious information that can be passed from mind to mind and is, therefore, gene-like in that it is capable of arranging for copies to be made of itself. Memes are things like jokes, stories, theories, food preferences, sound bites, habits, prejudices, clothing fashion choices, ways of doing things, ways of talking about things, even of the kind of beliefs and world-views you adopt. Anything cultural that can be imitated and is compelling enough or energetic enough or just lucky enough to get itself copied can justifiably be called a meme.

Just as with genes, memes didn't have to entwine themselves as larger and larger clusters of neuron-activating, -connecting and -orchestrating entities. But entwine themselves they did. Again, it happened with a vengeance.

The result is our magnificently complicated, multi-level storehouse of a mind. It brings with it the ability to pleasure itself by creating and responding to the most sublime music and art and architecture and literature. It can imagine elaborate technologies like the microchip. Fathom the atom. Develop the techniques to probe deep space. Figure out how its universe began and how it may end. Solve many of the mysteries of disease. And fashion elaborate blueprints for acting civil, communal, familial, humane—built around mercurial core concepts called love and altruism.

LINE IN THE SAND

When we put our arms around the totality of this astonishing two-headed apparatus, with all its Brobdingnagian implications, we can appreciate how proponents of the idea of the self as illusion might begin to have such a suspicion. A suspicion that all this prodigious activity and its supporting apparatus has somehow latched onto a means of running itself, without any qualitative assistance from a greater-than-the-sum-of-its-parts "centrality of consciousness" where it can be said definitively that the bucks stops. But when our scientific eminences leave the lecture hall, talk show or press conference where they have expounded on all this, the rest of us are left to confront the fact that they've left behind a far bigger issue than the one they have been seeking to explain.

They've glossed over, and completely failed to provide any convincing explanation at all for, why it unquestionably feels like there is a conscious, commanding, controlling self—an essential controlling essence—within us. Certainly, we *act* like we have a self. From all the moving, seemingly coordinated vehicles in the traffic stream of our awareness, it is difficult not to imagine that they are following such a route as the one we've traditionally called the self.

Of course, if we are little more than fascinatingly complex organic machines, then it is difficult to say that we are in charge of ourselves. If we are not in charge of ourselves, then it is hard to understand how we are responsible. If we are not responsible, then we are hard-pressed to preserve the notion of human freedom. It, too, is fast becoming to resemble an illusion. And if the self is an illusion and human freedom and responsibility are illusions, then, as far as we are concerned, *anything* can be an illusion—we'll never know, because we aren't capable of knowing.

We would end up being only a clockwork brain, a biological automaton, doing what we are conditioned to do by our evolving internal codes, that is, be a pliable host forged by genes, invaded by memes and programmed by both. And if we are deprived of the right to a self that is real, then the world is, too. Now and forever. In the words of Dr. Terrance Deacon, professor of biological anthropology at Boston University, "Then we have no hope of understanding our own consciousness, no hope perhaps of organizing a truly just and egalitarian society. No hope of moving beyond the sort of mean existence that we still live in."[3]

Absent a self, we can never assume to have our own sense of consciousness and being. We can forget about originating meaning or producing novelty that can be said to be uniquely our own. Irrespective of how dazzling or startling the results of our thinking, the credit must always belong to another, even if the "other" is only a mindless, directionless process that shuffles self-organizing components around in our heads like so many soulless dominoes until something wins or something clicks. After eons of development and learning, the seemingly wondrous faculties of the mind that appear to make us the only species capable of stepping back and marshalling perspective—of pondering the meaning of our presence in the world and what we might do differently or better—end up little better off than where they started. With bundles of neurons dancing hypnotically and robotically to the tunes of genes and memes.

To me, this is simply an unacceptable idea. Even if this narration of the mind-as-illusion argument that I've just voiced turns out to be a tad too alarmist or too overdrawn on my part, the fact that it is being seriously toyed with is already a nod too far in a direction too delusory. And because the influence of such an idea is spreading, I think it is time to draw a line in the sand. The buck must stop here and now—with you, with me, with Beta—on this issue of the self being a "folk psychology" invention of our gifted, perfervid, gene-and-meme-driven human imagination. There is simply more going on here than that, and we need to find a way to buy time for us to find out what.

NEW CHOICE-MAKER

In the interest of hiking to the top of a higher prominence for the purpose of accessing a better view, I want to propose something different. I propose the conscious acknowledgment of a *third* great replicator.

I have named it the *neinja* ("NAIN-jah").

The neinja cannot exist without the gene and the meme. However, it is both separate from and transcendent to both in ways that the other two kinds of encoding units can't begin to approach or appropriate on their own, not even after hundreds of thousands or millions of years (most genes) or thousands of years (most memes) of trying.

"Nein," of course, is the German word for no.

And "ja" is the German word for yes.

Our newest replicator is a search-oriented, evaluative-minded, no/yes-and-points-in-between choice-maker and decision-maker par excellence.

At the Beta level of the mind, it has formidable skills for challenging the hegemony of both the gene and the meme. It can marshal good judgment and moral defenses against unthinking outrages orchestrated by neurochemical onslaughts triggered by old, old gene-designed brain tissue patterns. And it has no compunction against calling a meme a meme. This frees it to move to dampen or even eradicate a meme's influences in the mind's developing finale of conclusions if its evaluations hint at impending danger, faulty evidence, bad ethics or the shadowy fingerprints of other parties' unjustified self-interest.

Let's say that your Beta neinja encounters something questionable, potentially harmful or simply mindless and of no use to us or our neighbors. When it recognizes such, this neinja does its best to say, "No, no more, no longer, not on your life, nary another time, non, nyet, *nein!*"—no!—and does all it can to reinforce and replicate the veto. And when it senses in our mind or environment anything useful or anything that represents new possibilities, novel convergences or emergences or anything that stands a good chance to improve the quality and the conditions of life, it says *ja!*—yes!—and does all it can to reinforce and replicate the endorsement.

The best aspect of this whole idea of the neinja replicator is that our representations, interpretations and expectations of the world around us can often be revised or replaced if they don't work well, or don't work well enough. We can reformulate our personal theories and hypotheses and run new personal experiments like the inquisitive scientist we all are at the core of our humanness.

Our Beta neinja also understands that there are more than a few times when we need to stand outside our logical structures with an attitude of curiosity and intrepidness and straightforwardness, not to mention humility and honesty, delayed gratification and judgment. We need to do so in the interest of providing a way around the high-voltage quibbles and conflict-points of explanatory attempts where there is little to be gained or lost or where the possibility of real progress or finality appears to be an absent quality. *Where we simply cannot, at this time or maybe ever, know.*

PRACTICAL PURSUIT

With the release of such "handcuffs of the mind," we are all encouraged to rejoin life where a river of tolerable ambiguity and openness to currently unexplainable paradox runs through it. From such a stance, something becomes immediately obvious that is otherwise probably obscured by all the rhetoric: by and large, we live life not in absolute assurance of much of anything. Rather, we live mostly "as if" things are true and real. As if the universe has meaning (the more we learn about at least the physical aspects of it, as one eminent scientist—a physicist, understandably!—has famously pointed out, the less it seems so). As if we have free will (maybe we do, but maybe, actually, it turns out we don't). As if there will be a tomorrow (for many of us there is, for some of us there isn't, and the day could conceivably come when there will be no tomorrow for anyone). As if we have a self (if we do, as we've noted in this chapter, we haven't nailed down the nitty-gritty mechanics for it yet and, in all honesty, may never quite manage to do so). Throughout it all, we need to remind ourselves frequently of scientist-turned-philosopher Michael Polanyi's memorable insight: "We know more than we can tell." More than we can explain. More than we can spell out explicitly, by today's scientific rules and ways and maybe by tomorrow's, too.

More times than we would like to admit, our circumstances are similar to those of the drunk who was found searching for his car keys under the streetlamp. Asked where he had lost his keys, he pointed to a darkened area down the block.

"So why," he was asked, "are you looking for your keys here under the streetlamp?"

"Because this is where the light is," he replied.

Somewhere down the road, as we look back with greater insight and experience and are able to move more of this subject of the self under the streetlamp, it's possible that the Beta neinja may turn out to be merely a super-meme. It may actually encompass pretty much the general qualities of the best of ordinary memes, plus something transcendent and exciting and self-organizing. Or we may discover that, with our theory of the neinja, we are much closer than we realize to the grand banana. The Beta neinja and all the neinjas of Alpha before it may actually be the elusive self that contemporary scientists can't seem to find any evidence for. If so, then it's been here all the time as the third great replicator!

Knowing if it is the former or the latter or something else altogether matters more to the scientists who have been looking for it than to the rest of us. Conceptual pragmatists on such issues that we are, what really matters is moving this subject under the streetlamp of practicality, not technicality, as quickly as possible.

Which is what I've been attempting to do.

What better use can we put the most powerful neinja yet—the Beta neinja—to than deploying it to explore the depths of the Beta mind itself?

That's what we'll do next.

Chapter 11: **Across the Great Divide**

AS THE EARLY generation of a new flavor of mind—one capable of harnessing the powers of a third great replicator—what kind of self do we Beta thinkers represent? What image, what manner, what sense of our own independent being do we offer the world? *How, exactly and descriptively, at the Beta level are we prepared to think?*

At this headwaters moment of this migration to a new kind of mind and a new variety of our human nature, it is important to provide the most authentic answers possible. And who better to know than those who have been doing the exploration and investigation? I've consulted seminar transcripts, books, articles, speeches, doctoral dissertations, Yahoo groups and research data from virtually every major academician, graduate student and practicing consultant in the past three decades who has seriously incorporated Clare Graves' theory and model into her or his work. Thanks to the exhaustive winnowing process of the Beta neinja, here is what—reduced to their fundamentals— Dr. Graves found, what these professional investigators have found and what I have found to be common thinking characteristics you can expect to see in Beta thinkers, yourself included:

In Beta:

■ *you have an unshakably hopeful stance of a very different kind than that usually called optimism.*

This rules out the kind of unbridled, macho-sounding "can-do" optimism we so often hear expressed by the Level 1.5 mind, especially from business people and sports figures. We can also rule out the kind of euphoric, "let's join together and save the world" feel-good optimism we often hear espoused by the Level 1.6 mind. In Alpha, when bad things happen, the motivational gurus and professional pick-me-up specialists generally tell you (1) it's only temporary, (2) it's not your fault, (3) it isn't like everything in your life is suddenly wrecked and (4) everything is fixable. In Alpha, optimism is viewed as a kind of all-purpose scab for swiftly covering up the wounds of setback and acting as if nothing has happened.

In Beta your fear of failure has been supplanted. In circumstances of setback or defeat, you can travel another road.

You can take time to gather your wits, assemble the facts, reflect, grieve, plan, adjust, be *realistic*. This way, the wounds of setback aren't glossed over. Beta's rationality sorts them out (maybe it *was* your fault and there is something important here to be learned and avoided in the future) and *then* the fast-act restoratives of the Beta spirit can move in to heal and repair.

Even for the short haul, Beta routinely encourages traveling the saner, more fully sentient, more fully informed and more personally honest—the pragmatically heightened—road.

In Beta, the kind of resilient, broad-ranging outlook that interests us is the kind that science fiction writer Ray Bradbury appears to have had in mind. "Optimism has only meant one thing for me," he wrote. "The chance to behave optimally."[1] The hopeful stance in Beta issues from one assumption: that in the overall scheme of things, humankind will have a chance to behave optimally—to deliver on the promise of its "genetic packaging," the brain included, and all that might lie beyond.

It is the kind of hopeful stance that can weather long stretches of turbulence and still maintain its belief in the ability of the human experiment to find its way forward.

The kind of hopeful stance that has an unshakable faith in its own personal compass for pinpointing meaning in the life being lived, even if at the moment there is not another single supporting voice of endorsement or encouragement.

The kind of hopeful stance that quickly returns the intellect to the task of looking for the gains available beyond pain, even when it appears that the human spirit may have sustained an appalling blow.

The kind of hopeful stance that doesn't need trophies, hand claps, headlines or the nonverbal accolades visible on the faces of kindred psyches in the communal group to maintain its strength of purpose and sense of direction.

The kind of hopeful stance that has roots so deep in your own psyche and tendrils extending so deep into the present and so far into the future at times that, incongruously, because of your seeming detachment, onlookers might wonder just exactly how you do feel and what your attitude toward it all currently really is.

The shift to Beta will be celebrated as one of the great psychological milestones of our species but don't look for it to be remembered primarily for revolutionary new thinking skills or novel "world smarts," extant and important as these kinds of gains are. Instead, I expect historians of the mind to point elsewhere when it comes to identifying the Beta mind's prime contribution to our growing humanness: *to the belief—and "hope"-timism—that committed, liberated minds can bring improvement to the most daunting kinds of world-class problems one by one, step at a time, and will do so.* No creature large or small should expect any less of a mind that understands this but that it will be devoted to such an effort all its days.

■ *you prefer to err on the side of information overload.* Complex amounts of potentially interconnecting data may easily spook the Alpha mind. But not the Beta user's.

Why not?

Because Beta is a more complex thinking environment.

Much faster than for minds in Alpha, in your mind, things will automatically seek out their own category of importance—will sort themselves for economy's and efficiency's sake.

For example, you may have a quick-referral category for information that you could call the "intolerably stupid" to which you automatically relegate things like road rage, child and spousal abuse, tobacco products, pornography or squandering one's personal wealth on costly objects that glitter and preen but otherwise sit dead and mute in the bloodstream of living endeavors. A "misguided or easily dispensable" category (for info on things like most public policies containing the words "zero tolerance," "reality"-based television programming, crash dieting and most fashion trends). And a "trivial or below-the-radar" category (for Howard Stern, mail-order techniques for enhancing breast and penis size, horoscopes, romance novels, drinking songs and the like).

Your Beta mind will quickly file away or dismiss information that doesn't relate to what you are interested in. This leaves your mind freer to grapple with the bigger picture and more complicated issues. In addition, your mind will resist being limited to or being fed oversimplistic or diluted information or no information at all.

What you can see from Beta is almost never boring and much more often is a glimpse of the earliest signs of something on the horizon momentously taking shape or struggling to take form. It may be something that you sense could acquire paradigm-shaking momentum. Or it may be something attention-grabbing because of a quality that the Beta thinker (and chaos-theory and complexity experts) recognize as "the simplicity behind the complexity." The Beta thinker never quite gets over just how much of value and usefulness is simply here for the viewing, for the *taking*, if only you could get people to look in the first place. And then get them to deal with what they see, responsibly, imaginatively and maturely.

■ *you are a "cognitive roamer."* In Beta, you are unusually sensitive to signals incoming from your operating environment. Deep down, you may suddenly realize that something seismological is going on. It's like those little pre-tremors that sensitive earthquake-sensing equipment can pick up, not to mention the animal creatures of the field and air, prior to a genuinely felt temblor. In Beta you can routinely expect to be sensitive to your environment in ways that in Alpha would have been unique and strange to your apprehension if they were apprehended at all.

When sensations quicken, you'll hear yourself saying, "Pay attention. Something is coming up." Or, "Listen up. Something is going down." Clues to the possibility of change, danger or developments that others may miss will cause you to begin to monitor events more closely. You may start assembling scenarios to see if any fit. You may ask: "What is morphing, disintegrating, metastasizing, mutating? What am I in touch with that could be nearing a tipping point—or a point of no return?"

I frequently experience this feature of the Beta mind while watching or reading about the news. Word tumbles in of an unexpected development—a slip of the tongue, a startling turn, a revealing pronouncement or indications of moral turpitude by a politician or other public figure; a dreadful disaster; something novel in consumer technology; a scientific breakthrough out of left field; a counter-intuitive voter polling result; an unanticipated counterfactual argument challenging the general consensus of how things are. You can never quite know what it will be. Only that, when it becomes visible, something happens to shift the Beta mind into a kind of (or so it seems) analytical hyper-speed, and suddenly you just simply *know*. Know that the world has changed and sense what some of the consequences are likely to be.

It's not so much a matter of thinking things through. Rather, it's more a matter of things falling into place for you in terms of recognizing patterns. This is why maximizing your access to quality, abundant information has such appeal to you. This is the most effective way to protect your opportunities to realize that something might be in flux or in play. And if it is, and if it interest you, for tracking its progress and perhaps becoming involved.

■ *you work with the world you find.* You understand that existence comes in only one basic model: life as it is. That life has always inched forward in fits and starts. You know better than most not to expect constant or unreasonable progress. That most times you can expect problems before there is a substantive gain, if there turns out to be any gain at all. That, usually, frustration precedes breakthroughs. And that a lot of people who win don't deserve it, and many who lose didn't have it coming. You tend to agree with writer Dennis Wholey: "Expecting the world to treat you fairly because you are good is like expecting the bull not to charge because you are a vegetarian."

When the going gets rough and you don't recognize any emerging pattern, you will tend to have a cuppa and see what happens next and decide what you want to do, given the circumstances. Few will be the times when you can't evaluate you own skills and abilities realistically and react accordingly.

This is usually the Beta thinker's prevailing interest: what is going to work in this particular situation? What will it take to do the right thing? Can I be of service? And, am I *interested* in being of service?

As one Beta thinker put it: "I have come to believe that the most important thing is one's independence since that gives you the freedom to accumulate and deploy resources as you see fit to move society in a positive direction."[2]

■ *you aren't easily spooked.* As I have already noted several times, users of the Beta mind have been released from many of Alpha's stranglehold emotional effects: feelings of numbness, abandonment, rage and shame, guilt and self-righteousness, fear of failing and inadequacy, sadness and loneliness and powerlessness. These enforcers or enablers no longer affect you as they do most others. This makes it much more difficult for anyone to use such fears to intimidate you. Or corrupt, threaten, compel or coerce you. Buying you off with promotions or more money or compliments doesn't work either.

■ *you mostly evaluate yourself.* External standards of personal evaluation often won't carry much weight with you. The review that is most meaningful to the Beta thinker is self-review because it's the only assessment with standards high enough, precise enough and realistic enough for you to respect.

You don't place much stock in exercises like the so-called 360-degree feedback process that industry likes so much, or annual reviews or any other kind of outside-of-yourself review. This is not to say, however, that you never listen to the opinions of others about how you might improve your behavior or your performance. You will, of course. You do so because you realize that being open to feedback is part of the process of being accountable. You'll listen to the janitor or the yard person or even your "weird uncle" or "crazy aunt" if he/she knows how to do something better than you and you see a possible use for the information or a way to learn from it.

■ *you can't be bought.* The traditional status symbols—big houses, cars, offices, expensive clothes, jewelry, perks, vacation homes or other kinds of standard big-ego signifiers—aren't turn-ons for Beta thinkers.

Not to say you never invest in top-of-the-line, upscale possessions. You probably like new electronic technologies that will enhance your thinking skills, for example. And you usually prefer things that work, that are functional, that respond when needed and perform when called on to get the job done. But in the comparative scheme of things, the trappings of success that so many work so hard to accumulate do little to turn you on. Your main interest materially is having enough, and if you don't have what you want, you will find ways to make do.

Your focus is on what is appropriate. You dislike conspicuous consumption, and you'll want to know if your clothes were made by slave labor in sweat shops, if your water is clean and where it comes from, if the purchase of a vehicle will contribute to the ozone problem or global warming. And you'll want to know the effects of your purchases on others upstream and downstream you will never meet. You care about them and are concerned about the consequences of your purchase.

■ *you don't take power trips.* Yours is the capability not to behave like the species you usually see at the zoo or on PBS jungle shows, sparring or warring over territory, sexual bragging rights, a perch on the top limb or first dibs at chow time. Since you tend to treat everyone as equals, traditional payoffs from gamesmanship don't interest you. That includes giving orders or controlling perquisites. Receiving obeisance or splitting hairs. Obfuscating the issues or secreting information, all as a means to being top gun and protecting your rank and your flank.

■ *hype, buzz and other forms of manufactured drama generally turn you off.* Those seeking to manage or influence you can forget appeals to artificial deadlines. Or to arbitrary "stretch" performance levels. Or to the other standard Alpha manage-with-adrenalin motivational techniques so widely used in business and sports. These simply don't fly with the Beta thinker. Neither do chicken-little bulletins or the lamentations of others about momentary setbacks, real or imagined, that are attempts to play on your emotions or herd you in one direction or another.

You are not unlike Anne, Robert Heinlein's character in *Stranger In A Strange Land.* When asked the color of a distant house, Anne replied, "The house is white on the side I can see." You usually would prefer that the people you communicate with simply stay with the facts as they know them or admit to their absence or their obscurity or unreliability if they don't.

■ *you don't have a lot of patience for shirkers or persons who refuse to learn.* You want to encourage people to understand that it is their responsibility to shape and guide their lives with the implements of their own judgments. You want them to understand that it is their responsibility to recognize on their own behalf the real dangers in life and act and react appropriately.

What you do when you come across stupidity—an inability or an unwillingness to learn—will vary with your mood, the importance of the situation, how it affects others, whether you think a reaction will be useful and whether it is worth the time to get involved.

If you think it worthwhile to get involved, you may point out to people that if they choose to go into business with dishonest people, they'll probably get taken. If they choose to do missionary work in the midst of lawlessness and fighting, they can easily die. If they return an obscene gesture to another driver, they may trigger road rage. If they leave their keys in the ignition, their car may be stolen. If they choose to drive through a crime-infested part of town at two o'clock in the morning, they may get shot. If they choose not to visit a dentist for years at a time, they may end up with a mouthful of cavities. If they choose to smoke cigarettes all their lives, they may get lung cancer or emphysema. If they choose to ignore an alarming condition in their body, they may end up in the hospital—or the morgue. If they choose to believe their investment counselor when she recommends that they invest heavily in kumquat futures, they may have nothing to retire on. If they choose to drink the tap water in a strange country, they may get sick. If they choose to ignore their boss's lies, they may end up jobless. If they choose to ignore a strange noise under their car, their muffler may fall off. If they choose to drop out of school, they may never have a very adequate standard of living. If they choose to run with a gang, they may end up getting a bullet. If they allow suspicious strangers through their door, they may be robbed or killed. If they keep piling up credit card debt, they may be plagued by bill collectors or go bankrupt. If they steal from the till at work, they may go to jail. If they choose to have unprotected sex, they may become a parent or a lifetime carrier of a sexually transmitted disease or a defendant in a paternity suit. If they choose to let someone else make their decisions for them, they may find that they have no life they can ever call their own.

Or then again, you may not.

In either case, your interest in the rescuer's role is greatly diminished the second time around. You do not tolerate lightly those who failed to learn and still wonder how it all went wrong.

■ *you accept without anxiety the possibility that we may be completely alone.* Admittedly, most of the people who have ever lived have felt otherwise. No matter where our minds are located on the spiral of the mind's development, and no matter whether the feeling is overpowering or something too vague to put words to, the sense that there is something greater than us doesn't seem to go away. As Poul Anderson says in *Goat Song*, "There is some undefined ultimate vagueness behind the measurable universe." Or to quote Princess Irulan in "The Sayings of Muad'Dib," (in Frank Herbert's *Dune*), "Deep in the human unconsciousness is a pervasive need for a logical universe that makes sense. But the real universe is always one step beyond logic."

Throughout Alpha, the mind has channeled such feelings into an estimated one hundred thousand belief systems: most frequently, religious systems, rituals and explanations. Even in Beta, the "greater power" question doesn't disappear. Because no matter how much we learn scientifically about the world, we will probably never be able to determine whether there isn't at least a *cosmological* God (a force needed to explain the existence of the biggest possible picture we can imagine) even though there no longer appears to be a need for a *biological* God (a force needed to explain us as living, functioning organisms).[3]

Whatever your thoughts and feelings about this issue as a Beta thinker, you aren't going to denigrate the sacred traditions of those who think otherwise. On the other hand, you'll not be caught looking to the gods to keep you safe or bail you out. Your belief structure simply does not have a category for cosmic rescue or a cosmic rescuer—at least not one that can be readily explained or summoned or dependably counted on. No other single thinking characteristic in Beta does more than this one to remind you to pay close attention to what's happening in the here and now, in *this* life, on *this* Earth, at *this* moment, to you and those around you (all six-plus billion of *them* and the umpty-teen jillions of additional other life-things). To anticipate ways you can get hurt or be harmed as a consequence of what is happening. To reject expectations that good things will result when, as any half-vigilant individual could see, the odds are high and getting higher that they won't. To avoid risks that (1) come wrapped in a package clearly marked trouble with no exit, (2) make little sense or (3) offer little expectation of a positive and meaningful outcome.

■ *you realize you aren't like everyone else.* You often feel alone, weird, like you don't belong. You know you are different and people don't always "get" you, much less always "dig" you. Yet you are not uncomfortable seeing yourself as part of an elite.

Not a dynastic elite like the Kennedys or the Hollywood "A crowd"-type elite. And not for the usual winner-take-all status or control motives and reasons so often seen with elites in the middle stages of Alpha.

Human nature is a natural builder of hierarchies, so there are many kinds of elites. Beta's elites are being formed to an unprecedented degree around high ethical and meaningful performance expectations rather than winner-take-all wealth, status or control. Credit Beta with, as did Dr. Graves, an existence ethic: if not always helping Mother Nature continue what she has started, Beta's elites at least focus on taking reasonable pains to avoid squandering her resources or bringing harm to her offspring.[4]

In Beta the reason you'll frequently find yourself in the company of elites is because they'll be your most consistent providers of competence. Of trustworthy information. Functionality. Flexibility. And a like-minded concern for focus and progress on issues that matter in personal lives and the larger polity.

■ **you aren't reluctant to turn to the internal allies within you.** It's always an intelligent comeback to match the character of your mind with the content of the occasion. Being Beta all the time, running flat-out at the top of your impressive capabilities during every waking moment, would be a sure-bet way to waste a nonpareil mind on issues and assignments best handled by the thinking of a different, earlier kind. So you aren't reluctant to pace yourself.

How do you do that? Regress, when it is the intelligent thing to do. Gear down, when it can have good consequences. Turn it over to the Alpha levels of the mind in you, and let a simpler side of yourself call the shots for awhile.

- *When you need the strengths, comfort and guidance that come best from blood bonds or bonds similar to them, you go to Level 1.2.*
- *You find a second wind, the extra surge, the adrenal push and the raw power and boldness you need in Level 1.3.*
- *You know that a return to Level 1.4 may be just the tonic if you feel the need to go home again, if only momentarily.*
- *You are never unaware of the value of Level 1.5's entrepreneurial skills, confidence and chutzpah.*
- *When you want your spirits to soar and your soul to luxuriate, even for a brief time, in pure harmony with all within you and all surrounding you that is good and beautiful and pristine and kind, then you know that there's only one boutique in your mind that can deliver the goods: Level 1.6.*

You are open to the reality that many will be the times when it is good and wise to relinquish the reins temporarily to less complex and less contemporary parts of yourself.

■ *you can be jarringly quick to say "no."* That Beta mind of yours can be lightning-fast in sizing up whether promises are being kept, whether the truth is being told, whether anticipated gains are happening, whether what might unfold is likely to be fair or whether you are being made privy to the total picture. Or at least to the part of the picture that impinges on or depends on your participation.

You make it a point to be honest and up-front in your dealings and expect people to be honest and up-front with you. So your decision to disengage when you assay that something may be rotten in Denmark can be brain-rattlingly abrupt. Hanging around to see if you can spot an insider's advantage if there is skullduggery afoot usually isn't a Beta thinker's style, either.

Also, with your knowledge of self and self-respect, you will say no to most situations that are uninteresting or where you suspect you can contribute little or nothing.

And yet, unlike the Alpha style, once you make up your mind, you are not averse to unmaking it if you receive new information from any source. People in Alpha—especially at Levels 1.4 and Level 1.5—tend to make up their minds very quickly: an "I'm right and I've decided and that's that" kind of attitude. And they cling to their position or decision come what may. In Beta, given new evidence, you will reconsider at any time. And yet ...

■ *when it matters to you, you want to be in play.* Beta tends to propel you into the thick of anything that effectively captures your interest. This isn't to say that you won't ever be a foot soldier or a bystander, content to go with the flow or the crowd. Beta's overweening expectation of human enterprises, big or small, is that they be as functional and proficient as possible. The question is, "Is this working?" If it is, you may stay close but not really be influential.

Projects, opportunities or enterprises—especially complex ones—that genuinely challenge you are a much different story, however. In these instances, the user of the Beta mind nearly always wants the conn or at least a seat near the planning and/or decision table.

You may or may not receive it. Much faster than most others, you are going to find yourself asking significant questions or, even more jarringly to any Alpha minds present, quickly pointing to solutions. This seldom sits well with the accomplished gamesmanship players of the organization—any organization. You may or may not be invited or permitted to stay. But you need to accept that this is now part of your new nature: your Beta nature.

Anyone wanting you to be a part of their team must learn to trust in the fact that you will put yourself where you are most useful, whatever the formal assignment or organizational chart. No action or intervention by higher-ups is necessary. With you, it's simply a natural, automatic thing to do. And others need to understand that while the results of your self-assignment may not be immediately apparent, they will eventually relate back to what you've agreed to do. And if this is not happening as you had anticipated, others need to realize that you'll quickly let them know and initiate adjustments or soon end it.

Let me share a "true life" example from my own experience. I have been issued a jury duty summons. As is my wont when directed to report for the voir dire process of jury selection and shepherded into a courtroom for questioning by the opposing attorneys, I soon get the judge's attention to explain that I'm happy to serve (true) but completely incapable of doing so (also true). For example, on this occasion, I point out that the state's attorney has not faced in my direction once since the proceedings began. Unable to read her lips, I comment, I have little idea what she has been saying. I don't tell him so, but ditto for his honor. He's seated magisterially about half-a-tennis-court away at the other end of the windowless, echo-prone courtroom. I can tell that he is moving his lips and hear that he's speaking, but I'm not at all sure that I've been understanding what he's saying.

As judges invariably do in my jury duty appearances, this jurist is quick to thank me for my public spiritedness and to explain that his hands are tied. By law I am duty-bound to serve if selected and he cannot excuse me. If I'm chosen for the jury, he assures me that he will provide an interpreter. I simply nod and let it go. This is no time to argue with a judge intent on hurrying the proceedings along.

The very first time I ever honored a jury duty summons, I learned that the legal system has no category and no solution for me. Since I don't know the sign language of the deaf, an ordinary interpreter for the deaf is no answer. I suppose the court could hire someone who produces "captions for the hearing impaired" for movies and TV programs and supply me with a rolling, scrolling text of the proceedings, but I know that it won't. So every time I am summoned, I follow this routine: I announce my problem without delay to the judge. Then, as soon as I see that I am again caught in the usual "Catch 22" about interpreters, I do the court, myself and the defendant a tidy favor: I set about making certain that no one will want me seated on a jury.

Since it is usually necessary to put someone in that role, on this occasion, I use the state's attorney as my foil. While most of the fifty-odd persons on the panel never say a word, I respond to nearly every question she asks about who we are, what we think, what our biases might be. Eventually, I'm even beginning to bore myself with my recitals. Finally, feigning innocence, I ask a question of my own. "All I know about sitting on juries comes from watching TV," I say. "Can a member of the jury ask questions during the trial?"

I expect the prosecutor simply to say no, you can't. But instead she launches into a spiel that, as best I can tell, has nothing to do with my question—or anything else being discussed. Obviously, she doesn't want the rest of the jury panel, especially those individuals who will be selected to hear the case, to conclude that she's easily pushed around. She speaks for nearly a minute before stopping. It's clear to everyone that I'm being ignored.

"But you didn't answer my question," I persist.

"No," she snaps. "Members of the jury are not allowed to ask questions."

That should do it, I say to myself. *Surely, the opposing attorneys are thinking that this guy's too unpredictable and obnoxious to risk including on a jury. Besides, act out much more and the judge may put you in the pokey.*

As it usually does, my strategy works. Soon, the names of those selected are called, and mine isn't among them. I've helped a system too inflexible and insensitive to realize it even has a problem find a solution by showing it exactly how, with a minimum of disruption to its proceedings, to handle me.

Now, I realize that my reader may chose to view all this more as petulant behavior on my part than as Beta-directed behavior. But if so, then I question whether you've ever had to deal up close with the sometimes maddening imperiousness and willful nonengagement with reality of the American court system (or most other countries' court systems, I strongly suspect). Sometimes, you just have to do what you have to do, no matter how petulant or capricious it may seem to someone looking on.

When all things equal out, being a Beta thinker means that you are going to have a better view of the forest than most others. Usually, when asked, you aren't going to mind pointing out which trees are most likely to fall in the paths of people or how all parties may find a better path through the brambles. Even if you are not asked and it matters, you are frequently going to respond as if you *had* been presented with a request to act or explain.

In the future, the way you think in Beta is going to be increasingly critical, even for those who don't think this way and never will. And those who do not think this way will include most of the individuals you are ever likely to have around you. Whatever else it chooses to do, the Alpha mind isn't going away, and neither, as we are about to see, are the challenges facing Beta because of this fact. Fortunately, among your new Beta capabilities are critical new skills for sussing out others quickly and doing near-instant analysis of how they think and what influence this might have on what they may do or don't do next.

Chapter 12: **People Clues**

OVERWHELMINGLY, this is still an Alpha thinker's world. Most individuals are no closer to Beta than they are to Mars. Where the Alpha mind is in—or is out of—control, things overall will almost surely get worse in many areas before they stand a solid chance of getting much better.

Over time, many individuals in Alpha will gradually wear themselves a groove—a groove of obsolescence—and then a rut, and then an abyss, and will hunker down at what could have been, under the best of circumstances, a learning experience only. Unless a person can find a way to extricate herself or himself from their Alpha-policed rut, they will find themselves blocked from Beta permanently. And yet, it is in the midst of such an over-whelming number of Alpha-arbitrated thinkers that the Beta mind must co-exist, search for answers, find its place and its way and be of assistance when and where it chooses to be and when and where it can be.

Fortunately, for such circumstances, Beta marshals some valuable new skills and safeguards, both preventive and pro-active, for interactions with people. For responding to them. And for entering into relationships, nominal or long-term, with them. It's time to take a look at these new thinking qualities.

One key skill lies with an ability to do quick size-ups when it comes to fathoming what people are, or are not, likely to think, or say, or do. This new orientation to people's behavioral habits and penchants should immediately make many of the people you meet less of an enigma and many of the circumstances involving people generally less of a crapshoot.

There is, of course, an important caution to be expressed and observed in making judgments about how anyone else is likely to think or what they are likely to do. It is a topic to be treated with great watchfulness and care.

In dealing with it, we need to be vigilant that we never drift any farther than necessary from the admonitory view expressed by one of the heroes of this book, the late Dr. Clare Graves. *People*, he said, *have a right to be.*

By that, I understand him to have meant that we need to err on the side of leaving others as free as possible to think with what they have and choose to think with.

That others generally have a right to be proud of how they think.

That others generally are entitled to the expectation that the rest of us, no matter how their minds happen to work, will be respectful of how they think. Will, at minimum, attempt repeatedly to put ourselves in the other person's shoes (or more literally, in the other person's head!).

That our assignment and responsibility as the comparatively mature persons we assume ourselves to be—as employers, managers, executives, educators, consultants, personal coaches and counselors, therapists, scholars, politicians, media participants, parents and all else—is, in a nutshell, to help those around us discover how best to cope and do end runs around their problems, whatever their thinking characteristics and distinctions.

I realize that these sentiments are idealistic. And that this is not a perfect world. Nevertheless, I endorse these ideals. And think they are usually the right thing to think and the right thing to do. Indeed, what other realistic, humane choices do we really have?

But viewing every human as deserving of respect *simply because of his or her humanness* doesn't ameliorate our growing understanding that the brain is not an island. It is attached with an acuity, a fidelity and an unbreakable symbiotic linkage as few other things are to the world around it. While this world and this brain are both serious works in progress, they also both have histories. A hierarchical history based in no small part on the fact that we are "bound into" a fundamental physical nature, inside and out, that is itself hidebound with hierarchies. While hierarchical histories do not always dictate to the future, they can and should be consulted for important clues to possible future circumstances and the odds that they will reappear. For the reasons we've been discussing in this work, there can no longer be any question but that both this world and this brain exert profound, often foreseeable influences on what the mind of a human can and will feel, can and does know, can and might do.

SINGLE-CLUE RISKS

Visit any National Football League game on a given fall Sunday. In the stands are sixty to eighty thousand people or more, many decked out in team colors, some of them even half-to-three-quarters naked and *painted* in team colors. And most all of them are shouting epithets calling for mayhem, gore, vanquishing, injury or even the demise of the opposing team's members, and that includes men, women and children ranging downward in ages to toddlers who have barely begun to walk and talk.

But it is also important to remember just what a slippery eel the mind can be.

It's likely that the Level 1.2 thinkers—mostly young children—are there because daddy (being daddy!) thought this would be great way to enjoy a little family togetherness. (Or else couldn't get a baby-sitter!)

Level 1.3 thinkers no doubt love the beer, the noise, the skimpily dressed cheerleaders (at least in the case of the males) and the violence on the field.

Level 1.4 users are fiercely loyal to their beloved Cowboys, or Steelers, or Seahawks, and wouldn't think of missing a game.

Level 1.5 thinkers may be playing host to a new business prospect, hoping it will help them cement a deal or a profitable new business relationship.

The Level 1.6 users may have come (if they have come at all) because the tailgate parties prior to and after the game, and the interactions during the game itself, can offer good camaraderie and fun.

(Frankly, I doubt that you're going to find many Beta thinkers in the crowd, although if you happen to see them at home you may catch them sneaking glances at the game on the television.)

The reasons why people go to the place of worship they do, attend the opera or theater, participate in weekend 4K or 10K runs, choose the restaurants where they eat or drive the kinds of cars they drive or select their friends and their mates can be just as iffy and confusing. This makes it risky to depend on a single clue in seeking to decide what level of thinking you may be dealing with. And yet, knowledge of *how* people think is an invaluable clue to *what* they might be thinking. So is knowledge of how they are behaving. And knowledge of how they see things is a dependable insight again and again into what they probably *can't* see.

Assume along with me for a little bit and we can gain insight into what can happen if we *don't* act on such assumptions....

*E*XTRATERRESTRIALS may be every bit as real and non-Earth-like as science fiction writers have portrayed them: as incandescent-light-bulb-shaped wraiths à la Roswell's, as little green folks from Mars or as strange-eyed spice miners on a water-starved planet far, far away. Or they may be merely the figments of extra-active, Earth-bound imaginations. Your guess is as least as good as mine.

But let's supposed for a moment that there are some very intelligent non-Earthlings somewhere. And let's suppose that they've made plans to touch down on our little planet and

demand access to its leader. Unannounced and thus far unnoticed, our very first extragalactic visitors have arrived at our
doorstep.

Our extraordinary visitors have big expectations for one of
the inventions they have in tow: their two-way All-Universe
speech interpreter and synthesizer. When they whisper "Xyciocjk
sxrsk oqkxvy" into it, the machine sounds exactly like former
American president Jimmy Carter when it says, "Take me to your
leader." And when Earthlings are doing the talking, the synthesizer can translate their words back into Kduyxos, the visitors'
native language.

When they had invited the device to give itself a name, much
to their puzzlement, it had chosen "Dymosthynes." And firing up
Dymosthynes marks the start of our alien visitors' problems.

TRY AND TRY AGAIN

On their first outing, they land in the middle of the Four
Corners desert, in the American Southwest, and haul out their
speech synthesizer. They soon meet a craggy-faced dude with his
hair tied in back like a pony's tail. He's dressed in jeans long past
their prime and a flannel work shirt with most of the colors of
Joseph's coat. He's wearing an outsized silver belt buckle, an
amulet-like thing on a string around his neck and old boots with
about the same amount of sole left as the tread-bare tires on his
pickup. Lowering the tailgate on his battered vehicle of many
miles, the taciturn gent sees his visitors settled in the back and
heads for Window Rock. As luck would have it, it's a protracted,
dusty ride for nothing: on this day, the chief of the Navajo Nation
isn't in his office.

That night, the strangers try again, and this time their navigational efforts steer them to south-central Los Angeles. The first
humans they meet are gang members. The 18th Street gang and
the Black P Stones are firing weapons at each other. Dymosthynes
manages to say only, "Take me ..." before the alien holding the
device is tattooed with 9 mm slugs. Back on their spaceship, the

dead alien's buddies pledge not to land anymore on the dark side of this planet.

True to their pledge to themselves, the visitors wait until high noon on the following day to land in Tehran. When their synthesizer says, "Take me to your leader" in perfect Farsi (if you ignore that it sounds like Farsi as Jimmy Carter would speak it), they are relieved that no bullets fly. But they are puzzled that they see no men and only a few small boys. When their synthesizer provides a translation from the only person they can get to talk to them, it sounds like, "It's Dhuhr. Our leader is at prayers."

Deciding that they might do better if they can find a location where the people at least sound like Jimmy Carter, they land the next morning in what they believe to be a beautiful park, with exquisitely shaped lawns and tiny raked sand beaches. They are encouraged by the thousands of people who have turned out to greet them. When their synthesizer booms, "Take me to your leader," a guy in a green jacket immediately summons little wheel-mounted space scooters for each of them and tells their drivers, "Take 'em to watch Tiger." On Hole 5 at Georgia's Augusta National Golf Course, front-runner Woods three-putts, but it's all Greek to the extragalactic visitors. If clubbing tiny white balls that take gigantic leaps as they try to escape the murderous swings of their predators is what leaders do in this strange place, then maybe they don't want to meet a leader after all.

Determined to try one last time, they set their sights on a landing in higher country. The next afternoon, not far from Boulder, Colorado, they ease their big spacecraft to a halt at the edge of a clearing in the mountains. Colorfully clad people are lofting kites, blowing iridescent bubbles and tossing what looks like upside-down dinner plates between them. Approaching a group near the center of the meadow, our aliens crank up Dymosthynes. No sooner has it drawled, "Take me to your leader," than hundreds of people link arms to form a big circle surrounding the visitors. Soon the synthesizer's Jimmy Carter is slowly singing along with the others to the late John Denver's

"It's About Time." The cadence is so catching that the alien holding the voice box soon puts it down and links arms with the circle. To the puzzlement of his colleagues, he is soon swaying back and forth, keeping up with the beat of the tune and the movement of the creatures around him.

It is at this point that the aliens' leader decides to call it quits and go home. Discovering who the leaders are on this weird planet has exhausted his patience. It is all too frustrating and mystifying for the uninitiated to sort out.

GOING BEYOND BEDROCK

The thing is...extraterrestrials or not, we are all aliens of a sort. Aliens trying to translate what the other person is saying and intending, planning and plotting. You are an alien to me, and I am an alien to you. There is always that "synthesizer" business going on between us. In every conversation, there are translators in operation. Your brain contains such devices, and so does mine. Even when we are trying to keep an open mind, it is the most natural thing in the world for one individual to assume that the other person's understanding of the world and what they are hearing and seeing and sensing is essentially the same—or ought to be!— as their own. And it's the most exasperating thing in the world that we are so often wrong.

In Beta, you are going to be forever on guard against this "bedrock miscalculation" that the mind makes over and over.

In Beta, you know better. You not only know that minds are not necessarily alike but also that from one moment to the next, the same mind may undergo confusing changes.

You know more. You know just how unalike minds can be.

You know clues. Many times, you know how to make an educated guess about the kind of mind a person may be using to shape their perception of the world at a given moment.

You know consequences. You know what is likely to happen when people try to interpret how you are thinking and what you are doing using a mind that isn't like yours at all. You know the good things that can come from how people view your mind as well as the dicey ones.

Most of all, you know that from one moment to the next, the world of Alpha is not at all a WYSIWYG ("What You See Is What You Get") kind of place. Without your Beta people-reading skills, you can easily end up feeling like everyone else. That is, like a loose load in the back of a 4x4 careening through a war zone. Let's look more closely at Beta's people-reading capabilities and how they can be useful to us and, often, to the other minds we're involved with.

Thinking about it, it would be ridiculous to assume that our mind is better equipped to handle many issues in today's world than most and then not involve that mind in pursuing outcomes that are important to us. Rule No. 1: is, "Don't do stupid things. Rather, do things alertly and conscientiously." Rule No. 2 is, "Be careful around situations that might cause people to behave stupidly." Rule No. 3 is, "Never surrender a psychological advantage without thinking it through."

Even with your impressive new "big picture" competencies, you will still need to pay close attention to what's happening in the shadows. Your world and mine are populated with enemies as well as allies, with non-performers, self-sabotagers and self-interested posers as well as people who keep their promises and perform up to their capabilities. It's important to learn to tell them apart and avoid those who distract you from your goals or put you at risk. It's also important to understand and monitor how asserting yourself in behalf of your personal agenda and choices may leave you vulnerable. And, above all, whatever the circumstances and wherever the action, it's important to pay attention to the kind of mind you appear to be dealing with.

This can be tricky.

Because the levels of mind we've been discussing are actually levels of thinking *in* people, not types *of* people. A person tends to think from one mind level more than any other but may also think at times from levels they have traveled through earlier rather than the one they currently prefer. For this reason, any of us can appear to have multiple personalities, and during the course of the day, we often do.

It's also good to remember that deciding who rightly and deservedly goes where on the Alpha/Beta mind model can be fraught with potential missteps. Even the Beta mind can be subject to technical difficulties (how to measure what may seem to be a moving picture). And to subjectivity difficulties (everything that I can ever conclude about how you think gets filtered through my brain, which is a very subjective place; you will encounter similar problems when you try and evaluate *my* level of mind). And to difficulties stemming from personal agendas and animosities (the more complex the world *and* the mind become, the more complex can be the reasons underlying our feuds, falling outs and interpersonal failings). But you can't afford to let such concerns shield you from this reality: if you refuse to view how people act as serious clues to how they think, then you may end up being essentially clueless as to how you will be treated by them. And those without a clue are not infrequently also soon without a prayer.

I think you probably know this already.

MINDS THAT MISLEAD

The business scene teems with people you don't want to do business with. Every election day, the ballot swarms with people you really don't want to vote for. If you are seeking a spouse or someone with whom to enjoy a long-term relationship, some of the very people you are attracted to most can be the very ones you don't want to take a chance on. When you are looking for someone to represent you in selling a house, handle your insurance, see to your legal needs, deliver your baby, keep your children or look after your aging parents, some of those who sound best qualified to see to your needs competently and professionally are instead precisely the ones you don't want anywhere near you or your loved ones.

It's not uncommon for individuals to intentionally mislead you about the mind they are coming from. Salespeople, for example. Why? It may be because it is their job to become chameleons and meet you where you are, then seek to take you to where they want you to go. Or it may be because they are, to put it plainly, not very honest people.

Many criminals—scam artists, armed robbers, purse snatchers, pickpockets, carjackers and other perpetrators of "crimes against people"—routinely present one mind's face when they want you to trust or ignore them and another mind's face when they want to control, influence or overpower you. The same can be said generally of lawyers, many of whom are also politicians, lobbyists, government executives and diplomats. Law enforcement officers need to be mentioned, too. The courts (including the U.S. Supreme Court) have given law officers the right to lie to you about which level of the mind they are using when they interrogate you, rightly or wrongly, about a crime they think you may have committed. Videotapes and transcripts of their interrogations of suspects have confirmed that they do so routinely.

When people pull a deliberate switcheroo of minds on you, the pattern on our model is often from left to right. The perpetrator's primary mind is either 1.3 or 1.5 but the mind that gets portrayed to you is usually 1.2, 1.4 or 1.6. For a time, they may pretend that you are one of them and that they are interested in staying on good terms with you, have your best interests at heart and want to help you. They need you to trust them, and they work to gain that trust by trying to convince you that they share your beliefs and values, that the two of you have common needs and are aiming toward common outcomes. Since they are often skilled at playing make-believe, it's too easy for you to assume that you share a common mind level unless you are being vigilant.

The reality can be something else entirely. You may be considered a mark, target, victim, object or suspect, and when the right time comes, the mind you may have thought you were dealing with becomes something else entirely.

Users of the Alpha mind may understand this in principle, having been a victim of such dealings, heard accounts from other victims, seen TV news "exposes" or read warnings in the papers or on the Internet. Nevertheless, they still keep visiting car dealerships where salespeople routinely lie to them or walking down dark streets alone in questionable neighborhoods. They still fail to protect their purse or pocketbook in crowds, fail to remove their keys from their parked cars or fail to lock their outside doors at home. They continue to vote for politicians who have lengthy public records of mendacity or double-talk. They assume that because lawyers are officers of the court that they can be depended on to be open, honest and aboveboard and always have their best interests at heart if they are their clients. And if they run afoul of the law or are suspected of such, they still take interrogating law officers and prosecutors at their word, even after being read their Miranda rights. It's amazing, because this clearly worded legal mantra of warning leaves no room for doubt about how nakedly vulnerable an individual in such circumstances is.

(I'm not expecting that the Beta thinker is going to be read Miranda rights very often. And I realize that there are arguments to be made, even if in most instances they may not be morally very defensible, for "the end justifying the means" when it comes to lying to persons thought to have committed serious crimes as they are questioned. At the moment, I'm simply reminding my Beta-thinking reader that it's a real world out there, and it has real consequences that always need to be held in mind and always taken into account.)

STOP, LOOK AND LISTEN

As a Beta thinker, how you respond to such potentially slippery encounters is going to be much different than many Alpha thinkers.

First, you'll look for congruence between what your senses are picking up on and what you are being told or shown. For example, car dealerships generally look, smell, sound, feel and—if you sample the free candies or the gourmet chocolate-chip cook-ies—taste like the kind of places where Mind 1.5 users hang out. It's hard to miss! And if you can't avoid such places entirely by buying a car from someone who doesn't hang out at a place that screams "competitive gamesmanship" at you when you walk in the door, you'll at least not mistake the salesperson's attempt at instant friendship for a sign that you are somewhere you really aren't. (Let me be quick to acknowledge that some participants in both the new and used car industries have made admirable strides lately in cleaning up their act. This new professionalism shows up as kinder, gentler environments [no outwardly smarmy salespeople since the sales staff is often on salary and off commission], more information and more honest information for the prospective client, better warranties and higher, all-around levels of integrity and dependability. May their numbers increase!)

Second, when you have no choice but to deal with a mind in Alpha that could put you at serious risk, bodily, financially, reputation-wise, influence-wise or whatever, you'll always bring with you a professional of your own who's experienced and adept at dealing with that level of mind. Your own lobbyist, your own bodyguard, your own lawyer, your own diplomat—yes, sometimes, even your own car selling (buying) expert or at minimum a trusted mechanic to check things out. You'll never assume you can beat the professional at his or her own game, regardless of the level of mind being used. Even lawyers seldom represent themselves when something truly substantial is at stake. (This is, of course, good advice for the user of any of the mind's levels. For the Beta user, to ignore it is simply nonsensical.)

Third, if you do find yourself suddenly confronted by an unmasked poser of the mind who represents a grave threat to you and those you love and value, your Beta mind is likely to start immediately plotting a way to protect yourself. The tactics of choice: if your life isn't in danger, just say no and go. If it is in danger and if you can, give them what they want. If you can't, watch for any opportunity to escape or take them out. Martial arts instructors will tell you this: if you are going to run away from a fight, you best run quickly. The Level 1.3 and 1.5 minds are often the tiger (attacker) stalking the crane (prey). Usually, the bad guy's attack is fierce and direct, and the surprised victim can be easily overcome.

The cautions I've been sharing are a mere smattering of the psychological insights that add up to the psychological advantage that accompanies Beta thinking skills. In most cases, I am telling you nothing that you've not already intuited, because once you make the leap, such understandings are swift to become second-nature with you.

It pays to remember that while people can be more compli-cated than what you can take in at a glance, they are seldom less so. If you suspect there may be a problem, never be reluctant to go from a flash of insight to a full-blown theory of possibility about how to protect yourself from the potential downside of how a person appears to be thinking.

Within moments of meeting one of my new carpenters, I suspected that he was a primary user of the Level 1.3 mind. I thought I could hear bottled-up rage in his voice, sense it in his choice of words and see it in his face and his body movements.

After chatting with him briefly, I took my wife aside.

"Be very careful around this person. I think he could easily fly off the handle."

I added: "It wouldn't surprise me if he hasn't been locked up at one time or another."

Because this individual was under the close supervision of one of our relatives and had come so highly recommended for his carpentry skills, we decided to run the risk of letting him help us with our remodeling project. Also, he'd just remarried and as we watched him around his bright young stepdaughter, we were impressed by the caring and love he was showing her. It was a close call. We let him stay, but we watched him carefully and walked on eggshells when we were around him. In the end, there were no problems.

Even so, there was plenty of reason later on to second-guess that decision. The last I heard of this individual, our handyman had absconded with a sizable down payment from a client for buying building materials. He was later found high on drugs. Eventually, we would learn that the reason for his Thursday afternoon absences on our project was because he was meeting with his parole officer. He'd been in the penitentiary on a narcotics conviction.

WHEN THE TIDE TURNS

On another occasion, I received a phone call from an individual I'd known but a short time and had communicated with only on the phone and via e-mails.

He professed to have a strong admiration for one of my products. He said it could play a perfect role in an ambitious start-up opportunity he was involved with. He didn't want to own my product or even pay me anything up front. He wanted a license providing him and his partners with substantial control—near-exclusivity—of my product in return for promised royalties on future sales. But he assured me it would be worth my while. In six years, according to his calculations, I could expect to be one of America's latest multi-millionaires.

This was wheeler-dealer kind of talk—-a hallmark identifier for Level 1.5 thinking. I was instantly alert to the likelihood that, should I decide to learn more, I was about to be inundated with the kind of cajolery, inducements and pressure tactics traditionally found to be appealing to the Level 1.5 mind.

How right that was: in a short time, my suitor and his colleagues were promising a barrage of Level 1.5 types of enticements and turn-ons.

Soon I was on an airplane headed west—at their expense. I listened as they described the IPO they planned within a year and how I would get sizable stock options on highly favorable terms. They spoke of an executive suite for me, with a substantial six-figure salary and a heady, double-take title like Chief Intellectual Officer (how many companies has one of those?) and a seat on the board of directors. They wined and dined me with panache. Before dinner one evening, there was a stopover at the local yacht club, a palatial affair at the edge of the Pacific, where I ended up yakking, not yachting—with one of the Beach Boys, who was sitting nonchalantly at the burnished wood bar when we walked in. Maybe he was there by happenstance, maybe not. You could see it in their eyes. Nobody, they were thinking, walks away from these kinds of goodies, especially when they've just fallen in your lap.

But I kept reminding myself, this was Level 1.5 terrain. *Pay attention!* When I did, what I soon detected in a ping-pong exchange of phone calls and e-mails with first one, then others, of my card-shuffling wooers was rapidly shifting, now-you-see-it-now-you-don't behavior.

Almost immediately, I realized that they were not viewing my product as a respected, top-of-the-line specialty creation, as they had first indicated, but more as a commodity, sure to be overshadowed by other branded products and by the main brand itself. And as much as they professed to want control of my product, what they seemed to be wanting even more was control of the model underlying the product. Once they had rights to my model, it appeared that they planned to use it to create other products and services but they had spoken of paying me royalties only on sales of the basic tool.

As the days passed, they continued to resist my requests that they describe specific uses they had in mind for my product even as they continued to push me to provide them with near-carte blanche authority to use it as they please—for "perpetuity," as they had brazenly specified it at one point in their draft documents.

They had based their financial projections on a low-end-of-the-range price that they said they intended to charge their customers for my product, a price that would significantly and directly impact the amount of my royalty payments each quarter. Yet they had arrived at this price with no consultation whatsoever with me while demanding that I rubber stamp their pricing decision. That feint in place, they then tried to complete their pick-and-roll by casually dropping the news that they had already arranged—or so they claimed—to substitute a better known product for my product if I didn't accept their offer soon.

Capping it all came the revelation that after thinking it through, they really didn't want me on the corporate board but had penciled me in for an advisory group instead.

"Run!" I heard myself say. "Run! Run! Run! Let this one go."

On this occasion, I used the "stay out" strategy advantageously. Within a few days of my withdrawal from the negotiations, I learned that the team that had been alternately schmoozing and head-butting me had imploded. They were bad-mouthing each other and splitting up. A few months later, the dot.com bubble burst, and all bets were off on the whole grand scheme.

How sweet it was not to be involved and at risk!

EVERYBODY'S SOMEWHERE

At the time you meet them or work with them or purchase something from them or bare your soul to them or play the best card that you're holding in your dealings with them, everyone you'll ever meet is operating somewhere on the spiral staircase of mind levels.

If it is at Level 1.2, you best take pains to stay in their comfort zone or you're going to be avoided or ignored. Once when I was employed as a writer for a Sunday magazine, I was dispatched into the Arizona desert to interview the famed "gandy dancers" on the Santa Fe Railroad. (The original gandy dancers were railroad track maintenance workers who moved metal in time to music.) Historically, gandy dancers had been African-Americans. But the gandy dancers I sought to interview were Native Americans. I'll not forget the experience. Suddenly, for reasons I could never identify, none would admit to speaking English. As an outsider, I had become a cipher.

If the mind you are dealing with is at Level 1.3, as was the case with my handyman, it's wise to guard your words and make no sudden moves. You may not know how explosive the Level 1.3 powder is, but it's always a good idea to assume that the fuse is short.

The Level 1.4 mind isn't nearly so prone to do you in with a fist, a gun or a knife but, if they have it in for you, with the rules or a nicely executed act of sabotage or put down. Example: Have you ever irritated a clerk in a government office who then fails to tell you that the previous Friday was the deadline for filing the papers that you've incorrectly filled out? You get to learn about the expired deadline on your *next* visit, after you have the now-useless papers correctly filled in. Or have you ever paid careful attention to how a Level 1.4 user reacts to your enthusiasm at being recognized for having achieved something outstanding. As a rule, the Level 1.4 mind does not like the individualistically minded winner and may react strongly against the success or enthusiasm of others. Australians call this "the tall poppy" syndrome. Any flower that sticks its head above the others gets chopped down. While growing up, I was frequently cautioned not to get "too big for my britches." If I had $10 for every time that happened, I could probably buy both of us a used Rolex.

Level 1.5 users are usually constantly calculating how much you really know and how much they need to let you know, even when you aren't part of any of their power games or sales schemes. They can't help it. It's simply something their mind does. Disappointing as that is, you may not be able to trust them fully because you must always assume that they may have held something back that might have influenced your decision or otherwise been helpful. Several protocols recommend themselves when you are dealing with Level 1.5 minds. Don't let them be the sole source of your information. Watch for the questions they are avoiding and insist on solid answers or find the answers anyway. Anticipate and sidestep their ploys ("a ploy perceived is a ploy denied"). Get everything that is important in detail and in writing. If you need to, let a lawyer speak for you at the first major signs of malfeasance or chicanery, especially if you can't get out or stay away. And remember that, given enough time and rope, the out-of-control Level 1.5 mind will nearly always engage in retched excess, overreach and overkill and screw up tactically. If they need to go, watch for your opening and when it arrives, pounce. Vote them out or fire them. Expose them. Isolate them. Take their resources. Destroy their influence and their reputation. If you can prove that they've violated the law, put them in jail.

The next level, 1.6, produces Alpha's most complex thinking. Recognizing where the user of this level is coming from, and deciding how to respond, presents a challenge of a different kind.

With some Level 1.6 thinkers, you may need to be prepared for—is there a better way to say it?—an invitation to play or hang out or dawdle. (Oscar Wilde wasn't far off the mark: "The problem with socialism is that it would take too many evenings.")

It's no big secret why users of this mind level might find play attractive: play is a direct route to feelings, and Level 1.6 is the purest of feelings territory. During such times, we need to acknowledge, the Level 1.6 mind can be highly creative. When you anticipate the Level 1.6 user's need for quality feelings time and your need for access to their creative energies and output, you can be more careful about scheduling, about your end of the commitment and about the likelihood that they will be able and willing to live up to their agreement.

On other occasions, the biggest challenge you may face from the Level 1.6 mind may not be playful at all. At this level, feelings can quickly turn sour.

Users of this mind level can become so fixated on what they want to happen that they lose touch with all perspective as to what is possible. For example, deeply and empathetically in sympathy with those who are disadvantaged and disillusioned or fixated on their own desires, they may find their minds going taunt with their own frustrations and impatience. At such times, their demeanor may become prickly, brittle, self-righteous or priggish. Their voices may grow shrill. Their sense of what is reasonable may all but disappear. Their expectations may soar beyond anything that is achievable, and their visions may degrade into tunnel vision. On some occasions, this is exactly what the world needs to experience from them because it will mean that *George Bernard Shaw's unreasonable person has arrived!* (The one, he said, who makes all progress possible.)

At other times, the Level 1.6 mind's insistence that things can only be viewed as it sees them and understood as it understands them can soon outlive its welcome. One begins to grow tired of this mind's users' frequent put downs and superciliousness and expressions of pique. Of their assumptions of innate superiority. Of their inability to acknowledge their own blind spots—to learn. So, one moves on, leaving them behind.

But whatever level of the mind you think you are dealing with, there's one cautionary aspect to remember:

Don't expect to be right every time in your assessments. As much as you'd like your Beta mind to be a vigilant cat always on the trail of stereotyping's mouse—that is, as much as you'd like always to characterize people accurately and fairly—there will be surprises. You can watch for months and still have doubts as you attempt to ascribe a mind level for some individuals. This makes having as wide a variety of clues as possible a very desirable state of affairs. Realistically, we will seldom have all the clues, or even the kind of clues, we'd ideally prefer. This makes paying attention to the emotional and behavioral clues we do have all the more important.

With your Beta thinking skills, you are better equipped than ever to recognize when and how to help people change or deal with their "life structures" so they can quit sabotaging themselves and others (you included), Rule No. 1: Use Beta's increase in "aperture power"—in the amount of the world's complexity that your mind can functionally admit and process. Rule No. 2: Use Beta's skill for removing bottlenecks and helping people (and things) be as competent as possible as much of the time as possi-

ble. *Rule No. 3: Use Beta's skill for detecting changing milieus and intervening in ways that help spark and shape new possibilities.*

The information in the chart that begins below can be used to help people work on their contexts, strengths, ability to contribute and the amount of satisfaction they derive from doing things well. All this adds up to a pretty yeasty mix. Once you accept the power of thinking this way about how minds work, you will find that you possess a remarkable set of operating insights for members of the human species.

OPERATING INSIGHTS
FOR THE LEVELS OF THE MIND

Level 1.1 (Alpha)
"One breath, one step, one moment at a time."

Practices moment-by-moment survival.

Sees a basic stimulus-and-response world almost totally focused on hour-by-hour physical needs and desires.

Can be unresponsive, irrational and difficult-to-read or can behave in other random or inappropriate ways. Depends on instinct and automatic body/mind processes to stay alive. A person can be susceptible to deadened or numbed feelings or can feel remote emotionally. Eyes and mind may be blank. Attention may be attracted to immediate stimuli and movement and go elsewhere at any time.

No moral justification of behavior is attempted by this mind's user.

You can help by:
• Seeing to their basic needs: food, water, shelter, medical care, etc.
• Viewing and responding to them as a person, not something less.
• Avoiding threatening gestures or movements.
• Expressing interest, affection or love—reassurance—by gentle, careful caressing, stroking or handling (if appropriate).
• Communicating to the basic senses.

Level 1.2 (Alpha)
"Be one with my kind."

Safeguards the tribe, clan, family—their people.

Sees a naturalistic world dominated by life cycles and seasonal events. Maintains an automatic allegiance to closest "blood ties" with a deep respect for traditional explanations and accumulated wisdoms inculcated in elders.

"Blood is thicker than water" behaviors

A person can be susceptible to feeling vulnerable and abandoned. May be prone to fatalism, sacrificial violence, withdrawal and/or depression.

Moral justification of behavior: "It's in the hands of fate."

You can help by:

- Praising their strong sense of family and tribe—their people—in a way that acknowledges their ties to their kin.
- Respecting their rituals, ways, customs, elders, ancestors and sacred grounds.
- Guarding against rapid changes, ambiguous moves, uncertainty.
- Making gifts of appropriate goodwill tokens and tangible belongings.
- Going the second mile in seeking to understand them.

Level 1.3 (Alpha)
"Hold on in a hostile world— alone."

Practices being a "world of one"—to hell with everyone else.

Sees a put-down-prone, impersonal, autonomous, egocentric and threatening "survival of the fittest" world. Invests energies and awareness almost exclusively on activities and situations where he/she can be viewed as standing tall, can talk tough and can avoid shame at all costs.

Detonates in your face a lot.

The emphasis is on raw adventure, risk-taking and mounting challenges to any attempts at control by others—all without feelings of guilt. A person is unusually susceptible to feeling rage and shame. May be prone to retaliation, violence or sabotage. Lack of sensitivity to the feelings of others. Perhaps cold, ruthless, given to dictatorial action.

Moral justification of behavior: "It's a hard, cruel world."

You can help by:
- Producing immediate payoffs, prizes and rewards.
- Offering opportunities to demonstrate power, daring and prowess.

- Praising them for their willingness to undertake daring, perhaps dangerous, projects (where risk-taking is necessary).
- Being careful not to shame them or cause them to lose face, invade their turf unbidden, portray them as weak or demean them privately or publicly.

Level 1.4 (Alpha)

"Protect the truth."

Safeguards personal beliefs, the rules one lives by, stability, community, institutions.

Sees a regulated, orderly world of hierarchical absolute laws and relationships. Seeks to live faithfully and securely within a firm understanding of what higher powers require and will reward and to contribute toward a stable community and environment.

Steady, salt-of-the-earth behaviors.

A person can easily be susceptible to feeling guilt and self-righteousness. May be prone to deep grieving and may search for support from authority, litigation and/or sabotage.

Moral justification of behavior: "There is duty, and there are orders—always."

You can help by:
- Praising their loyalty, sense of duty and honor, high standards of service and preparation, disciplined response, good behavior and punctuality.
- Seeing that their world is as orderly, stable and predictable as possible.
- Avoiding slights to their religion, patriotism, ethnic ties and other objects of loyalty and devotion.
- Honoring rules, procedures, customs and historical beliefs important to them.
- Being on time, being fair, being "moral" and ethical, being respectful.

Level 1.5 (Alpha)

"Win as much as I can."

Practices the skills needed to attain and maintain recognition as someone who is successful.

Sees a highly individualistic, "Newtonian" (predictable clockwork-like) world, full of opportunities that can be manipulated into status, control and payoffs. Pursues ever-expanding personal influence, status and wealth, chiefly by working to become more and more skilled at negotiating, timing, strategies, tactics and other key skills of gamesmanship.

Usually schmoozing and cruising for advantage.

A person can be susceptible to fears of being materially poor and personally inadequate. Acts for personal good first, acts to cut general losses second. Believes life to be largely a game filled with status, payoffs and more opportunities for players who compete with savvy, energy and persistence. Prone to tough negotiation, testing of limits, litigation and strong gamesmanship behaviors.

Moral justification of behavior: "There will always be losers."

You can help by:
- Providing them with opportunities to succeed and symbols suitable for a "winner."
- Acknowledging skills at gamesmanship, persuasion, strategizing, competing, negotiating, staying fashionable, "keeping up with the Joneses" and keeping up with the state of the art.
- Arranging for them to be in the company of big-name personalities, players and VIPs.
- Letting them in on the action and providing quick advancement, material rewards and plentiful recognition for success in meeting goals.

Level 1.6 (Alpha)
"Get well, balanced, whole."

Safeguards groups and causes; wants the ideal of "the natural, wholesome life" for everyone.

Sees a world that should be caring and supportive all the time for all participants. Is devoted to participating with others in good feelings, healings and "the natural life" and sharing the benefits of such outcomes.

Behaviors that reflect a desire that all be one.

Seeks to have everyone included except for those who refuse to adhere to the requirements of inclusion. During emotional times, the individual may be susceptible to feeling sad, lonely and powerless and acts to soothe the pain where possible. May be prone to attempt to push your "guilt" buttons and to mount public protests, group litigation and/or group sabotage as it seeks an equitable balance and outcome for all. Believes that the world is filled with just causes and higher needs. To live fully, believes you can personally benefit from getting closer to people in groups, from getting in touch with your feelings, from healing old wounds and respecting new ones—and from committing to the needs and best interests of the larger good.

Moral justification of behavior: "We have to try."

You can help by:

- Praising them for being egalitarian, participative, democratic and inclusive.
- Arranging for them to work with a team and conditioning their pay and rewards (at least in part) on the team's performance.
- Avoiding actions that would be harmful to people's feelings, destructive of the environment, demeaning to any ethnicity, intolerant of the consensus-building process, damaging to a sense of community or construed as elitist.
- Understanding their need for the means to heal, express feelings, be playful, humorous and tolerant, demonstrate social responsibility and support people-oriented causes.

Mind 2.0 (Beta)

"Get real"

Practices making a complicated world work as realistically, functionally and fairly as possible.

Sees a relativistic world filled with new complexities, many of which are going to require new approaches and solutions. Expects the world to endure and move onward, with both rueful times and celebratory times to be experienced time and again. Demonstrates strong personal competence by tapping into the strengths of all earlier mind levels situationally and innovating frequently; routinely aims—and downloads— ahead of most other participants.

Behaviors that can help make complex things happen appropriately.

A person feels whatever is appropriate and may feel any of the emotions of Alpha but usually for much briefer periods of time than when they were an Alpha thinker. Acts to facilitate appropriate response using realistic and functional choices. Believes in looking for innovative ways to solve problems that are of interest and/or that are important for creating new competencies and a more functional world. To the extent possible, wants this world to serve the needs of all living creatures, now and later. Prone to try for a win/win-type outcome where possible. If not, on many occasions, will get out. Uses litigation only as a last resort although is not hesitant to use it as a tactic against sharks and scorpions when necessary.

Moral justification of behavior: "The rules can be ambiguous, and so can the world's needs and challenges."

You can help by:
- Responding to their need for autonomy, resources, information, privacy, personal freedom and the ability to choose their opportunities, agendas, strategies, tactics and venues for involvement.
- Providing for fluid, flexible boundaries and relationship dynamics based on functional needs.
- Providing for self-determination of goals and schedules.
- Acting in principled, ethical manner.
- Not being punitive, repetitive, dysfunctional, closed-minded, cute, tart, buck-passing, rank-pulling, bullying, rules-rigid or untruthful.

In Beta, we like to be able to trust people, to believe in them. We want them to be able to trust and believe in us. And we'd like to be able to trust them to know their own capabilities and limits—the capabilities and limits I've just been describing—and convey them to us honestly and work well within them. Yet, if followed indiscriminately, these expectations can be recipes for trouble. When we allow ourselves to forget how the Alpha mind works—or on many more occasions doesn't work—we've neutralized much of our Beta mind's advantage.

I've learned the hard way not to let the worker raking the leaves in my yard go into my residential bathroom and shut the door. This was how my wife's high school class ring, the first charm bracelet I gave her and our first child's baby spoon disappeared from a keepsake "type tray" display we'd assembled and put on the bathroom wall. How could I not have foreseen this possibility, knowing I was working with Level 1.3 of the mind? Well, I had foreseen this possibility but had a good history of taking risks with it. I'd let yard workers use our bathroom facilities for years without a problem. Should I have seen something that I missed in the individual who did the thieving or have done something different this time? Obviously.

I've learned not to expect that the plumbers charging me $85 an hour are as adept as I am at getting the city's plumbing inspector out to my house to approve their repair of a gas leak. That's why I handle all dealings with the city inspector's office myself. It's faster, cheaper. Less frustrating.

I don't automatically assume that my busy personal physicians read as widely as I do in all areas that might impact all the medical care I need. That's why when I go to the doctor, I bring up possibilities, ask questions and run through my own personal checklist alongside my physician doing his or her own workup. And why in the emergency room, I'm sometimes prone to inquire about certain drugs and certain techniques the average visitor isn't likely to know about. Usually, my doctors are right on top of the latest information in any area of interest or importance to me. But occasionally, they haven't been. I never want to run the risk that they may not be, especially on that one occasion when it could matter.

I don't assume that the veterinarian who cares for my pets, the mechanics who maintain my cars, the graphics designers who do my artwork, the printers who produce my print products, the computer technicians who help me with my Web site and my other vendors or professionals care as much about my animals, property or projects as I do. Or will plan for them in the same detailed way that I will. Or monitor them as closely. They may, and often they do. But when it matters to me, I'm a micromanager of other thinkers' involvement in my personal affairs and those involving my family. And almost always, my involvement is largely based on my advanced reading of their thinking skills.

Once you've experienced and experimented with what can be done with methods of scarcity and what can be done with methods of abundance, often simultaneously, in your dealings with people, I'd be very surprised if you ever wanted to go back to your old way of thinking about why people do what they do. Why they believe as they believe. And why they so often insist on making their way through life with such an unrelenting commitment to a few compelling benchmarks that define who they are and what they can accomplish and what they can become. These ideas set the stage well for where we're headed next: looking at how Beta changes the way we play the game.

Chapter 13: **The Game**

I **HAVE COME TO** see that how the game is played is probably the most revealing single feature of the Beta thinker's mind—the quality that most quickly and definitively distinguishes Beta thinking from other kinds of thinking.

The game is about how people make things happen—or delay or prevent the building or making of them. About how wealth and power, access and opportunity, get boosted. Or rearranged. Or destroyed.

So much in life and at work, in the serious hours and the after-hours, depends on how effective we are at participating in the game. At how skilled we are at navigating alertly amid the issues and personalities important to leveraging our resources and creating the solutions we need to help make our life and other lives, and the world, better (or at the least, no worse). More than anything else, excelling at game strategy and execution is what makes achieving the leap out of Alpha worthwhile.

For example, one of the new personal behavioral qualities for me in Beta is that, while I still have a temper, I am no longer nearly so temperamental. The shift has been an astonishment and a joy for, among others, my wife and daughters. Seeing dad wait nearly an hour for his meal in a restaurant that has experienced a total service and kitchen meltdown without seeing him bark, spark and fume—well, "the new dad" quickly became the talk of the table. This is not to say that I stood by passively. The manager was summoned and questioned. The details of the problem—a computer breakdown followed by employee confusion—were solicited. But I managed to absorb the information congenially, once it was clear that people were working urgently on a fix. The scene amounted to solid evidence to some of those who know me best that I'd changed how I play the game.

As a Beta thinker, you understand with a clarity not available at any other level of the mind that *life is thoroughgoingly gamy!* Unless we are the most committed kind of hermit, we are constantly at the game. (And it can be argued that the deliberate, ongoing isolation of the hermit from others of her or his species is, in itself, a game.)

Games are played anywhere the issue boils down to this: to get your desires and needs met, you must go to, through, around or away from someone else who is trying to get his or her needs and desires met. When one person interacts or fails to interact in behalf of a goal with another, or one company with another, or one nation with another, or any other group with another group, or a group with an individual, most likely a game is involved.

This doesn't necessarily mean a contest or competition intended to produce winners and losers, although this is not infrequently the case. There are cooperative games, too. And many games that involve features of both. (Or, for that matter, neither.) Games can, and often do, grow tangled and vexing very quickly.

While hardly the most earthshaking denouement of changes in the mind, the fact that I now use my temper differently says loads about the Beta thinker's approach to the game. The difference can be summed up in a very few words: *the user of the Beta mind very rarely allows himself or herself to get caught up <u>by</u> the game.* As long as you are using your Beta skills, even as you are participating in the game, you will nearly always make a special effort to stand free and clear of its choice-foreclosing dynamics, particularly when they are needlessly and heedlessly destructive. (Maybe that makes us all subscribers to the revered American sportswriter Grantland Rice's approach to keeping tabs: "The one Great Scorer in the sky marks against your name, not whether you won or lost, but how you played the game.")

For certain, nothing else comes close to matching the contributions that competent skills in the game can make to this triumvirate of Beta-styled hopes: (1) Billions of years in the making, the game that nature has been playing with all its creatures, great and small, will continue for as many species as possible. (2) In the future more persons will do well at playing games that lead to cooperation than has been the case in the past. And, (3) when it matters, we as a species will continue to make progress toward replacing finite games (played for the purpose of creating winners and losers) with infinite games (played for the purpose of continuing play or, as business people like to say it, "expanding the pie").[1]

This is not to say that users of the Alpha mind have no solid game-playing skills. Plainly, that would be wrong. Game skills in Alpha can be formidable, which is why, at the Beta level, we must pay such close attention to our participation in the game. At Level 1.4, for example, most games are forced—by the Alpha mind—into one generally all-consuming format: one where players are viewed either as Good (Desirable) or Bad (Evil). As the twenty-first century has lost no time in demonstrating, such a mental template continues to pose great dangers because it continues to be adopted by so many for general usage. In this new century, from the World Trade Center towers to Jaffa's Clock Tower to the sniper towers of Baghdad to the towering monuments of Washington, D.C., the games characterized as good versus evil have not slowed an iota.

BETA'S BIOLOGICAL SECRET?

Go a mind level higher, and, if you are fortunate enough, the leading edge of the game metamorphoses into "co-opetition"—cooperating when it comes to creating a pie and competing when it comes to dividing it.[2] (The trick, of course, is knowing *when* to cooperate and then *when* to switch back to competing. Hence the great value, or so accomplished Level 1.5 gamespersons will almost surely argue, of deliberately operating much of the time in a self-generated fog of vagueness, confusion or deception. This way, other participants in a game may not be able to tell what you are doing. And this may be time that you need to try to figure it out yourself.)

Advance one more level, and the mind assumes that there is really only one game—an infinite one—and that it is often hurtful to assume or act as if there's anything else. At Level 1.6, the belief is widespread that all participants in this single game are uniformly entitled to equally shared power and the benefits thereof.

Realistically, however, there are all sorts of "below the surface" forces and competitions and acts of sabotage and sleights of hand present in the game as Level 1.6 users play it. Therefore, it isn't actually an infinite game at all. As with "life its own self" elsewhere, finite games are ubiquitous at Level 1.6. Users of this level of the mind are usually loath to acknowledge and talk about the subterranean realities of their supposed "infinite" game *because so many of the behaviors you find taking place aren't supposed to be there!* Why, we ask, *are* they there? Often because of the errant expectation generated by the Level 1.6 mind that, over time, the good (cooperation) will nearly always automatically drive out the bad (defection). Such, lamentably, isn't the case.

With the arrival of Beta, there is, once again, something powerfully and unexpectedly new. I strongly suspect that there will come a time when we have a neuropsychological explanation for why the Beta thinker is especially so alert for, and often so adept at participating in, games. Perhaps we already know one of Beta's biological secrets. Many researchers believe the brain has what they call a "mentalizing" module. This clump of cerebral tissues has a specialized purpose: figuring out what other people believe, feel or might do next. That is, with quickly developing a workable theory about what's on someone else's mind. Predict this with only partial accuracy and consistency, and many times you'll have a formidable leg up in the game.

There is a observational technique called functional magnetic resonance imaging (fMRI)—the laboratory version of medical MRIs—which takes pictures of brain parts and activity at work. Thanks to fMRI studies, we know where mentalizing activity is centralized in our heads. Given that we have centralized Beta on the left-brained side of our model of the mind, it is of more than passing interest to note that the brain's mentalizing specialty— one so vital to skilled game strategy—is localized in the *left* medial prefrontal cortex and not the right.[3]

BOOKSTORE ADVENTURE

But whether it is the Alpha mind's participation that we are tracking or the Beta mind's, a major challenge for any of us when it comes to games is their complexity.

Because a game can involve many moves and multiple layers, time lines and parties, neuroscientists suggest that one problem when it comes to strategizing at games may be a person's working memory. An individual can only keep so much on his or her mind at one time. Usually, that amounts to about two rounds' worth of this kind of strategizing, if there's any strategizing going on: "If she does A, then I should do Z. But she knows that I would do Z, and so she would do B instead. But, knowing I would do Y, she would do C...."[4]

Another challenge the game often throws at us is the element of surprise. We never know when it is going to hit us full in the face without so much as a warning beep. It happened to me just the other morning at, of all places, a used bookstore. And of all times, at a time when I had my mind on a half-dozen more urgent tasks and was, visibly, in a hurry. And over, of all things, three grocery sackfuls of discarded books I'd had for weeks in the back of my aging Jeep.

I have shopped frequently at the "half price" bookstore in our neighborhood (and despite what I'm about to tell you, I will no doubt do so again). The typical customer will buy books from the store for half the original publisher's price. However, I'm probably not typical. When I see a book that has strong appeal, I may pay the store's full price (which is actually half price). But usually, to satisfy an insatiable craving for reading books that I've fed since childhood, on most visits, I buy books at the place by the sackfuls. I select them from the bargain racks, most of them marked at 25 or 50 cents apiece. And it was by and large these kinds of books in my sacks.

For this reason, I'd almost tossed all three sacks of books in the trash. But ever the questioning student of how games are played, I was curious about how the used book business works in my neighborhood. Especially at the "We Buy Books Here" counter at the place where I so often shop. I was quite sure that while the book dealer sold books at half price, he bought them back at mere pennies—and maybe *a* penny—on the dollar. What I wasn't prepared for was how suddenly I found myself engulfed by a game of got'cha. As in "Now, I've got you, you son-of-a-b****."

I was still several feet away from that location when I heard a shout: "Is this everything you've brought?" Was that me being snapped at? It was. I looked up to find myself peering into the empty face of a clerk. I say empty because his face—and his voice—was flat and devoid of emotion. That said one thing: he was being careful with what he revealed of himself, and I'd not even arrived yet at his counter or exchanged a word.

Without waiting for an answer, he pointed to a table. "Put your books there and go look around the store," he said curtly. "I'll call you in about 20 minutes. Tell you if I'm going to make an offer."

"No," I suggested helpfully, "I think I'll come back later today,"

"You have to stay on the premises," he snapped.

Maybe in used bookstores in New York City people are habituated to being barked at like a stray mongrel about to pee on the table leg, but not in my city. The game was on! And in a flash, I understood that this was a game where I had absolutely no leverage. Unless I happened to have a first edition of *Gone With the*

Wind in my sack, which I didn't, or knew the founder of the bookstore chain (I did, but he died), the clerk could care less whether he bought my books or not or how much he paid for them.

In another instant, I knew that he knew that I considered the books of almost no value to me.

And besides that, he knew that I was in a hurry, and I knew that he knew I was in a hurry.

If I wanted to wait around for the better part of a half-hour, he'd probably fork over a little pocket change for my books. On the other hand, I represented little to nothing of added value to him. He was virtually floating in books—they surrounded him in piles like stalagmites half as tall as he was. Did I want to lug my books back to the car? Absolutely not. One of the bags had even ripped down the side on the way in.

I quickly selected two or three hard-back copies in one sack that maybe I'd give to someone some day. And, without saying a word, abandoned the rest. He knew that I probably would. It was a game he played several times an hour. And he was never the loser. One way or another, he always ended up at the end of the day all the books he needed, virtually for free.

And he'd even looked like someone from New Jersey who could have easily have worked in a used bookstore in New York!

Next time I will donate my sackfuls of throw-away books to the Salvation Army Thrift Store. (Not that the Salvation Army hasn't been known to play a game or two itself.) Or put them in the trash.

PLAYING WELL MATTERS

We humans have been playing the game—as humans—for many millennia. We've been aware at least since Plato that we usually play the game like a charioteer driving two horses: reason and emotion. And we've been aware at least since Sherlock Holmes that usually the more information we have, the sharper our game can be ("Data, data, data! I cannot make bricks without clay," fumed Conan Doyle's prickly, impeccably logical detective in "The Adventure of the Copper Beeches"). But whatever the game and how well or poorly we play it, this is where, in the affairs of love, the family, sports, business, politics and the wars of gods and men and women, outcomes are largely, consistently, often irreversibly determined.

Sometimes, you can find yourself boxed into a corner, and it isn't worth the hassle it would require to participate further in the game. Maybe all you stand to lose is the value of three sackfuls of books you almost threw in the trash anyway. So you toss in the towel—who cares? Other times, you may stand to lose something very dear—perhaps even your life. On still other occasions, you may be able to make a move that, startlingly, brilliantly, converts a win/lose game into something altogether different. And sometimes, you can do something so unexpected and artful and strategic that it takes a finite game and turns it into an infinite game. In finality, as a Beta thinker, it matters greatly how you play.

So let's look more closely at the game. And waste no time honing your already ample Beta skills at playing it. Because nothing is more important for you and for the world outside your door, for as distant as your imagination and influence can be stretched and your Beta thinking applied.

IN ONE SENSE, almost every sentence I've written thus far in this work has, in one way or another, been about how the user of Beta plays the game. Here's a recap.

The Beta thinker:

• offers the latest example of the brain's continuing to harness its natural powers for upgrade. It isn't too much to say—and I have said it—that the wiseheartedness and operational processing spurt underlying the Beta thinking qualities have opened the door to "the mother of all personal breakthroughs."

• is uncustomarily attuned to the consequences of his or her behaviors, decisions and actions. (And anyone else's, too, if it appears that what they are doing or thinking of doing might have serious costs or spin-offs later on for Planet Earth and its occupants.)

• demonstrates an adroit new kind of ability and willingness to choose what he or she will be responsible for, then be steadfastly responsible for it.

• proves to be remarkably well-insulated from many of the traditional fears, cat-killing-like curiosities, allures, blandishments, causes of confusion or missteps that rob so many thinkers in Alpha of their momentum, resources and hopes.

• has heightened pattern-finding abilities that are further evidence that, at the cutting edge, the brain continues to rewire and redesign itself to keep pace with an evolving, changing world.

• shows evidence of having experienced a notable increase in "aperture power"—the amount of the world's complexity that the mind can functionally admit, process and respond to.

• brings new abilities to bear for discerning what other minds may be basing their current and future conclusions on. Not always but often enough to be of value, these Beta skills of anticipation can provide a window on the world of others and on its own user's world that can be little short of prescient.

• has much to offer the aggregate community of brains with its tracking and signaling abilities at a time when firm, dependable navigational benchmarks are increasingly hard to come by. Action verb that it seems to be, the Beta mind appears to thrive at performing one of the hardest tasks of our times: keeping up with dissolving borders and newly emerging boundaries and understanding the possible implications of a world in flux.

If you know where to look and what to watch for, it is not impossible to spy many of these character-constituting qualities of the Beta thinker through keen-eyed observation. But for the most part, they are external signposts. What I want to do now is to take a more *behind-the-scenes* look at how the game is played in Beta. Let's look at the critical internal assumptions that every Beta thinker brings to the context of human interactions. And especially in those game situations with these characteristics: where the outcome is anything but a foregone conclusion. Where there are power issues to be resolved. Where the value or nature of what's at stake may be in dispute or plainly unknown. Or where "the pie" is in play and what happens is going to determine how it is divided up and whether it is diminished, left the same or given a chance to grow.

It's a desire to find, participate in and promote infinite games as opposed to finite games that so often separates how the Beta thinker plays the game from the way others are playing it.

"[Infinite] and finite play stands in the sharpest possible contrast," says former New York University religion professor James Carse, the author of *Finite and Infinite Games.*[5]

How true!

Finite games must be won by someone, and when they are, the game is over. Players of finite games know when their game began, and they know when it is complete. Players of an infinite game can't actually say when their game started, nor do they really care. And they aren't marking time until it is over. Their intention is to keep the game from ending—to keep everyone in play.

In the Beta thinker's mind, the important thing to keep in mind is whether it makes sense to pursue an infinite game in a particular situation. Or whether, given the circumstances, you are limited to or best served by a finite game. Or whether you are actually indifferent to what kind of game it turns out to be because it doesn't really matter that much.

This is why Beta users can often be heard describing game situations in terms that originated with professional game theorists and strategists.

For example, we Beta thinkers have come to view most of the games that are played in Alpha as zero-sum games. Initially, at least, there are only winners and losers to be found in such games, and few genuine win/win opportunities (although if played well strategically, sometimes a zero-sum game can be imbued with "a touch of the infinite" in that it can be used to promote an eventual win/win outcome). Moreover, in such games, little if any real wealth gets created for the universe or the participants. Instead, wealth simply trades hands (or bank accounts). Usually, following one of Mother Nature's most implacable and calloused rules, "those that hath will have it more abundantly, whilst those that hath not will have even that which they hath taken away." Zerosum games, then, are finite games.

One of the Beta user's most prized thinking qualities is the ability to recognize immediately the tell-tale signature of the zerosum game. Frequently, it has "shark" written all over it (as was the case for me at the bookstore). Then, to select a strategy early-on for ending or participating in or steering clear of the game in the most advantageous manner possible.

WEIGHING WHAT'S NEEDED

It isn't at all unusual for a Beta thinker simply to surrender, for example. In fact, this was the strategy I chose to use at the used bookstore. There was next to no concern on my part for a payoff. Winning offered me little. Playing to win or at least negotiate a compromise (and win something) would have consumed time that *was* valuable to me. So once I saw the game, I immediately gave in and left. I had things to do that were much more important to me.

Now, there is this caveat. Because you are being put in an inferior position, giving in is not something you want to do all that often. Give in or give up too frequently, and you begin to give up too much. And staying in an inferior position over the long haul does nasty things to your self-estimate and self-esteem. Occasionally, though, giving in can be very powerful, even for the one who surrenders. Even lead to a win/win, yet. Like when you let someone triumph in an argument and then the moment they have the victory, their resistance falls apart, and life can go on more cooperatively. This way, now that the way has been cleared for yet another game, both of you may win.

Nor is it at all unheard of for a Beta thinker simply to take over once he or she has weighed what's needed. The danger, of course, with "now hear this—I'm in control!" strategy is that its focus, emphasis and effect are overwhelmingly aimed at the here and now. By and large, such a strategy ignores what political scientist Robert Axelrod has so aptly called the "shadow of the future." That is, the "what goes around, comes around" possibility that you may have to deal with a party again, and next time you find your actions coming back to haunt you. If this is the case, you'll want not to have burned your bridges or damaged your standing or used up all your capital with that party.

The take over player intends to dominate, control, win. And this invites drama—retaliation, strong emotions, sabotage. If played too often, over the long term, this strategy can threaten your survival. Eventually, a stronger power may show up and take you out. Or you'll run out of victims and with no one remaining to join you in the game, have invited your own extinction.

Take over is definitely the strategy-of-choice for bullies. And yet, even so, there's a time and place for it.

At Disneyland one sunny afternoon, I was suddenly, roughly shoved to one side. My adrenaline kicked in. Swiftly, I turned toward the person who had bulldozed me, ready to defend myself. But that was before I realized I had been about to step abroad a departing ride that was already moving. The young attendant who had pushed me so indecorously had probably kept me from being injured or even killed. On this occasion, take over had been a good coping strategy for him and for me. I was removed from harm's way, and he had done his job. There are times when there is an emergency and no time to explain. Or when your authority needs to be emphasized and heeded without any further delay. Or when you know what needs to be done and it matters that it is done instantly. This is when the Beta thinker isn't reluctant to take over or see others take over, even though, at least initially, it definitely produces a finite, zero-sum game.

The idea of rushing into a compromise—engineering and accepting a trade-off, a barter—isn't necessarily all that appealing to the Beta thinker, either.

Finessing the "art of the deal" is, of course, the big, big thing in, for example, the world of business.

You've probably heard it said numerous times that a realistic deal is one in which both parties are unhappy with the outcome. The reason for their unhappiness isn't exactly rocket science. Both parties are unhappy because neither received what they wanted or got their needs fully met. Compromising is another zero-sum game. It is intended to produce something you can live with—but usually little to nothing that is calculated to make you feel more alive. By its very nature, a compromise nearly always produces second-best outcomes all around.

No wonder that most managements and unions end up hating each other. Or that people who are facing an outcome that forces them to accept less than they need or deserve turn to terrorism. Or that systems of meditation or arbitration so seldom produce outcomes completely pleasing to anyone. If you consistently win less than you need or want, your relationship with the people on the other side of the table or those in the middle is going to be impaired. Moderation—compromise—is a good strategy for drinking. But for much else in life, if used repeatedly and exclusively, this zero-sum strategy almost assuredly and steadily reduces the quality of your life as it stands sentinel against larger payoff potentials.

I should add that the Beta thinker is hardly so naïve as to think that you can get your needs fully met in every game situation. That you'll never need to compromise. This is why any Beta thinker is at least as interested as anyone in Alpha in the strides that have been made in game theory studies and research in the past fifty years.

For the uninitiated, probably the most recognizable name in game theory is that of John Forbes Nash Jr. (And the reason is not so much Nash or his work in this area but rather Russell Crowe and his portrayal of "the mad genius," a victim of schizophrenia, in the movie, *A Beautiful Mind*.)

Nash won the Nobel Prize in economics in 1994. The reason was an eye-brow-raising, door-opening contribution to game theory that had occurred to him many years earlier, prior to the onset of his devastating illness.

If rational parties are playing a "nonconstant sum" game, Nash had postulated, they will act like opposing physical forces in nature—say, the wind against waves in the ocean. They will keep testing and pushing and changing how they are dealing with each other until there is simply nothing else that a participant in the game can do to improve her or his outcome. When this point is reached, a game has reached an equilibrium: *Nash's equilibrium*, it's famously called. The creator of the Web site gametheory.net says, "Players are in equilibrium if a change in strategies by any one of them would lead that player to earn less than if she remained with her current strategy."

But Dr. Nash's equilibrium isn't a one-trick pony. There can be, and often is, more than one Nash equilibrium in a game.

And things can grow even more sticky. Some games will have numerous equilibria, maybe very stable ones or maybe not, while others will have *no* equilibrium (for example, the notoriously unpredictable "Dollar Auction" game published in 1971 by Martin Shubik, a colleague of John Nash's at the RAND Corporation in the early 1950s, and popularized at MIT[6]).

Moreover, in game theory, equations—math!—are flying everywhere. Even professionals in economics, management studies, psychology, political science, anthropology and biology who have flocked to the subject because of its wide applicability and mathematical precision can sometimes find themselves in disagreement or lost at sea about what it all means. For example about how far to the right of the decimal point you need to go in making measurements (sometimes it's hundreds of places). Or how many iterations—repeated rounds—of a game you need to include to genuinely understand what happens at the end.

One of the largest chasms, however, has opened between "standard economics" and, as I will be mentioning again later in this chapter and the next, "neuroeconomics."

Though they didn't talk about it in such terms, what generations of economists before John Nash Jr. were attempting to do—and in most cases, today's economists still are—was turn numbers into feelings. Their argument was that the ultimate arbiter of every individual's economic decisions was access to happiness or pleasure. And that the simplest way to predict and track this outcome was to follow the money. Thus they have chosen to assume that a person acting in the marketplace—that is, making economic decisions—is always focused on maximizing his or her dollars or francs or yuans. But it has become clearer and clearer that turning numbers into feelings isn't the way to predict the outcome of people's economic decisions. What economists need to be doing *is turning feelings into numbers*—and as the new neuroeconomists expand their skills, tools and insights, this is what has begun to happen. These cutting-edge inquirers have realized that the best and most accurate currency for studing personal economic decisions—which is frequently the focus of game theory and experimentation, to begin with—is not money but brain chemicals. And, while the definitive studies are early, it is already clear that brain chemistry doesn't always follow the money. And when it does, the path it takes may be counter-intuitive, difficult to trace and almost endlessly nuanced.

LEARNING FROM BUSINESS

As researchers like the new neuroeconomists move game theory deeper into the brain, the subject matter is also beginning to be moved out of the ivy-clad, math-infested Halls of Esoterica and sat down in more generally useful domains. Dr. Colin F. Camerer, a professor of business economics at Caltech and a leading voice in neuroeconomics, has noted, "Simply mapping social situations into types of games is extremely useful because it tells people what to look out for."[7]

"What to look out for"is one of the key elements of strategic thinking. Mention improvements in strategy, of course, and, among others, you'll soon have business people prowling the scene like paparazzi. They'll be talking in plain English, no less, about what game theory can teach you about avoiding, for example, being forced into a corner or having to accept an unwanted or unfair trade-off.

Here are strategies that business types have distilled from game theory for getting their needs met that the Beta thinker can use, too—in or out of business[8]:

1. Remember that when someone enters a game, the game changes. You can never join a game and expect it to be the same game you saw before you entered. Think of it this way: you can't walk into a room without being in the room. And once you are in the room, the room isn't the same any longer. Same way with a game. Physicists call this the Heisenberg ("uncertainty") principle: anytime you interact with a system, you change it. So there's never a change-free entry (exit, either, for that matter). Not in a business situation. Not in a family argument. Not in a neighborhood conflict. Not in a sexual liaison, licit or illicit. Not in volunteering to help out or providing someone with charity.

When you or someone else enters a game, you need to ask Cicero's question, *"Cui bono?"* Who stands to gain? If, for example, someone benefits from your being in the game, they owe you something. For this reason, there are times when you should even expect to be paid to play. If you can't find a way to get paid, then you may want to sit this one out. Or think, as we see next, about finding a way to add more value to your having shown up.

2. Power in the game mostly comes from adding value. It's easy to find out how much value, or how little, you bring. You take the size of the pie when you are in the game and subtract the size of the pie that remains after you have departed the game. What's left over is the value you add. (Sometimes, it's a pretty humbling amount for any of us.) What you can take away from the game primarily depends on your value in the game. The other participants are unlikely to let you take away more than you bring because this reduces the amount left for them to divide. Even researchers into personal relationships have found this to be true. They note that "the person who has the most to offer or the most to withdraw from a relationship will obtain the outcomes he or she desires more often."[9]

Increasing your added value is what improving yourself or your product is all about. And usually, it's hard work. Basic work, mostly. Tending to fundamentals. Find ways to improve quality. Discovering and promoting new uses. *Protecting your added value* is all about creating and protecting relationships with those who respond to the fact that you add value (your customers) and those who help you add value (your suppliers). With a relationship, you open the door to adding even more value. That's because you always offer something unique to a relationship: yourself.

3. Rules can be a source of power, too, and so can changing them. Generally speaking, the people with the power make the rules. Many rules have been around for a while—as well-established laws and customs. Violate them consistently, and you can end up with no one to participate with you in the game. The rules found in contracts can carry the day, too. Where rules are the issue, four things matter in a game: (1) You need to be creative in generating rules that are right for you and imaginative in envisioning how those rules might be used by you and others. (2) You need mastery of the details of those rules. (3) You need to remember that any strategy based on a rule is risky if your control of the rule is shaky. (4) And remember that any rule you were counting on may be renegotiated, overturned or ignored, especially if you lose power. (The law is "the law" only as long as those who make, enforce or interpret it agree that it is "the law." After that, what the law books say really doesn't matter.)

The older the universe grows, the more obvious it becomes that rules are ambiguous. A rule almost never turns out to be *the* rule. So don't blindly follow rules. You can be assured that few of

the other participants in the game will, especially if they are experienced.

**4. Much of what goes on in a game is about perceptions—
tactics.** What people are perceiving in a game and how they interpret it determines how they'll behave in a game. So a skilled game
player pays careful attention to actions likely to influence the perceptions of other participants. Typically, tactics are intended (a) to
make things clearer for the other party or parties (b) keep things
murky or (c) make them even murkier still. Therefore, many
games, and not only in business, are deliberately played in a fog.
A fog of confusing information, of partial information, of *dis*information intended to help shape the perceptions of others.
Everything you do and everything you don't do sends some kind
of signal to the others. Likewise, you need to pay attention not
only to what you are seeing and hearing but also to that which
you haven't seen or heard. ("Is there any point to which you
would wish to draw my attention?" "To the curious incident of
the dog in the night-time." "The dog did nothing in the night-
time." "That was the curious incident," remarked Sherlock
Holmes in the "Silver Blaze.")

It won't surprise me one whit if the whole topic of playing
zero-sum games ranks pretty far down on my Beta reader's list of
favorite pursuits. If so, I can identify actively with the feeling.

One of the least appealing aspects of my entire career, and
never more so than lately, has been having to deal with single-
minded zero-sum players doing their closed-minded zero-sum-
producing things and thinking. But we have no choice but to
monitor the lives, times and activities of zero-sum gamesters—
and more often than we'd like, deal with their real or artificial
dramas and often wasteful, unfair ways of time-structuring and
dividing the pie. Deal with their webs of deception, machination
and confrontation. Deal with their games of chicken and other
forms of brinkmanship play. Zero-sum games are destined to
remain as ordinary to our collective existence as anthracite to a
Pennsylvania coal mine. Ranging from soap operas to Grecian

tragedies to the wildest of wide-screen extravaganzas (witness the never-ending conflicts of the Middle East!), such dramas of the human condition permeate the landscape of the Alpha mind. This is why dexterity and boldness at playing an intelligent zero-sum game need to remain part of our Beta skills kit.

CHOOSING YOUR EXITS

Joseph L. Badaracco Jr., a professor of business ethics at Harvard Business School, says we should celebrate the fact that there are "quiet leaders" around who excel in sorting things out and getting problems solved in the everyday world of what I have been calling the zero-sum game. He seems to think—and it's difficult to argue with him—that for every superstar in the leadership firmament there are thousands of bit players who keep civilization from grinding to a halt expressly because of their pluck, luck, skills and not infrequent courage in moving things along and getting problems resolved in what is essentially a zero-sum environment. He has studied the participants in the game assiduously, celebrates them and offers this advice:

"Count your political capital and spend it carefully. If your situation is uncertain or hazardous, find ways to buy time before you do anything. Use the time not to moralize or preach, but to drill down into the technical and political aspects of your situation. Search hard for imaginative ways to bend the rules. Instead of moving aggressively to solve a problem, try to nudge, test and escalate gradually. Finally, don't dismiss compromise solutions— quiet leaders see the crafting of creative compromises as an invaluable practical art and the essence of responsible leadership."[10]

If Professor Badaracco's advice doesn't work, you may want to remember my final words on this subject: *with surprising frequency, the best answer to a zero-sum game is a negative-sum strategy!* Anytime you see that you don't need to have a dog in the zero-sum hunt, just leave. Withdraw, disappear, vamoose! Take your laptop, disconnect your answering machine and go hole up in your cave until you can find a more suitable, more rewarding, more constructive game to participate in.

(Well, I do have one more comment on this subject. That's to remind you of a thought shared in the previous chapter. If there is a better strategy than *get out*, it might be *stay out*. If you don't get in to begin with, then you won't have the worry of deciding when would be a good time to leave. Or as the political obiter dictum reminds us: "It's easier to get into something than get out of it.")

The games ideally preferred by the Beta thinker are those designed to help everyone be a winner. The best prospects for such an outcome—or so Beta thinkers will argue, based on escalating evidence—lie with non-zero-sum games, in which the accounting is not static.

In this kind of game, you and I may win together, or we may lose together. But we don't compete against each other. We don't even have to be in sight or in touch with each other. For that matter, we don't need to know each other. Or actually even cooperate. What we are doing is conducting ourselves in a way that, if we should ever have the opportunity to cooperate, the world, ourselves included, will benefit because we are preserving the non-static features and qualities of what has been called a condition or state of non-zero-sumness.

The scientific/policy essayist and researcher Robert Wright defined the term, which he may have invented, in *Nonzero: The Logic of Human Destiny*:

"Non-zero-sumness is a kind of potential. Like what physicists call 'potential energy,' it can be tapped or not tapped, depending on how people behave. But there's a difference. When you tap potential energy—when you, say, nudge a bowling ball off a cliff—you've reduced the amount of potential energy in the world. Non-zero-sumness, in contrast, is self-regenerating. To realize non-zero-sumness—to turn the potential into positive sums—often creates even more potential, more non-zero-sumness. That is the reason that the world once boasted only a handful of bacteria and today features IBM, Coca-Cola and the United Nations."[11]

When non-zero-sumness is available, the chances are heightened for positive-sum outcomes. This would make it possible for everyone to win because the way is clear and the ingredients are available for wealth to be added to the universe. That explains the Beta thinker's standard approach to winning: "When it matters, I want us both to win—and win elegantly and resoundingly—no matter what the odds or the difficulties or the time it takes."[12]

In difficult negotiations, I've had to remind myself more than once of those words. Because producing a positive sum outcome can be much like making dim sum: many different elements are usually in play, requiring a lot of arduous, time-consuming work. That's why when I'm negotiating, I much prefer to have only Beta thinkers at the table. In fact, I was involved in such discussions not very long ago. Here are some of the things that, as Beta thinkers, we *didn't* do on that occasion as we all sought to keep non-zero-sumness and its potential positive-sum payoffs alive.

• *Stonewall.* Silence isn't golden when it is being used as a weapon. I have to agree with the authors of *Crucial Conversation: Tools for Talking When the Stakes Are High,* who argue that silence can be devastating. "It's almost always done as a means of avoiding potential problems, and it always restricts the flow of meaning."[13] When people we have issues with disappear on us even momentarily without explanation, problems don't get solved; instead, they tend to be compounded. Our imaginations go into overdrive, and it is all too easy for the accusations bolting through our heads to burst into real view. In most exclusive-to-Beta negotiations, there is a minimum of this, I'm happy to say. In the discussions I'm recalling, even the most innocuous-seeming hiccup—such as a shipment delay caused by missing a FedEx cutoff time—was promptly explained by one party to the other, usually by e-mail. We all considered unhampered, free-flowing, quality communication a necessity.

• *Play the time scarcity card.* We established deadlines for ending our talks, but only as goals. Three deadlines came and went and each time we established a new target. Neither side tried to make its offers seem more compelling by threatening potential—or permanent—unavailability.

• *Try to force consistency on each other.* There was little "but you said this before" or "you've already agreed to that." During our discussions, we each repeatedly shifted directions, junked scenarios and invented and improvised on the spot, even concerning issues and outcomes on which we'd already agreed—or so we'd thought at the time—to put to bed. What we were searching for was not a way of entrapping, wearing down or putting fear into the other. We were searching for something that would work for all parties. This was true even on minor issues, since we viewed the little things in our relationship and mutual dealings in the same way that it is sometimes suggested that God is in the details.

• *Ignore what the others were feeling.* Throughout we communicated our feelings in detail, believing feelings to be a reflection of something important that perhaps hadn't even been articulated yet or had been communicated by one party to the other in a damaging way. When strong feelings materialized, each of us immediately set about rearranging the deck furniture of our negotiations, not wanting them to become an underwater relic.

• *Attempt to hide information that in most standard business negotiations would probably have been considered confidential and privileged.* We never got to the point of exchanging P & L statements, but we probably would have if anyone had expressed the opinion that this would have been helpful. What we did do many times was speak frankly to each other about, among other issues, mutual operating costs and comparative values, revenue histories and marketplace financial realities.

• *Damage our basic trust of each other.* Talk about a Gordian knot! These were complicated issues on the table. Sizable sums were at stake. My native culture and that of the other party are as different as a camembert and a cheddar. Their natural language isn't mine, and vice versa (although they are fluent in mine and I hardly know more than a word or two in theirs). There were also markedly different business plans and approaches, not to mention unusually strong personalities, in the mix. But to our good fortune, real trust issues were never a factor. Everyone's fundamental integrity was assumed. Freed from the temptation to inject basic character or other ad hominem issues, we could stay focused on factual issues involving mostly procedures, processes and thresholds. When your goal is protecting non-zero-sumness, preserving the trust you have of each other can save vital time, energy and resources—maybe save the day.

• *Insist that it was our way or the highway.* When it appeared all might be lost, even for Beta thinkers, I tried something drastic. "Because I'm the licensor, the concept of the future we've been working within may have too much of me in it," I told the party on the other side of the table. "As the licensee, you've usually been forced into a reactive mode. Let's put the shoes of this kind of control on your feet. I invite you to abandon my framework completely and design a framework where you are the primary conceptual architects." After considering it, though, the other Beta thinkers in the loop decided that their conceptual framework and optimum agreement wouldn't be all that different from mine. I was thanked for my suggestion, and they declined the offer. This helped all of us to see that there were only a few remaining issues left to resolve, and we disposed of those quickly.

This experience obviously addresses the value of trust in a major way. And once more, the neuroeconomists I mentioned earlier are paying close attention to this reality using their new research tools—in this case not fMRI procedures but blood analysis studies. At Claremont Graduate University, for example, Dr. Paul Zak has discovered that trustworthy participants in game situations enjoy higher levels of a neurochemical called oxytocin. This is a hormone linked closely with pleasure and happiness. When a trustworthy person gets an enviromental signal that he or she is dealing with other trustworthy persons, the oxytocin levels in their blood climb. Because of this fact, Dr. Zak goes so far as to suggest that there is an important ratio between oxytocin levels in people's blood and the economic health of their society. That is to say, (1) the higher the trust levels between people (2) the higher their oxytocin levels, (3) the higher their happiness levels and (4) the higher a country's economic well-being. "Trust is among the biggest things economists have ever found that are related to economic growth," he says.[14]

As a Beta thinker, whether around the negotiating table, the boardroom table, the pool table or the dinner table, you are forever going to be doing your part to help people benefit from a fresh, compelling and potentially powerful perspective on the omnipresent issue of who's winning and who's losing—and who is trustworthy. At such times only this is a certainty: if people's serious needs and futures are on the line, you won't be declaring anyone a loser or aiding anyone in becoming a loser unless and until it is their own exit strategy of choice and you can simply find no way around it. After all, helping people stay around is the way you play an infinite game.

Because your preference for win/win outcomes is probably known and appreciated, people will tend to think that you will automatically walk the win/win talk on every occasion. So it can come as a jolt roughly akin to jogging full tilt into a bridge abutment...in the dark of night...while listening to Sibelius on the Walkman...when others realize that there are times when you have no compunction against doing unto them as you have just been done unto.

It's called reciprocity. We look next at this and other Beta strategies for wading into the affairs of a world increasingly in need of intelligent persons with a new psychological awareness and ambition and a commitment to betterment on Earth for the greater good. And promoting a doctrine of reciprocity is likely to be merely the beginning of your agenda for a world that is increasingly in need of Beta thinkers.

Chapter 14: **Crossings**

STUPIDITY, DR. EINSTEIN reminded us, is doing the same old thing in the expectation of getting a different result. The Beta mind has materialized in substantial part, I've already suggested, because an ever more observant human nature has realized at the cutting edge that it can't keep doing the same old things without getting the same disappointing results.

To get to the Beta level, as we've seen, you must start with a healthy, suasible, concerned mind. Then you need that mind made sufficiently ready by our twenty-first century "thought galaxy" of technological tools and the new information universe this makes possible. Finally, you need that mind to glom onto how much thinking habits need to change to deal effectively with today's issues and challenges and to make some important choices. When all that happens, this mind nearly always gets out of Dodge. Even before it may fully realize what has happened, it's on the other side, looking back. In between, there is that major psychological phenomenon that we've styled "the gap."

We've spent a lot of time in this book examining the world-affecting, person-changing path that the mind travels as it heads toward the gap. Then we sought to understand the psychological prerequisites, energies and choices that may get someone hovering at the brink across it. After that, we took a detailed look at what the crossing signifies for a person. Now, I want to close out our discussion of Beta by looking at some of the realities that are

going to call us back across the gap repeatedly in the days immediately and intermediately ahead.

It is my prediction, in fact, that you are going to find yourself returning to Alpha as a regular habit. Because the need for
audacious, strategic, wisehearted Beta thinking and doing is
never going to be extinguished—not in this universe, not on this
planet, not in your lifetime or mine. Even though I strongly suspect this to be the case, if I attempted to urge on you any kind of
agenda, I'd be demonstrating just how little I understand about
how your Beta mind actually works. The door doesn't need to be
told how to use the hinge! You'll set your own highly stylized,
highly individualized—and no doubt highly effective—agenda.

But here are some critical issues and assignments where I
think we may run into each other, and a bunch of our other Beta-
thinking colleagues to boot.

A hyperspeed future

For certain, we *do* seem to be looking into the yawning face
of a growing tidal wave of technological change. Change *is* accelerating. It is difficult not to take seriously the claims of seemingly
off-the-chart forecasters such as engineering/inventing wun-
derkind Ray Kurzweil that technology is itself an evolutionary
process that will soon out-"evolutionize" biological processes.
Before too very long, Kurzweil foresees the arrival of—you're
probably no more ready for this than I am—*the Singularity*. By
Kurzweil's description, the Singularity will be a super-Rubicon of
a breaking point at which time technological change will overrun
and shove aside human ascendancy, control, leadership, thus
elbowing aside our very history. A time when, essentially, gifted
machines arriving from beyond the far edges of our imagination
will begin edging us off our perch at the top of the pecking order.
To put it bleakly, should Kurzweil's Singularity actually happen,
our machines will have begun to outthink us, and having out-

thought us, begin to outdo us on most every other important front.

Impressively, Kurzweil has tracked change all the way from the opening billionths of a second of the Big Bang. So he deserves to be taken seriously when he says that not only is change accelerating, but also the pace of change. "So we won't experience 100 years of progress in the twenty-first century, it will be more like 20,000 years of progress (at today's rate), " he forecasts.[1]

As you might expect, there are other opinions on all this. In a special issue of the *Philosophical Transactions of the Royal Society of London* published in the summer of 2003, a group of prestigious scientists with a visionary bent stop short of expecting "a singularity." These forecasters argue that machines will remain an alien species to us because of a "personhood gap." Machines, they say, will continue to lack "human levels of insight, sensitivity and an ability to handle great uncertainty," not to mention an adequate counterpart to human emotions, which they correctly view as an important aspect of our reasoning ability. And yet, dating from that December day in 1788 when James Watt's assistant created a schematic for a device to control engines that came to be known as a Watt governor, machines have been steadily ramping up to "supply virtually all the knowledge and labor" in our economies, they point out. Our intelligence, they say, will be our last redoubt even as our own limitations in that department prevent the development of a "full-blown intelligence economy...in the foreseeable future." The bottom line: humans and their increasingly capable, knowledgeable machines must learn to live together, share control and complement each other in "the co-evolution of a Society of Agency." "There are immense possibilities and great dangers," these experts conclude. "We face an awesome prospect."[2]

To both of these predictions, our Beta mind says, "Okay."

Just that.

Okay.

Okay, so we humans are staring at the approach of serious waves of change. And wondering if they will swamp us. And, okay, so we've been here before.

Have you ever read any of William Bradford's *Of Plimoth Plantation*? Bradford was one of the Pilgrim Fathers and governor of the colony for twenty-eight years. In his book, he describes the debate of the Pilgrims over their decision to go to America. (The quote is longer than most in this book but well worth wading through, I'd suggest.)

> Others again, out of their fears, objected against it and sought to divert from it; alleging many things, and those neither unreasonable nor improbable; as that it was a great design and subject to many inconceivable perils and dangers; as, besides the casualties the sea (which none can be freed from), the length of the voyage was such as the weak bodies of women and other persons worn out with age and travail (as many of them were) could never be able to endure. And yet if they should, the miseries of the land which they should be exposed unto, would be too hard to be borne and likely, some or all of them together, to consume and utterly to ruinate them. For there they should be liable to famine and nakedness and the want, in a manner, of all things. The change of air, diet, and drinking of water would infect their bodies with sore sicknesses and grievous diseases. And also those which should escape or overcome these difficulties should yet be in continual danger of the savage people, who are cruel, barbarous and most treacherous, being most furious in their rage and merciless where they overcome; not being content only to kill and take away life, but delight to torment men in the most bloody manner that may be.[3]

More than thirty years ago, physicist-visionary Freeman Dyson quoted from Bradford's book at length in a prestigious lecture at Birkbeck College, London. Dyson concluded that humanity always seems to be faced with these three devils: disunity, shortage of funds and fear of the unknown.[4]

And that humanity usually has a way of muddling through and making the feared future work by relying on virtues like toughness, courage, unselfishness, foresight, common sense and good humor. Such qualities will be needed again and again in the centuries to come, Dyson concluded. Obviously, I agree.

The future I see personally from Beta looks like more of the same stuff that the Pilgrims faced. I could say "only more so," but I'm not sure of that. Every level of the mind has, in effect, faced a kind of singularity—that is, a time when the human experiment could have ended. The user of Mind 1.1 went up against an attacking tiger armed only with a stick. Relatively speaking, I can't really say that circumstances were any less dire for the future of humankind then than when we might be about to create machines more intelligent in important ways than we are.

This circumstance seems (to me) to be ongoing: we humans have some qualities that are worth preserving, that serve us well in dealing with prospects we don't understand or didn't expect. We can see these more clearly than ever using the Beta mind. Best we see to it that, to the fullest extent of our abilities, they are preserved and put to good use.

Again.

Immaturity, etcetera

I think we'll all readily agree that *mature* minds do not:

• Ignore the brutality rampant in the world against girls and women and the need for better care for them. Five hundred thousand women are dead each year in pregnancy or childbirth. One hundred million women and girls are "missing" because they were aborted or killed at birth for being female or because food or adequate medical care has been denied. One hundred thirty million girls have been genitally mutilated. Between one and two million—who can really know?—girls and women are trafficked into prostitution annually.[5] And countless millions more are condemned to die or live lives of misery because of someone else's "cast the first stone" religious or cultural scruples or their being

drugged with the cocaine of indifference cut with the talcum pow-
ders of ignorance and arrogance. These are victims dead or in misery from AIDS. From bearing children they can't support and
have no skills for raising. From ostracism and abandonment for
sins real or imagined.

• Drag their feet in moving against a growing planet-wide
trade in so-called exotic pets that epidemiologists say can, at any
time, loose devastating disease-causing viruses, bacteria, parasites and who can say what else against a hapless, defenseless
human population. Given the laxity of tax import/export laws
and enforcement and the consumer's blithe naiveté while shop-
ping at the pet store, about all the experts can lamely recommend
is that you wash your hands often.[6]

• Tolerate pandemic lying by the people at the top and their
media supporters. The problem is particularly acute at the
moment in America. When the news of the day is reduced to
stereotypes, caricatures and sound bites, says *New York Observer*
columnist Joe Conason, it is all too easy to "substitute invective
for argument and images for facts. The technique is unscrupulous
and almost foolproof. It's the big lie, repeated and repeated, until
the truth is obliterated and the lie is legitimated."[7] Even where
there is supposedly a "free" press, the news media are increasingly impotent to ferret out the truth because they are increasingly
owned and controlled by and sympathetic to—yes—the very
people at the top who are doing the lying.

• Condone an age of narcissism in which hubris fuels out-
of-control egos to the point where it is almost commonplace for
people who are already overachievers to cheat and dissemble to
appear to be even more than they are.[8] Examples in America: the
executives of Enron, Arthur Andersen, WorldCom, Adelphia
Communications, Global Crossing, Tyco and HealthSouth, who
were caught cooking their books or in other questionable activities. Baseball player Sammy Sosa, who was caught corking his bat.
Jayson Blair, the *New York Times* reporter, who was caught invent-
ing and stealing stories. And the managers of numerous mutual

funds who engaged in mendacious chicanery, wholesale fraud and ripoff-quality manipulations at the expense of their small investors.

• Turn a blind eye toward the quality of justice and the need for skilled handling of the criminal. Even in a country supposedly as advanced as the United States, penny-pinching, "get tough on crime" legislators have reduced prison budgets so much that only about 15 percent of state prison inmates are enrolled in academic or rehabilitation classes. Within three years of their release, two in three commit another serious crime.[9] Then comes the news that in states that use lethal injection as a means of execution, at least thirty-one are using a drug—pancuronium bromide—that can leave a wide-awake inmate paralyzed and unable to speak or cry out as he slowly suffocates.[10] It is difficult to imagine a more cruel and unusual punishment. And evidence is growing that before an inmate ever arrives at a prison, he or she is victimized by widespread prosecutorial misconduct in the American criminal justice system that goes almost totally unpoliced, unexamined and unpunished.[11]

• Vandalize, poison and junk up our planetary home by dumping the artifacts of our immaturity onto its surfaces and into its depths, heights and people. After World War II, entire ships full of munitions and poisons like mustard gas, arsenic, lewisite and sarin were sunk in the Baltic Sea and eastern Atlantic. An expert says, "It's an illusion to think we can clear up this mess."[12] And we haven't begun to mention the polluting of the air, soil contamination, nuclear wastes and a host of other deep troubling and dangerous "problems of the leavings."

• Create public debts so huge that they bankrupt their country and then act to suppress this information. In the United States, an updating of generational accounting has shown that the true obligations of the U.S. Treasury are ten times larger than the Treasury debt held by the public. At this writing, the mind-numbing figure of unfounded government obligations is $43.4 trillion, which compares to a net worth of all American households of $39 trillion. *The supposedly almighty financial giant of the world is broke!* Yet the highest levels of the elected government ordered this information withheld from its constituents so it could get Congress to pass another huge tax cut.[13]

• Make vituperative and inflammatory statements about the religion of others at a time when much of the world is already in substantial danger because religious passions are inflamed. An American evangelist whose family name is a household word called Islam "a very evil and wicked religion." Topping that, another well-known U.S. church leader characterized Islam's founder and prophet, Muhammad, as a "demon-possessed pedophile."[14] If we are looking for equivalent acts of recklessness and indifference to the dangers, then perhaps we should consider lighting a match in a room filled with paint fumes or shouting fire in an overcrowded auditorium with few exits.

• Build extravagant "luxury fever" homes at a time when the poorest one-fifth ("the bottom billion") of the world's population receives less than 3.5 percent of the world's income: Example: A retired cell phone magnate and his wife built a 48,000-square-foot French-styled chateau near Denton, Texas. It sported a tea-room modeled after New York's Tavern on the Green, a two-story closet, a fifteen-car garage, a two-lane bowling alley, a reproduction of a fireplace from the movie *Titanic* in one of the men's dressing areas and 130 tons of air conditioning. (The lady of the house admitted, "It was a dream, and it probably should have stayed a dream. I was being a bad steward of God's funds.")[15] And the cost of this prodigal Texas pad didn't begin to approach the $98 million Bill Gates spent on his 66,000-square-foot home on the shores of Lake Washington.[16]

For people involved in the "politics as usual" activities of Alpha, a list replete with these kinds of tragedies and screw-ups is vulnerable to being denounced as knee-jerk observations of so-called progressives or others on the "left" side of the political spectrum. From Beta, though, you and I see and call it differently. The spectrum involved isn't one that runs from the political right to the political left. The spectrum that concerns us runs from that which describes still eerily animal-like behavior and choice-making quality to that which is seriously imbued with qualities like good judgment, humaneness, fairness and reasonableness that we like to label distinctively human. This spectrum runs from a decided lack of human maturity to a marked improvement in human maturity, and all of the examples just cited are much closer to the bottom of this spectrum than the top.

And any of these abysmally soul-searing, gravely hazardous, immeasurably wretched or unspeakably dumb activities and many others I could also have mentioned can benefit from a puissant dose of Beta thinking. Go in where you choose to go in intent on summoning all the audacious, strategic and wisehearted power of the Beta thinking skills you can muster. For we are faced with a worldwide immaturity crisis in our thinking. It's another gap, and it's growing.

It's a gap that can sneak up on us when we are least expecting it. When we are well-pleased with ourselves. When all looks good, safe, maybe impregnable.

Let me tell you quickly about my experience with the school superintendents of Oregon, for example.

It was their annual retreat. We were gathered at Salishan Lodge, a beautiful place at Siletz Bay on the Pacific coast. I was their keynoter. And from the moment I arrived, it was a white-water ride.

Because there's no way to be kind about it—these school leaders were prideful and full of themselves. In a word, arrogant.

As they were quick to remind me, the Oregon public school system was considered one of the country's elite. By most standards, the taxpayers of Oregon had funded the needs of most of their districts lavishly. That evening, in introducing me, the group's president startled me with his assurance that anything I'd have to say about how the brain works would be passé in his school district. Making no effort to hide his cockiness, he reported that they had "covered all that kind of thing" years ago. Well why,

I immediately wondered, had this outfit invited me to spend two days with them?

Before breakfast the next morning, word of a general rebellion was dispatched to my guest suite. Overnight, the discontent had grown. Obviously, it was time to have a no-holds-barred showdown with the school superintendents of Oregon. And that's what occurred during in my one remaining appearance at Salishan.

Looking and sounding as stern as I felt, I faced down the school chiefs and quickly got to the point: "If you want to make good use of my being here, you can consider me a wake-up oracle. A messenger from a future that is about to sweep down on you. It is a future about which you are clueless. But this is my prediction: Schools in Oregon are probably no more than five years away from an apocalyptic meltdown. The world is about to change, and you aren't paying attention. You are coasting on empty laurels, and trafficking on yesterday's momentum. When it comes, the biggest crunch for you is going to be financial. Five years from today I want you to remember that you heard it here first. Your school systems in Oregon are soon going to be so starved for money that even your personal pensions may even be in doubt."

I left Siletz Bay, and Oregon didn't fall into the sea. I'd long since forgotten about my disharmonious encounter with the cavalier school superintendents of Oregon until one day about five years later when my eye happened to fall on one of Bob Herbert's columns on the Op-Ed Page of *The New York Times*.

Dateline: Hillsboro, Ore. Subject: The looming disintegration of Oregon's schools. Herbert wrote, "The Oregon public school system was terrific, one of the best in the nation. Now, suddenly, it's speeding along the road to ruin, the victim of a bad economy, and, more than anything else, the radical antitax fever that has gripped so many Americans. The idea that American kids in 2003—first and second graders, juniors and seniors in high school—could be forced out of their classrooms because the public will not come up with the money to pay for them is astonishing."

The president of the Hillsboro Education Association was quoted as saying: "People are starting to refer to Oregon as the Mississippi of the West."[17]

Let me hasten to note that there was nothing psychic about my comments at Salishan that morning. Had the opportunity arisen, a year or two later, I'd have made similarly pointed remarks to the board of directors at Enron Corporation. And shortly after that, to the governors of the New York Stock Exchange. And after that, to shuttle flight managers and top officials at NASA. And that by no means exhausts the list of deserving, top-drawer candidates for pointedly-worded wake-up calls in recent years.

This kind of speech is a good one for a Beta thinker to make to any group that is too full of itself and not paying attention. Any group that is blinded to other possible rhythms and scenarios, to their own irrational exuberances and to ultimately unsupportable or unsubstantiated conceits. *Any group whose immaturity gap is showing!*

The sharks and the scorpions

Economist Ken Binmore of London's University College describes how the psychological sharks in our midst differ from the non-sharks:

"The outsiders who lurk in dark alleys with rape and mayhem in their hearts are neither nice nor forgiving. Nor do sharks only cruise in murky waters. They also swim in brightly lit boardrooms and patrol the corridors of power. Such upper-crust sharks show beautiful teeth as they prey on our bank accounts and raid the pension funds of elderly widows. [We] would be the fools they take us for if we returned the smiles with which they try to convince us that they are nice people like ourselves."[18]

We must watch out for the psychological scorpions, too.

The scorpion meets the frog along the stream bank and solicits a ride to the other side. "How do I know you won't sting me out in the middle of the stream?" asks the frog. "Because if I do, I will die, too," the scorpion answers. The frog is mollified, and they push off. Somewhere near the middle, the scorpion attacks. "Why?" asks the soon-to-be-dying frog. "Because it's my nature," replies the soon-to-be-drowning scorpion. Gandhi succeeded because the British were not scorpions and refused to destroy him and his followers. The Nazis *were* scorpions, intent on preemptive first strikes, and in the Holocaust, millions of Jews died even though they almost always cooperated.[19] In the long-running Israeli-Palestinian conflict, both sides have too often acted like scorpions in that neither has demonstrated any genuine, intelligent, lasting intention of letting the other side be a winner, too.

Our design as humans brings with it a cruel and egocentric capability for being the cause of others' suffering or for being indifferent to their fate. Sharks and scorpions are merely among the most dangerous manifestations of this condition. As a Beta thinker, you will forever be alert to ways and means to limit, neutralize or nullify sharks and/or scorpions if you can or to stay free of their deadly crunch-down jaws and poison-spewing tails if you can't.

For example, we need a Death Index. To have it, we will need a supercomputer and some hefty funding from a gutsy, far-sighted foundation (or perhaps several), but it can be done. You see, the sharks who have political control long ago realized that they do not have to worry about long-term consequences of their decisions. Who can say what the final impact of a quarter or a half or a whole trillion-dollar tax cut will realistically be? Or the elimination of a government-funded housing or educational or child-care support program? Or dumping poisons in the environment or selling a subtly defective product that regulators and legislators have turned a blind eye toward.

If you are an elected official or a lobbyist, you usually don't have to worry. By the time anyone figures it out, if anyone ever does or even gets around to wondering, you'll have gathered your rewards and be long gone.

But not if we had a Death Index. A Death Index would calculate the human toll from important political decisions from the get-go. And announce it right away. And that would make a difference right away. Because a large number of the decisions that political leaders make end up costing lives. Since it is usually our money that they're betting with at the human craps table, we all deserve to know what the odds are that it is our life that may be ended or shortened. Or one of our children's. Or our neighbor's. Or a homeless or mentally ill person's. Or that of a nine-year-old desperately poor child harvesting cocoa beans in the Ivory Coast.

Also, we need to rethink the legal profession. The law is the only major occupation awarded legitimacy by civilized societies for deliberately producing huge numbers of sharks and scorpions and little else. On his first day at law school, one lawyer told me, he and the other students in his freshly matriculated class were told, "We're going to teach you to view the world from the asshole up." When I look at the legal profession through my Beta lenses, I generally see an industry that needs to be deeply shamed. Then, taking a page from Dr. Atkin's diet on the value of ketosis, starved. Then reconstructed from the ground (and the a**hole) up. The profession is a growing cancer on public and private priorities and possibilities. And a huge hindrance to the fair, prompt, affordable resolution of disputes, the equitable allotment of humankind's resources and the intelligent determination and handling of its choice-making options.

As previously admitted on these pages, there have been times when I've resorted to lawyers when I've bumped up against a shark in the pool. It will probably happen again. And I realize that not all lawyers are sharks or scorpions and not all shark or scorpions are lawyers. (There are some lawyers who actually battle the kinds of actions and actors that thwart the dignity, fairness, utility and integrity of the law and even support the underdog on occasion. I don't think that kind of lawyer will object to my desire to curtail the pernicious influences of the other kind. And I should add, I've had good friends who are attorneys. And we also have lawyers in the family, very good ones, who are probably going to want to argue with much if not all that I've been saying about their profession.)

But my research tells me this. In the United States, resolving disputes fairly is a rare goal for most of today's lawyers, especially those who litigate. (This ceased to be the primary purpose of the profession's litigators decades ago.) And so is using the law as the law was usually meant to be used. If you read the Federal Rules of Civil Procedure or many of the state procedural codes, I'm told, you find well-written, well-reasoned rules for getting legal problems resolved fairly and expeditiously. But the process has been corrupted by the only "rule of law" that counts any longer: winning.[20] At any cost. Tucker Carlson, the cable news commentator, sums it up for most of us. "I've never had a pleasant letter from a lawyer," he says.[21]

What can a Beta thinker do? This is the thought I have: Thwart and infiltrate. Thwart and infiltrate. Cut the lawyer out (resolve your own disputes and use a lawyer only when you absolutely must.) When it's worth the effort, expose lawyers for who they are, what and how they think and the damage they cause (gather your facts and sow your truths). Act at every worthwhile opportunity to keep their pernicious, expensive, destructive shark or scorpion influences at arm's length and out of the decision-influencing activities of any organization or group where you have clout (simply tell your colleagues that there are solid alternatives to a lawyer—and prove it).

I do actually think such activities might make a difference? Oh, yeah, I do. I really do. I've seen it too many times. When the right "tiny difference" finds itself implanted in the right "initial conditions," the "amplification" can end up being "exponential."

But first, we always need that tiny difference. Lots of them. It helps if they are all over the place.

Thwart and infiltrate.

Follow the neurons

Let's put it this way: If you can remember when Sputnik was launched, you can probably recall the Platters, those masters of dulcet tones and ultra-harmonized bob-bob-a-bobbin' beats. In one of their platinum hits, they sang, "Oh-oh, yes I'm the great pretender, Adrift in a world of my own." Well, the brain is a crooner, too. It sings, accurately, as it turns out: "Oh-oh, yes I'm the great pretender, interpreting nilly-willy as I go along."

The brain often simply doesn't understand what it is trying to do or just done, or why! It just does its utmost to act like it does.

From one moment to the next, the brain "does not have perfect access to the output of [other internal processing] systems, and exaggerates the importance of processes it understands when it attempts to make sense of the body's behavior."[22] As neuroscientist and experimental psychologist Michael S. Gazzaniga says puckishly, "I like false memories. Some of my best memories are false."[23]

Gazzaniga is an expert on the brain's dirty little secret, which he explains this way:

"The brain, particularly the left hemisphere, is built to interpret data already processed. Yes, there is a special device, which I call the interpreter, that carries out one more activity upon completion of zillions of automatic brain processes. The interpreter, the last device in the information chain in our brain, reconstructs the brain events and in doing so makes telling errors of perception, memory, and judgment."[24]

For example, Dr. Gazzaniga's interpreter gets input from a humor processor in the brain.[25] Then it has to figure out why that thicket of tissue has just caused its user to giggle. There is a processor that can produce intense religious feelings when stimulated, even in irreligious people![26] Other processors automatically deem faces as "attractive" or verbal remarks as "sarcastic" or "idiotic" a half-second or so before the brain's interpreter manages to cobble up a logical substantiation as to why it thinks this is so.[27] In fact, most of the electrochemical activity that undergirds our behaviors involves default modes of brain operation so antediluvian that they are not directly accessible by higher forms of brain functioning—the higher, distinctive human kind![28]

The bottom line is that people frequently haven't the remotest idea why they believe what they believe. Or why they have chosen to treat information as they are treating it. Or why they are reacting as they are reacting. We are always and forever off balance and slightly behind the curve, seeking somewhat tipsily to explain ourselves, most of all, *to* ourselves.

Even when individuals get better, later information, it is often impossible for them to reverse what they have already concluded because "the physiological processes that produce learning are not reversible."[29] Repeat any message often enough, and people tend to believe it even if, each time they hear or see it, they recognize that it is false.[30] Provide people with definitive evidence that the basis on which they arrived at a belief is false, and they will persist on holding to that belief anyway.[31] And then there is this curse of the neurons: once people know something to be true (or false), they have an exaggerated sense of the degree to which others may share the same conclusion.[32] Where the brain is concerned, nothing, it seems, is quite as it seems. Consequently, where the world is concerned, nothing, it would appear, is quite as it appears.

Even in Beta, the best we can do much of the time is resort to "playing the averages." On average, this is why I think I've concluded that you have a pretty face or an ugly one. On average, this is why I think you are just short of saintly or are incorrigibly evil. On average, this is why I think that you should not be charged or why you should be given probation, locked up for thirty years or put to death. *On average*, this may be why I've fallen in love with you but then again, it may not be that at all.

In Beta, above all, we want to be forever intent on remembering that our mind is at best a jury of its peers. And we want to remember that the prosecutors of the old brain processes may never have gotten around to asking the right questions or may have suppressed the very information that could have benefited our understanding most. Every day, researchers are discovering more and more ways that the brain's older processes corrupt the integrity of the newer brain processes. Realizing this, we want to stay eternally vigilant against detrimental, ill-fitting, unsubstantiated qualities in our thinking.

Our main thinking advantage in Beta is that we have a new kind of internal permission to step away from the averages—and to ask, "What is the brain's real agenda here? What are the averages omitting? Disguising? Distorting? Really afraid of? Seeking to satisfy? Intent on preserving, thwarting or augmenting?"

Then we can, or so we are pledged to, pursue more accurate, meaningful answers to such questions as these:

- Why do people persist in repeatedly acting against their own best interests?
- Why can people as a group hate that which as an individual they might be able to love or accept?
- Why do people in power lie so easily and so often?
- Why do people not in power succumb so effortlessly to the lies?
- Why do people place such emphasis on being better off than someone else—on leaving the Joneses in the dust? That is, why is it so difficult to say, "Stop, I've got enough, I don't need to amass anymore wealth, resources, square footage, horsepower, diamond carats or whatever"?
- What blinds those who control the means to see justice done to so much injustice?
- What is really behind the psychology of the bubble— the irrationality of "the supra-rationalizing mob"?
- Why does the quality of your planning so closely track the quality of your anxiety?
- Why is sadness often compounded by more sadness?
- Why does anger lessen the risks that people can see?
- Why is it so easy for us to decide what we would *like* to happen is what is *going* to happen?

- Why are we so quick to blind ourselves to the rights, the needs, the suffering or even the very existence of "the other"?

When we use our Beta thinking skills to look closely at these kinds of issues, they remind us one more time just how dangerous and difficult life on Planet Earth continues to be. And how tricky it may be to do anything generally substantive about much of it anytime soon.

And yet our Beta mind will not permit us to shirk the opportunity that this kind of information affords. There is no alternative to doing what you can think of that might make a positive difference, as frequently as you can think of it. Because of the way our Beta brain functions, we have no choice but to agree with Dostoevsky, who wrote in *Demons*,

> Liza! What was it yesterday, then?
> It was what it was.
> That's impossible! That's cruel!

Yesterday can be our instructor, our inspiration, our fascination, our caution. But as we follow the neurons, yesterday is not good enough for our tomorrows.

The world we find

I've never thought that there's anything profoundly advanced about the physiology underlying the Beta mind compared to the Alpha mind's. Nothing all that new has been invented—there's simply not been time for anything radically different to have evolved in our brain biology. There's not been time for an evolving nature to invent super-neurons, concoct new brain chemicals or roll out a massive cerebral redesign. Nor is there anything metaphysical involved that I can sense—little to no increase in outright spiritual adeptness that I can see—although each new level of the mind does seem to shuffle the spiritual card deck.

What has happened has had to happen on the fly. It's simply that the brains of some adults have somehow finagled a way for their neurons to stake out a very interesting perch for watching and platform for involving themselves in a world that is now moving so fast that it is beginning to gasp at times for breath.

Because you can see changes and you can see complexities and you can see consequences better than most, I'd guess that one of your main roles is going to be sensing, announcing and responding to patterns. Intuiting possibilities and opportunities for suasion or invention. Experimenting with new blends of resources and information. And then infiltrating or involving yourself in circumstances that interest you and doing the things you can think of to remove or "hot-wire" around the rot and indifference, the arrogance and hubris, the ignorance and miscomprehension, the bad luck and the wrong turns and the dangers, all in the hope that more and more non-zero-sum games can be encouraged and kept going.

Looking on from Beta, I personally am going to be watching to see how realizations and developments like these I am about to mention affect who we are as a species, as peoples, as individuals. And what can be done with this knowledge and intelligence to protect and fortify the lives we are, the lives we lead and the lives still to come.

■ *The world we inhabit is forever and incorrigibly chunky, so we need to get used to it.*

Our understanding of the universal drama that we are an integral part of is never going to be complete because it is all impromptu—it is being invented as it goes along. We are not ever going to catch up to it fully or get it to sit still long enough for us to name all the parts and figure out how, or even if, they are interrelated. Science can forget about a "theory of everything." Ain't going to happen. The more complexity we have, the chunkier things get. New systems of organizing keep appearing that follow their own novel principles. A new kind of science has to be invented each time to talk and think about them adequately.[33] As Clare Graves was one of the first and best to observe, we humans are embedded in this maelstrom of restless, ceaseless creation in which spontaneous, completely new properties keep emerging. So don't think that, in finality, we are ever going to figure *us* out, either. Ain't going to happen. The best we can do is what we've been seeking to do in this work: zero in on the chunks of our psychology and physiology that are already here and partially understood—and keep adding to them as we can—and put this knowledge to the most adroit and constructive uses we can think of.

■ *The hole in the ozone isn't the only hole we need to be concerned about.*

Many of us who study stages of psychological development have always harbored a deep chariness of the Level 1.5 mind.

Far and away, the most prevalent psychological feature of this stage of the mind—both its bane and its gain—is its sense of calculation. How much can it get away with? How far and how fast can it manage to do so? What gains can be locked in before it triggers resistance that threatens its control or returns? And how is the most effective way for it to accomplish all this? The person who thinks this way is forever testing the waters in an effort to find out.

In the three centuries or so since this mind debuted, there have often been meaningful barriers to a runaway Level 1.5. Influences that helped to keep the lid on have included geographical limits, finite markets, bad publicity, offended moral voices, incensed public opinion, limited communications capabilites, limited information processing capabilities and political and governmental controls. These counterbalances couldn't be depended on to work immediately, or completely, or always. But, in the main, they acted as a brake on many of Level 1.5's excesses.

Then, in the late twentieth and early twenty-first centuries, explosive gains in information, communications, trade, transportation and technology collectively blew a hole in the ozone safeguarding us from the ultraviolet rays of Level 1.5's natural and unrelenting avariciousness and acquisitiveness. Suddenly, the user of this mind level hardly needed to be concerned at all about calculation or caution. In an historical blink of the eye, and especially in America, Level 1.5 broke out and went hog-wild.

The result?

Wholesale corporate corruption. Utter fiscal irresponsibility and unconscionable moral indifference by politicians and regulatory officials at the highest levels. Brazen deceitfulness and casual, indiscriminate lying by many with power and authority. An almost complete abdication of concern for the losers by the winners in society. And a widescale replacement of the skills and the humanity of the employee by dehumanized technology and rigid, cookie-cutter planning. (Sociologist George Ritzer has called it "the McDonaldization of society," which he defined as the creation of a tightly controlled, highly scripted, hyper-rational delivery system that maximizes efficiency.[34]) There is a surfeit of rank Level 1.5 arrogance extant in the circles of people calling the shots and controlling the purse strings today.

And there has been serious damage done.

Some of our civilization's best and brightest ideas—like James Madison's warning in "Federalist No. 51" that government has to control the governed and then it has to control itself and Clare Graves' discovery that the minds come in flavors and must be treated accordingly and some of the very bedrock principles of a liberal democracy itself—are under siege or being poorly utilized. I think ours is a world that has been put in considerable difficulty because of this. Even the ultra-pro-business editorial writers of *The Wall Street Journal* observed after the U.S.-Canadian electrical blackout of 2003, "Markets are a great way to organize economic activity, but they need adult supervision." [35] Yea, verily!

So there's a lid to be rebuilt. A hole in the psychological ozone to be filled in. Important work to be accomplished in the name of progress for the greater good. For as novelist David Morse pointed out in a compelling critique of the Bush-Cheney

Administration's efforts to fight a war in Iraq with a McDonaldized "McArmy," we are seeing graphically that "the profit motive does not always serve the public good."[36] Hopefully, with regard to the current remaining superpower, with this eruption of retched excess, we will have gotten at least part of this juvenile component of our national character out of our system. Sown some wild oats that will not require a reprise, so to speak. In this country, we have been fast losing the idealism expressed by Saul Bellow's character in *The Adventures of Augie Marsh*. We no longer seem to believe that America represents the "universal eligibility to be noble." But things will change. I'm a staunch believer in the words of the late Herbert Stein, chairman of the Council of Economic Advisers in the Nixon Administration: "Things that can't go on forever, don't." I predict you'll find Beta thinkers in the thick of the search for what has gone missing and for ways to learn from the experience and help minds change because of it.

■ *Beta has arrived at a "universal belief" that works well with all mind levels.*

As a consistent strategy for living, no one can afford repeatedly to turn the other cheek or roll over and play dead. This invites the sucker's payoff.

This insight explains the enthusiasm of the Beta thinker for a robust behavioral ethic whose standard defense when it comes to handling a defection that matters (and in one way or another, most defections do) is not all that far removed from that ancient retaliatory dictum: "Eye for an eye, tooth for a tooth." But with a nontrivial modification.

I have phrased this Beta viewpoint thusly:

My most basic belief about you and me is that my future and yours, and the future of life itself, are best served if my intention is to do my best for you, just past the point where I can no longer see you demonstrating that it is your

intention to do your best for me. At that point, my inten-
tions and my actions toward you will likely change.

This is a "belief" because it is a meta-representation arrived at after much reflection on how-the-world-might-be (at-its-best), given what we currently know and what the world currently is. And this is a telling moment-by-moment "strategy" that anyone at any mind level can use humanely and intelligently with anyone else, if he or she so chooses. Call it, if you want a name, a belief in the value of "delayed-action reciprocity."

You might think that this is a belief and a strategy appropriate for use only with the bully, the thoughtless, the unscrupulous or others who refuse to be fair, honest or responsive on issues of any substance between you and them. But the core message within such an attitude may need to be transmitted even in the most loving or committed relationships. This is especially true when there are so many things going on that may divert our attention away from our responsibilities to each other.

On such occasions, the message you want transmitted to the transgressor, speedily and convincingly, is this: "I won't defect on you first. But if you defect on me, you need to know now that I nearly always view defecting as a serious matter, and I nearly always do something about it. When we are defecting on each other, we can't cooperate. And if one of us lets the other get away with it once, it may happen again. So you can count on me letting you know that this isn't the way I do life or relationships or business."

In Beta, this modified "tit for tat" approach to dealing with people and power comes close to defining a way of life. Consequently, because we are using something so universally and frequently applicable, there is always the need to be cautious, inventive and appropriate in our actions. Here, then, are some concerns and possible degrees of response when you are using delayed-action reciprocity:

- See if you can identify a way of reciprocating that stops short of running the risk of permanently damaging a relationship. (For example, can you leave room for your defector to save face or find a route back into the relationship if he/she proves to be conciliatory?)

- Use "the morning after" test. How important and effective is the act of retaliation you have in mind going to appear to you tomorrow? (By then, sleep and the emptying of your short-term memory will have performed a cleansing of your reasoning and emotional faculties, and you may see things differently.)

- Is there a way to retaliate that essentially moves matters back toward zero, or where they were when the defection occurred? (For example, can you demand that the defector restore things to where they were before?)

- Apply the "shadow of the future" rule. The more you are likely to need someone's cooperation in the future, the more important it is to do what you can to keep your retaliation from closing that door.

- Be alert to possible ways your defector may counter-retaliate, prejudging as best you can your vulnerabilities and taking steps to protect yourself. (For example, if you sue, what is the likelihood that the defector will counter-sue, setting the stage for a destructive and never-ending pure tit-for-tat dynamic?)

- Consider how your retaliation may impact innocents if they are present when you act. (For example, delivering strongly worded grievances to grown-ups in the presence of children is usually not a good idea.)

- What are others going to consider appropriate in the circumstances involved? (If others know about it, a retaliation that is appropriate will usually enhance your reputation in the circles you move in. However, a retaliation that doesn't fit the crime can do just the opposite.)

- If the defection has damaged or poses a threat to the community-at-large, then you may want to get others involved in the retaliation. (Lone voices speaking up in favor of the commons can end up being more lonely still if no one else rallies to the cause of just, responsible action.)

The basic fairness of delayed-action reciprocity makes it a candidate for adoption by most mind levels. That's why I like to refer to it as a universal "justified true belief." I view it as the most intelligent, most robust, most ethical and most humane action available as a general behavioral strategy.

If you truly understand what makes it so "justified," so "true" and so "universal," you can understand the empathetic power that resides in such a stance as I've been describing. Initially, at least, it puts every encounter with another living entity, human or otherwise, on this footing: "At the moment it comes down to only you and me." I don't mind at all if you choose to view such a primal force as the most basic, non-sexually constituted form of love. During the intervals when we are at our most receptive and reflective and under the influence of such a force, these may be the kind of thoughts that help to define our awareness of the other:

> *In a flashback, I've sensed the point where our biologies were one.*
>
> *I've seen my heartbeat in your face. And can feel yours in mine.*
>
> *I can feel your emptiness in the cave in my chest.*
>
> *I want to know your experience and, at minimum, be able to walk a ways in it.*
>
> *I want to augment your life here: show me how.*
>
> *I believe life is extraordinary. I don't want you to die before your time. Or to experience pain or distress unnecessarily. Especially if there is anything I can do to prevent it.*
>
> *It comes down to this: you and I are here to optimize you and me until it is no longer possible, responsible or humane to do so.*

We can say and embrace and act on all this even if "the other" is only a spider, a bird, the ugliest beast in the cage or the lowest member on the totem pole. Such an awareness is, I believe, fundamental in the Beta emotional character.

*A*S WE CONTEMPLATE the future for Beta, and the future of a world with Beta, I'm reminded of a special antecedent in our species' thinking life that was called to our attention by philosopher Daniel C. Dennett in his book, *Kinds of Minds*.[37] Our situation today is surely not all that unlike that time when neuron messages from, say, the kidneys zipped up the spinal cord only to tumble into the Grand Central Station of nerve impulses at just the same moment a flood of messages were arriving from a host of other points on and within the body. Back then, the brain had no real means realistically to separate one category of what-is from another, or prioritize its responses intelligently, or reflect imaginatively on what-might-be or what-should-be. All in all, very messy circumstances. How was such a brain to think?

Then certain brain tissues began to function without being interfered with by the myriads of messages pouring in from sensors and the nerves in other parts of the body. Certain parts of the brain had finally finagled a way to interact exclusively with certain other parts of the brain, all the while uninterrupted by incoming messages. When that happened, at long last the brain had a place—and a way, and a time—where it *could* go to think!

My sense is that the arrival of the Beta mind compares well both metaphorically and literally with Professor Dennett's prized evolutionary moment when the lights actually went on for the first time in the brain's own private study. Don't you think when Professor Dennett's counterpart of the future looks back at the gap, she or he is going to say, "It was a long time in coming, but finally the brain managed another epic turning point for itself. First, it found itself a study and got it lighted. Then, at long last, it began to get its study smart-wired to deal with the new kind of world knocking at its door."

As I noted in Chapter 1, Dr. Clare Graves urged us to recognize that *the post-self-actualization era is here!* It's here whether or not Clare Graves had ever recognized it. Or whether I had ever recognized it. Or you. Or most of the rest of humanity ever manages to. And it is of such a profoundly different character that, however you wish to define it, it requires a momentous leap to get your thinking to it. For there is a gap in the way.

Moreover, Dr. Graves stressed that this revolutionary new dimension is more than a mind, it's also the totality of everything else: it's the world we currently live in, warts and all. Therefore, context is as important as the organism that does the contextual computation. Graves was also among the first to finger the arrival of, and to describe in depth, and to argue for the desirability of, protean new conditions for living and working.

This emergent new context-moving-across-the-gap can now be detected at work around the globe, around the clock, in the form of puissant new technologies, planet-encircling electronic networks, re-ignited tribal juices sometimes called neonationalism, uncertain economic fault lines that may carry no passport, rampant if often poorly understood threats to the green and blue of our physical environment, a worldwide health care crisis—you name it. There is much, and much of it new, to name, digest and respond to.

Every passing moment, this new mind and this new world are altering the shape and nature of our surroundings, complicating and indelibly changing our family life, work life, cities, culture, societies, technologies and physical surroundings to an almost nonstop, metonymic rhythm. So even if a person never succeeds in acquiring these new thinking skills we've been discussing or maybe never even realizes that they exist, he or she probably won't elude the need to deal—in a major way—with this question: *What are you going to do with the world that these thinking skills are a part of, now that it's here?*

And guess what?

Anyone who chooses to argue for their limits will most assuredly get to keep them!

Acknowledgments

OUTRAGEOUSLY HEALTHY ego notwithstanding, writing a serious book is never a one-person task. As with raising a child, it takes a village. A community. And I've been blessed with unselfish support from numerous individuals in my personal community, each of whom has gifted me repeatedly with their thinking talents, insights and resources—and often a considerable amount of their time as well.

As she has for more than four decades now, my life and business partner Sherry Ann Lynch fulfilled her usual invaluable tripartite role cheerfully and competently: (1) chief sounding board (2) chief copy editor and proofreader and (3) chief arbiter of good judgment and taste. This is our fourteenth book-length project together. Each and every time, she's helped me be a better thinker and make a better book. And not once during the countless hours that we spent discussing how to handle the editorial mechanics and the marketplace politics and the applications of the theory involved in producing *The Mother of All Minds* did she say to me, "Why don't you just finish the blankety-blank thing?"

For the first time on a book project, I found myself turning often and confidently to our daughters Kimberly and Mendy for their ideas and guidance. Both provided logjam-breaking insights at crucial times. This is a more honest and coherent book because of Kimberly's highly acidic revulsion to anything rickety or disconnected—and her skill at fingering literary solutions, even to the point of sitting down at the computer more than once and showing her dad how to write his way out of his predicament. Mendy proofed and critiqued and did triage on needful prose. How proud I am of both their minds—and how appreciative of their interest in me and my work, and for their valuable assistance!

Once again, Etta Lynch, my talented aunt, waded into my thicket of words and masterfully sorted out the King's English for me. Never mind that she'll be eighty on her next birthday. Or that she was busy finishing her long-delayed college degree at St. Edwards University. Or teaching her own advanced creative writing classes at Texas Tech University. It's a godsend to have a top-notch writing coach in the family. (I've never caught her in a grammatical mistake, so any that you spot on these pages you can be confident I engineered on my own after she'd done her editing.)

To my delight and benefit, I also gained a skilled assist in the wording of things from an unexpected source. Dr. Natasha Todorovic is a leading authority on the theories of the late Dr. Clare W. Graves. She was generous and forthcoming when I had questions and issues on Dr. Graves' groundbreaking "biopsychosocial" model of human thinking skills. But until she began to burnish my prose as she checked over my facts and interpretations, I had no idea how accomplished she also is at the writer's craft. I'm grateful to her for the time she spent improving and correcting my copy. (And she was kind enough to do so even though she and I have some disagreements in theoretical areas).

Also, my son-in-law John Stytz read several chapters. I thank him for flagging issues and wording in need of further work and for his suggestions. (And for his skilled attention to keeping my computer systems and equipment updated!)

There have been those who responded, often multiple times, when I asked them for information and insight. Without exception, their generosity exceeded any reasonable expectation. Dr. Todorovic and her colleague, Christopher C. Cowan, maintain a one-of-a-kind Web site (www.clarewgraves.com) that catalogues available materials on the life and research of the late Dr. Graves, but their assistance went much beyond that. I can't thank them enough for sharing their proprietary materials and responding to numerous e-mails in rich, helpful detail.

Dr. Sean Brophy of Dublin, Ireland, faxed me many pages on the work of the late Dr. George Kelly, a contemporary and in many ways a close ideological soul mate of Dr. Graves. Also, Dr. Brophy shared his paper based on my observation of similarities between Dr. Graves' theory and that of Dr. Elisabeth Kübler-Ross. Dr. Alistair G.J. MacFarlane was quick to provide me with copies of key articles in the special issue on information, knowledge and the future of machines that he edited for the *Philosophical Transactions of the Royal Society of London.* Cheryl Thomas of Results Performance Management in Victoria, British Columbia, provided several detailed reports on her use of the Brain Technologies tools and models in the MBA program at Royal Roads University. Dr. Alan Rae of Executive Studio, Ltd., Hounslow, Middlesex, United Kingdom, was generous in discussing his personal and professional use of the Graves theory. Brenda Reynolds quickly forwarded her Graves-theory-based master's thesis, "Optimizing the Alternative Dispute Resolution Process in Fisheries & Oceans Canada." The late Kenneth L. Adams, a long-time friend and colleague, provided extensive documentation of his facilitation of the groundbreaking Collaborative Process involving remediation of the former Amoco Refinery site in Casper, Wyo. Also, through the years, Ken served repeatedly as a sounding board for my ideas about the Gravesian corpus of materials. (Ken's untimely death during the writing of the book has deprived us all of a uniquely valuable mind and spirit. He is sorely missed.)

In addition to those just mentioned, my thinking as reflected on these pages has been significantly influenced by the work of any number of other accomplished and successful individuals who share my interest in the brain studies, mind research, psychology, personal and organizational development, philosophy, religion, cultural change, futurism, management studies, politics, neuroeconomics, game theory or other topics.

I can't begin to name them all, but because I have spent substantial time studying and reflecting on the work of a goodly number, I want to name these (in no particular order but with thanks to all for being influential in my personal thinking and idea development): Buckminster Fuller, Peter Koestenbaum, Paul Tillich, Ernest Becker, Michael S. Gazzaniga, Steven Pinker, Howard Gardner, Colin Camerer, Robert Wright, John Brockman, Steve Brams, Robert Kegan, Jonathan Wallace, Freeman Dyson, Robert Axelrod, Stephan Jones, Fritz Perls, Thomas A. Harris, Paul Krugman, Edward O. Wilson, Richard Feynman, Ken Wilber, Ray Kurzweil, Daniel C. Dennett, James Carse, David Neenan, Paul L. Kordis, Don Beck and, of course, Clare W. Graves. Also, as my reader has no doubt already noticed, I enjoy science fiction, and none more than the writings of Frank Herbert, Ray Bradbury, William Gibson and Robert Heinlein. Reading them aerates my imagination (and sometimes supplies me with an apt quote)!

Another group vital to our work at Brain Technologies is comprised of our most active distributors. I want to thank these individuals for their loyalty and support and acknowledge the brain power they represent in the world community of change agents and developers of new thinking skills and leadership talent: Michèle Carrier, Charles Boulos, Perla Rizalina M. Tayko, Pamela Wakefield-Semmens, Cheryl Thomas, Bob Farnquist, Bruno Schulze, Charles Widmer, Peter Hodel, Jacques Groenen, Andrea Gould, Paul Morgan, Julieann Myers, Brian Lundquist, Asma Fayyad, Kat Barclay, Ron Braund, Ian Musk, Mila P. Mendoza, Jim Rush, Judy Suiter, Lucille Ueltzen, Vicki Poels, Ram Chandran, David Cox, Sallie Suby-Long, Joanna Murray, Sean Brophy, Marjan Bolmeier, Alan Rae, Shahrill A.J., Grace Lim, Sjirk Loogman and Tanis Helliwell. And then I couldn't be more grateful for the quiet contributions of good friends and neighbors kind enough from time to time to ask "how's the book coming?" and then to do tangible things that help it come together. A warm "thank you" to these folks: Stanley Levenson, friend, colleague and confidant for twenty-five years and a doyen in the American public relations industry. Herman van Beek, my across-the-alley neighbor and MC scow-racing afficionado, who never fails to appear when asked to come bail me out on Web site and computer matters—and never fails to have the fix required. Larry Lourcey, my across-the-street neighbor and a gifted portrait photographer who makes me look far better than I have any right to expect. And Linda and Larry Hahn, who over three decades have endured hours and hours of opinionated discussions with Sherry and me—and what do they get for it but another book filled with more opinions! Thanks, too, to the talented Robert Aulicino for getting the cover design right from the very first and to Manish Sahu for handling our Web site design needs so well.

And then there are several wonderful people who have been instrumental in many helpful ways, some of them recently and others not so recently. These individuals have made contributions that I would be derelict to leave unmentioned: Claus-Peter Leonhardt, Johannes von Stosch, Dieter Brandli, John Ludtka, Dave Shafer, Mike Koury, the late John A. Jackson, the late Gordon Greaves and the late Mildred Downs.

I say it again: it takes a village—a global village, in this instance—to make a book. My village is very full and talented and supportive, and I treasure it.

Notes

Chapter 1: Out of Alpha

[1] Daniel C. Dennett, "The Bright Stuff," *The New York Times*, July 12, 2003, available at http://www.nytimes.com/2003/07/12/opinion/12DENN.html

[2] Personal communication to the author from Alan Rae, founder of Executive Studio, Ltd., Hounslow, Middlesex, United Kingdom, January 27, 2003.

[3] Don Edward Beck and Christopher C. Cowan, *Spiral Dynamics: Mastering Values, Leadership and Change*. Blackwell Publishers, 1996, p. 48.

[4] Clare W. Graves, "Human Nature Prepares for a Momentous Leap, *The Futurist*, April, 1974, p. 72.

[5] Graves.

[6] Graves, "Levels of Existence: An Open System Theory of Values," *Journal of Humanistic Psychology*, Fall 1970, Vol. 10. No. 2, p. 141.

Chapter 3: Beta Blockers

[1] Howard Smead, *Don't Trust Anyone Over Thirty: A History of the Baby Boom*, published as an e-book by iUniverse.com, 2000, excerpts of which are available at www.howardsmead.com/boom.htm

[2] Smead.

[3] Charles Dickens, *Oliver Twist; Or, The Parish Boy's Progress.* Bantam Books, 1980, pp. 183-184.

Chapter 4: The Ways of the Will

[1] From Dr. Steven Hyman's opening chapter, "Susceptibility and 'Second Hits,'" in *States of Mind, New Discoveries about How Our Brains Make Us Who We Are*, edited by J. Allienna Hobson and Roberta Conlan, (John Wiley & Sons, Inc., 1999), available at http://search.barnesandnoble.com/booksearch/isbninquiry.asp?userid=6TGBLGZA99&isbn=0471299634&pwb=1&displayonly=chapter

[2] Dr. Sean Brophy, a gifted counselor and business consultant in Dublin, Ireland, has made available to me his own writings on the remarkable similarities between Clare Graves' model and that of Dr. Elisabeth Kübler-Ross, and I thank him. I also appreciate his acknowledgement of my primacy in noting this similarity. He has made a number of presentations on this topic to doctors and hospital administrators and staff in Ireland, among others.

Chapter 5: Accepting the Power

[1] From the Population Reference Bureau's web site: www.prb.org/Content/NavigationMenu/Other_articles/July-September_20001/How_Many_People_Have_Lived_On_Earth.htm

[2] Graves, *The Futurist*, p. 81.

[3] Quoted in *The Pleasure of Finding Things Out: The Best Short Works of Richard P. Feynman.* Perseus Books, 1999, pp. 24-25.

[4] Peter J. Gomes, author of the introduction to Paul Tillich's *The Courage to Be*, Yale University Press, 2000, available at www.yale.edu/yup/chapters/084714chap.htm

[5] Tillich, p. 164.

[6] This quote is one of Umberto Eco's best known and is found on numerous "quote round-up" Web sites. I found it at http://www.quotationspage.com/quotes/Umberto_Eco/

[7] David H. Barlow, *Anxiety and its disorders: The nature and treatment of anxiety and panic.* Guilford Press, 1988, p. 12.

[8] Graves, *The Futurist*, p. 81.

[9] I don't know which of John Clute's books contains this quote—and neither does he. An anthology-maker included it but without noting where he found it. In an e-mail, Mr. Clute assured me that it sounded like something he's said more than once. But he couldn't put his finger on the exact quote location.

[10] Graves, *Journal of Humanistic Psychology*, p. 152.

Chapter 7: Free to Be

[1] Kevin Kelly, *Out of Control*, Chapter 24, "The Nine Laws of God," available at http://www.kk.org/outofcontrol/ch24-a.html

Chapter 8: Alpha's Chassis

[1] Robert Kegan, "Grabbing a Tiger by the Tail," March 23, 2000, available at http://www.dialogonleadership.org/Kegan-1999cp.html

[2] George A. Kelly, *The Psychology of Personal Constructs*. Norton, 1955, p. 6.

[3] Quoted in Ben Ratliff's "Johnny Paycheck Dies at 64; Hard-Living Country Singer," *The New York Times*, national edition, Feb. 20, 2003, p. A29.

[4] James P. Carse, *Finite and Infinite Games: A Vision of Life as Play and Possibility*. The Free Press, 1986, p. 33.

Chapter 9: Alpha's Chassis, Con't

[1] Jill Conner Browne, *Sweet Potato Queens' Big Ass Cookbook (And Financial Planner)*. Three Rivers Press, 2003, quoted in "Lard bless us all," *The Dallas Morning News*, Feb. 16, 2003, p. 10C.

[2] Quoted in Annie Layne's "Four Power Plays," *Fast Company*, November, 2000, available at http://www.fastcompany.com/lead/lead_feature/act_greene.html

[3] This documentary film was released on May 11, 2001, produced by D.A. Pennebaxker, Chris Hegedus and Jehane Noujaim and co-directed by Noujaim and Hegedus.

[4] Quoted in Jean-Jacques Taylor's article, "'Fear of failure' motivates Parcells," *The Dallas Morning News*, May 7, 2003, p. 3C.

[5] Quoted in Warren G. Bennis and Patricia W. Biederman, *Organizing Genius: The Secrets of Creative Collaboration*. Perseus Publishing, 1998, available at http://search.barnesandnoble.com /booksearch/isbninquiry.asp?userid=6VP668PIM1&isbn=020133 9897&pwb=1&displayonly=chapter

[6] Bennis and Biederman.

[7] Jane Spencer and Cynthia Crossen, "Why Do Americans Feel That Danger Lurks Everywhere?" *The Wall Street Journal*, April 24, 2003, p. A1.

[8] All quotes in this and the previous two paragraphs are from Norah Vincent's "Enabling disabled scholarship," *Salon*, August 19, 1999, available from http://archive.salon.com/books/ it/1999/08/18/disability /print.html.

[9] The original meaning of this phrase as proposed by Ernst Haeckel a century ago isn't true at a basic biological level nearly as often as Haeckel thought it to be: sometimes embryonic development (ontogeny) does repeat (recapitulate) the pattern of evolutionary history (phylogeny), but then again, in many instances of development it doesn't. For more information, see the lecture notes for Biology 391, "Organic Evolution," at The University of Tennessee at Martin, available at http://www.utm.edu/~rirwin/391OntogPhylog.htm

Chapter 10: Neinja

[1] All the quotes in this paragraph are from Daniel C. Dennett, "Are We Explaining Consciousness Yet?" a research paper available at http://ase.tufts.edu/cogstug/papers/cognition.fin.htm

[2] Richard Dawkins, quoted in a transcript of a debate, "Is Science Killing The Soul," between Dawkins and Steven Pinker, available at htttp://www.edge.org/3rd_culture/dawkins_pinker/ debate.html

[3] Terrance Deacon, quoted in a transcript of the Australian Broadcasting Company's ABC Radio National series, "The Descent of Man," Episode 3, "Is Anyone in There?" available at http://www.abc.net.au/science/descent/trans4.htm. The series was aired Dec. 17-20, 2001.

Chapter 11: Across the Great Divide

[1] Ray Bradbury, "Beyond 1984," 1982, reprinted in the anthology, *Yestermorrow*. Capra Press 1992, p. 174.

[2] Personal communication from Alan Rae.

[3] Wilson, p. 241 and 244.

[4] Graves, "On the Theory of Ethical Behavior."

Chapter 13: The Game

[1] Carse, p. 3.

[2] Adam M. Brandenburger and Barry J. Nalesbuff, *Co-opetition*. Currency-Doubleday, 1996, p. 4.

[3] Paul Fletcher, Francesca Happe, Uta Frith, C. Baker, Ray Dolan, Richard Frackowiac and Chris Frith, "Other Minds in the Brain: a functional imaging study of 'theory of mind' in story comprehension," *Cognition*, 1995, No. 57, pp. 109-128.

[4] Niall M. Fraser, book review of Steven J. Brams' *Theory of Moves*, in *Interfaces*, March/April, 1995, p. 91.

[5] Carse, p. 6.

[6] William Poundstone offers this description of the rules for the Dollar Auction in *Prisoner's Dilemma* (Doubleday, 1992), pp. 280-282: "A dollar bill is auctioned with these two rules: 1. (As in any auction) the dollar bill goes to the highest bidder, who pays whatever the high bid was. Each new bid has to be higher than the current high bid, and the game ends when there is no new bid within a specified time limit. 2. (Unlike at Sotheby's!) the second-highest bidder also has to pay the amount of his last bid—and gets nothing in return."

[7] Camerer, *Behavioral Game Theory: Experiments in Strategic Interaction*. Princeton University Press, 2003, p. 7.

[8] The examples and insights that follow on this and the next two pages are adapted from Adam M. Brandenburger's and Barry J. Nalebuff's popular book, *Co-opetition*. Colin Camerer, the Caltech economist and game theory expert, praised *Co-opetition* for drawing "attention to the barest bones of a game—players, information, actions, and outcomes." And he praised Brandenburger and Nalebuff as "brilliant theorists who could have written a more theoretical book. They chose not to because teaching MBAs

and working with managers convinced them that teaching the basic elements of game theory is more helpful." (*Behavioral Game Theory*, p. 7.)

[9] Felicia Pratto and Angela Walker, "Dominance in Disguise: Power, Beneficence, and Exploitation in Personal Relationships, in *The Use and Abuse of Power: Multiple Perspectives on the Causes of Corruption*, edited by Annette Y. Lee-Chai and John A. Bargh. Psychology Press, 2001, p. 97.

[10] Joseph L. Badaracco, Jr. *Leading Quietly: An Unorthodox Guide to Doing the Right Thing*. Harvard Business School Press, 2002, p. 8.

[11] Robert Wright, *Nonzero: The Logic of Human Destiny*. Vintage Books, 2000, p. 339.

[12] Some of my readers will recognize this statement as one that Paul L. Kordis and your author used in *Strategy of the Dolphin®: Scoring a Win in a Chaotic World* (Morrow, 1989).

[13] Quoted in John Langone's review in *The Dallas Morning News*, March 25, 2003, of Kerry Patterson's, Joseph Grenny's, Ron McMillan's and Al Switzler's *Crucial Conversations: Tools for Talking When Stakes Are High*. McGraw-Hill, 2002.

[14] Quoted in Tom Siegfried's article, "$$igns of activity: When game theory meets brain imaging, a new approach to economics is born," *The Dallas Morning News*, October 27, 2003, p. 4E.

Chapter 14: Crossings

[1] Ray Kurzweil, "The Laws of Accelerating Returns," available at http://www.kurzweilai.net/meme/frame.html?main=/articles/art0134.html?

[2] The quotes in this paragraph appeared in a special issue, "Information, Knowledge and Technology," of the *Philosophical Transactions of the Royal Society of London*, August, 2003, in articles by the issue's compiler and editor, Dr. Alistair G.J. MacFarlane.

[3] Quoted in Freeman J. Dyson, "The World, The Flesh and the Devil," available at http://www.impearls.blogspot.com/2002_11_10_impearls_archive.html #84429829

[4] Dyson.

[5] Nicholas D. Kristof, "Bush vs. Women," *The New York Times*, national edition, August 16, 2002, p. A19.

[6] Denise Grady and Lawrence K. Altman, "Beyond Cute: Exotic Pets Come Bearing Exotic Germs," *The New York Times*, national edition, June 17, 2003, p. D1.

[7] Joe Conason, *Big Lies: The Right-Wing Propaganda Machine and How It Distorts the Truth*, Thomas Dunne Books, 2003, quote available at http://www.salon.com/opinion/feature/2003/08/18/conason_one/print.html

[8] Bill Marvel, "When the top isn't high enough, *The Dallas Morning News*, June 10, 2003, p. E1.

[9] Fox Butterfield, "Study Shows Building Prisons Did Not Prevent Repeat Crimes," *The New York Times*, national edition, June 3, 2002, p. A11.

[10] Adam Liptak, "Critics Say Executive Drug May Hide Suffering," *The New York Times*, national edition, October 7, 2003, p. A1.

[11] Michael J. Sniffen, the Associated Press, "Prosecutor misconduct studied," in *The Dallas Morning News*, June 26, 2003, p. 7A.

[12] Marlise Simons, "Discarded War Munitions Leach Poisons Into the Baltic," *The New York Times*, national edition, June 20, 2003, p. A8.

[13] Scott Burns, "Facts got cut prior to taxes," *The Dallas Morning News*, June 1, 2003, p. D1.

[14] Laurie Goodstein, "Seeing Islam as 'Evil' Faith, Evangelicals Seek Converts," *The New York Times*, national edition, May 27, 2003, page A1.

[15] Joshua A. Baugh, "Couple's dream come true is yours for a price," *The Dallas Morning News*, Feb. 16, 2003, p. A31.

[16] See "The Gates 'Ecology House" at http://www.zpub.com/un/bill/ecology.html and "Bill Gates' house tidbits" at http://www.netscrap.com/netscrap_detail.cfm?scrap_id=528

[17] Bob Herbert, "Teaching Kids a Lesson," *The New York Times*, national edition, May 1, 2003, p. A33.

[18] Review by Ken Binmore of Robert Axelrod's *The Complexity of Cooperation* in the *Journal of Artificial Societies and Social Simulation*, Volume 1, Issue 1, 1998.

[19] The observations about Gandi and the Jewish victims of the Holocaust were borrowed from Jonathan Wallace, "An Ethnic Based on the Prisoner's Dilemma," at www.spectacle.org

[20] I found Wallace's article, "Litigation," in *The Ethical Spectacle*, to have many valuable insights about lawyers. (Wallace is a lawyer.) The article is available at http://www.spectacle.org/995/liti.html

[21] Quoted in "Your Biggest Fan," an excerpt from Tucker Carlson's *Politicians, Partisans, and Parasites: My Adventures in Cable News*, Warner Books, 2003. Available at http://www.salon.com/books/feature/2003/09/13/carlson_excerpt/index.html

[22] Camerer, "Neuroeconomics: How neuroscience can inform economics," p. 3.

[23] Quoted from Michael S. Gazzaniga's *The Mind's Past*, University of California Press, 1998, in "An Interpreter Knows Its Past, Fleabyte: "Thinking with Computers," June 15, 1999, available at http://www.fleabyte.org/flb-10.html

[24] Gazzaniga.

[25] Itzak Fried, "Technical Comment: The Hippocampus and Human Navigation," *Science*, 282, p. 2151.

[26] Michael Persinger and Faye Healey, 2002, "Experimental facilitation of the sensed presence: Possible intercalation between the hemispheres induced by complex magnetic fields," *Journal of Nervous and Mental Disease*, 190:8, pp. 533-541.

[27] Timothy D. Wilson, Samuel Lindsey and Tonya Y. Schooler, 2000, "A Model of Dual Attitudes," *Psychological Review*, 107:1, pp. 101-126.

[28] Camerer, p. 9.

[29] Camerer, p. 13.

[30] Daniel T. Gilbert and Michael Gill, 2000, "The momentary realist," *Psychological Science*, 11, pp. 394-398.

[31] Lee Ross, Mark R. Lepper, Michael Hubbard, 1975, "Perseverance in Self-Perception and Social Perception: Biased Attributional Processes in the Debriefing Paradigm," *Journal of Personality and Social Psychology*, 32:5, pp. 880-892.

[32] Colin Camerer, George Loewenstein and Martin Weber, 1989, "The curse of knowledge in economic settings: An experimental

analysis," *Journal of Political Economy*, 97:5, October, pp. 1232-1254.

[33] Such a viewpoint was discussed at length by John Ziman, Emeritus Professor of Physics of the University of Bristol, in an article, "Emerging Out of Nature into History: The Plurality of the Sciences," in a special issue of the *Philosophical Transactions of the Royal Society of London*, August, 2003.

[34] George Ritter, *The McDonaldization of Society*. SAGE Publications, 2000.

[35] Quoted in Bob Herbert's column," Home Alone," *The New York Times*, national edition, Sept. 1, 2003, p. A17.

[36] David Morse, "Rumsfeld's McArmy goes to war," Sept. 18, 2003, available at http://www.salon.com/opinion/feature/2003/09/18/mcarmy/

[37] Dennett, *Kinds of Minds: Towards an Understanding of Consciousness*. Perseus Publishing, 1997.

*I*ndex

Dudley Lynch

...has consistently demonstrated his ability to create leading-edge thinking skills models and tools and equip others to benefit from them in highly effective ways. His professional career spans more than four decades.

As president of Brain Technologies Corporation of Plano, Texas, he has personally trained nearly 1,000 thinking skills professionals in twenty-one countries in his techniques for helping individuals and organizations be better thinkers.

He is the creator of cutting-edge self- and group-assessment instruments now being used in six languages. These include *Asset Report, the Book of You®; The BrainMap®* and **Path***Primer®*.

He was lead author for one of Europe's best-selling business books of the nineties. He has been a frequent presenter on the international business and thinking skills development lecture tour.

He has used his own thinking skills to create numerous public relations/public affairs strategy plans and documents for Fortune 1000 companies in partnership with major Dallas public relations firms.

He has written fourteen books and hundreds of magazine articles, including cover articles in *Business Week* and by-lined articles in *Fortune, Reader's Digest, The New York Times, The Economist* and more than 225 other periodicals on six continents.

He has a Bachelor of Arts degree from Eastern New Mexico University and a Master of Arts degree from the University of Texas at Austin.

"Leaping free" tools and aids

Up-to-the-minute information about our Brain Technologies Corporation people, products and services is always available at www.braintechnologies.com.

- **Assessment tools**
- **Workshops**
- **Training for certification as a BTC/ Beta thinking skills expert**
- **Books and facilitation guides and aids**
- **Presentations and on-site consulting by Dudley Lynch**

And you are wecome to e-mail us at any time at to discuss your special needs. Send your questions and inquiries to info@braintechnologies.com.